HOME INFORMATICS AND TELEMATICS: ICT FOR THE NEXT BILLION

IFIP – The International Federation for Information Processing

IFIP was founded in 1960 under the auspices of UNESCO, following the First World Computer Congress held in Paris the previous year. An umbrella organization for societies working in information processing, IFIP's aim is two-fold: to support information processing within its member countries and to encourage technology transfer to developing nations. As its mission statement clearly states,

> *IFIP's mission is to be the leading, truly international, apolitical organization which encourages and assists in the development, exploitation and application of information technology for the benefit of all people.*

IFIP is a non-profitmaking organization, run almost solely by 2500 volunteers. It operates through a number of technical committees, which organize events and publications. IFIP's events range from an international congress to local seminars, but the most important are:

• The IFIP World Computer Congress, held every second year;
• Open conferences;
• Working conferences.

The flagship event is the IFIP World Computer Congress, at which both invited and contributed papers are presented. Contributed papers are rigorously refereed and the rejection rate is high.

As with the Congress, participation in the open conferences is open to all and papers may be invited or submitted. Again, submitted papers are stringently refereed.

The working conferences are structured differently. They are usually run by a working group and attendance is small and by invitation only. Their purpose is to create an atmosphere conducive to innovation and development. Refereeing is less rigorous and papers are subjected to extensive group discussion.

Publications arising from IFIP events vary. The papers presented at the IFIP World Computer Congress and at open conferences are published as conference proceedings, while the results of the working conferences are often published as collections of selected and edited papers.

Any national society whose primary activity is in information may apply to become a full member of IFIP, although full membership is restricted to one society per country. Full members are entitled to vote at the annual General Assembly, National societies preferring a less committed involvement may apply for associate or corresponding membership. Associate members enjoy the same benefits as full members, but without voting rights. Corresponding members are not represented in IFIP bodies. Affiliated membership is open to non-national societies, and individual and honorary membership schemes are also offered.

HOME INFORMATICS AND TELEMATICS: ICT FOR THE NEXT BILLION

*Proceedings of IFIP TC 9, WG 9.3 HOIT 2007
Conference, August 22- 25, 2007, Chennai, India*

Edited by

Alladi Venkatesh
University of California, Irvine, United States

Timothy Gonsalves
Indian Institute of Technology-Madras, India

Andrew Monk
University of York, United Kingdom

Kathy Buckner
Napier University, United Kingdom

 Springer

Home Informatics and Telematics: ICT for the Next Billion

Edited by A. Venkatesh, T. Gonsalves, A. Monk, and K. Buckner

   p. cm. (IFIP International Federation for Information Processing, a Springer Series in Computer Science)

ISSN: 1571-5736 / 1861-2288 (Internet)

ISBN: 13: 978-1-4419-4470-2   eISBN: 13: 978-0-387-73697-6
Printed on acid-free paper

9 8 7 6 5 4 3 2 1
springer.com

Acknowledgements

We gratefully acknowledge the support of the National Science Foundation - USA (*POINT Project - Grant No. IRI 9619695*), various academic units of the University of California, Irvine (*CalIT2, CRITO, The Paul Merage School of Business, Center for Ethnography, Office of Vice-Chancellor for Research*), IFIP Head Office, Austria (International Federation for Information Processing), the Indian Institute of Technology (IIT)-Madras, India and the TeNet Group (IIT-Madras).

Preface

This volume represents the papers reviewed and accepted for the HOIT2007 conference held at the Indian Institute of Technology Madras (IIT-M) in the city of Chennai, India, in August 2007. The conference, entitled "Home/Community Oriented ICT for the Next Billion," addressed many major themes of current interest in this field. In particular, the focus was on community-based technologies. The conference was organized by IFIP working Group 9.3-Home Oriented Informatics and Telematics (HOIT), in association with the TeNeT Group of the Indian Institute of Technology, Madras. The conference papers cover a wide range of topics that transcend local/national themes and engage us in global issues. This was the first time the HOIT conference was held outside Europe or North America, testifying to the growth and development of other regions of the world.

The conference included paper sessions, panel discussions, special keynote speaker presentations, and poster sessions. The topics were grouped under different themes. Following are the five basic themes of the conference and a brief description of the papers that appear under each theme.

Empowerment and Digital Divide
In their comparative analysis of South Africa and India, Joseph and Andrew show how ICTs can have dramatic impact in two key areas—alleviating poverty for rural women and achieving socio-economic development goals. In the next piece, Malhotra and co-authors discuss "DesiCrew" as a unique business process outsourcing (BPO) initiative in the context of rural areas in India. Directly addressing community-oriented concerns, Pitula and Radhakrishnan propose an "inclusive technology" that permits greater participation of rural communities and minimizes the digital divide between rural and urban dwellers. The setting in their study is Peruvian Amazon. Gonzales and co-authors transport us to a different setting, in Mexico, and describe in detail the emergence of a low-income community that has broadband Internet access and other ICT-related features.

ICT and Learning
Sarma and Ravindran demonstrate how intelligent tutoring systems have been developed using artificial intelligence techniques to teach autistic students. The next article is an elaborate case study by Harishankar and co-authors on active teaching and learning strategies that have become the hallmark of the TeNet online tutorials developed in collaboration with IIT-Madras. This is followed by a paper written by Javed Khan and co-authors on how awareness systems can support communication between busy parents and young children at school.

ICT-Emerging Communities and Societal Issues
Dinesh and Uskudarh extend the community-oriented theme to the school environment and discuss a community knowledge management system that facilitates ongoing interactions between the school administration and the local community. Vyas and co-authors shift their focus to work environments and propose a system that mediates casual

and engaging encounters among employees and leads to meaningful and pleasurable experiences. The idea is to make the work environment less monotonous.
Parmar and co-authors discuss a health information system sensitive to the needs of rural communities, elaborating on the design challenges in developing such a system. Subramanian raises an important issue of growing concern whose significance cannot be ignored: as new economies emerge based on information revolution, how do we protect information privacy laws? The context is India but the topic has a wider appeal.

Home Applications and Family Uses

One of the central issues facing users of new technologies relates to the quality of their everyday experiences. Clark and Wright propose a scheme for on-line grocery shopping based on their survey of consumers. In their study of daily domestic life, Swan and co-authors perform an analysis of how families manage clutter and design a scheme for domestic management. This is followed by a design-oriented analysis in the domestic setting by Sondhi and Sloane that focuses on digital photo sharing among family members and friends. Extending the notion of family experiences directed toward fun, Monk and Reed examine recreational use of the telephone focusing on many-to-many situations as opposed to the normal one-to-one approach associated with telephone use. Darbari and Agarwal offer some practical ideas that incorporate end-user requirements in sharing and experiencing digital photographs.

ICTs in the Home – Usability and Design Issues

Monk and Lelos extend our traditional concepts of usability by delving into the domain of aesthetics. They raise the question of whether digital products can be both useful and aesthetic. Fitzpatrick and Stringer examine the nexus between home, school, and work and show how such an understanding is critical to the development of next-generation technologies. As new technologies provide opportunities for social interactions, there is a growing interest in designing suitable devices for this purpose. Petersen and co-authors discuss CASOME (context-aware interactive media platform for social computing in the home), which they propose as an interactive system for family use. Leitner and co-authors go into considerable detail concerning design issues that have occupied our attention on smart home systems and provide some answers. Choi takes a close look at the notion of domestic objects by suggesting that the current approach neglects people's diverse functional uses and comes up with a more inclusive design.

Editors
Alladi Venkatesh – University of California, Irvine, USA
Timothy A. Gonsalves, Indian Institute of Technology-Madras, India
Andrew Monk, University of York, UK
Kathy Buckner, Napier University, UK.

Table of Contents

[A]. Empowerment and Digital Divide

1. Convergence opportunities and factors influencing the use of internet and telephony by rural women in South Africa and India towards empowerment - *Meera. K. Joseph and Theo. N. Andrew*   1

2. Untapped Resources! Amazing Potential! TeNeT's Rural BPO Initiative - *Saloni Malhotra, P.Rathi, Timothy A. Gonsalves, Ashok Jhunjhunwala and Thejus Giri*   21

3. A Set of Heuristic Measurements for Evaluating the Inclusiveness of a Technology - *K. Pitula and T. Radhakrishnan*   35

4. The Tech-Enabled Neighborhood: Findings from an experience in Tecámac, Mexico - *Victor M. Gonzalez, Kenneth Kraemer, Luis A. Castro and Alladi Venkatesh*   49

[B]. ICT and Learning

5. Intelligent Tutoring Systems using Reinforcement Learning to teach Autistic Students - *B. H. Sreenivasa Sarma and B. Ravindran*   65

6. Teaching - Learning Strategies in Interactive Education – A Case Study - *V Bharathi Harishankar, Archana Ghode, Alankar Bandyopadhayay, Maryma Scotlin, Hema A Murthy, Timothy A Gonsalves and Ashok Jhunjhunwala*   79

7. On the role of awareness systems for supporting parent involvement in young children's schooling - *Vassilis-Javed Khan, Panos Markopoulos and Berry Eggen*   91

[C]. ICT – Emerging Communities and Societal Issues

8. Community Software Applications - *T. B. Dinesh and S. Uskudarli*   103

9. Being Social @ Work: Designing for Playfully Mediated Social Awareness in Work Environments - *Dhaval Vyas, Marek R. van de Watering, Anton Eliëns and Gerrit C. van der Veer*   113

10. Shaping social beliefs: A community sensitive health information system for rural India - *Vikram Parmar, David V Keyson and Cees deBont*   133

11. "Can we trust the Indians with our data?" An examination of the emergence of information privacy laws in India - *Ramesh Subramanian*   145

[D]. Home Applications and Family Uses

12. Off Their Trolley -- Understanding Online Grocery Shopping Behaviour - *Lillian Clark and Peter Wright*   157

13. Containing Family Clutter - *Laurel Swan, Alex S. Taylor, Shahram Izadi and Richard Harper*   171

14. Digital Photo Sharing and Emotions In A Ubiquitous Smart Home - *Gaurav Sondhi and Andy Sloane*   185

15. Telephone conferences for fun: experimentation in people's homes - *Andrew F. Monk and Darren J. Reed*   201

16. Enliven Photographs: Enriching User Experience - *Akshay Darbari and Pragya Agrawal*   215

[E]. ICTs in the Home – Usability and Design Issues

17. Changing only the aesthetic features of a product can affect its apparent usability - *Andrew Monk and Kira Lelos*   221

18. Exploring technology influences between home, work, school: implications for managing ubiquitous technologies in the home - *Geraldine Fitzpatrick and Mark Stringer*   235

19. Designing for Co-located Social media use in the home using the CASOME infrastructure - *Marianne Graves Petersen, Martin Ludvigsen, Kaj Grønbæk, Kaspar Rosengreen Nielsen*   251

20. Usability – Key Factor of Future Smart Home Systems - *Gerhard Leitner, David Ahlström and Martin Hitz*   269

21. Lessons from the Life of Domestic Objects:
Design Considerations for UbiComp Devices for Home - *Youngmi Choi*   279

Convergence opportunities and factors influencing the use of internet and telephony by rural women in South Africa and India towards empowerment

Meera. K. Joseph and Theo. N. Andrew

University of Johannesburg, 17011 Nind Street, Doornfontein Campus, Johannesburg, 2028, Republic of South Africa

Abstract. Access to Information and Communication Technologies (ICTs) can have dramatic impact on poverty alleviation for rural women and for achieving socio economic development goals. Rural women need to treat ICTs as an empowerment tool and a means to a living. The use of mobile communication devices and internet are changing the way agricultural activities are managed by farmers nowadays. Rural women's lack of mobility and less hands-on computer experience might hinder women's welfare and empowerment. This paper analyses how use of the telephony (both cellular and land line), internet and other ICTs can benefit rural women in educational, business and economic sector. Women in rural India and rural South Africa were marginalized partly due to their lack of ability in being vocal when it comes to empowering themselves using ICTs due to cultural norms in India, and apartheid in South Africa. Over the years, unlike other developing countries, the above-mentioned countries have its unique ICT projects meant for empowering rural women. This paper is driven from the authors' commitment for rural development and rural women empowerment. It highlights different low-cost ICT initiatives and strategies taken by women's organizations, various companies and other non-governmental organizations (NGOs) for rural women empowerment. The paper also highlights various factors influencing use of internet and mobile phone adoption by rural women. Various bottlenecks for the community projects, factors de-motivating the use of mobile phones and internet by rural women and possible solutions for these are also mentioned.

Please use the following format when citing this chapter:

Joseph, M. K., Andrew, T. N., 2007, in IFIP International Federation for Information Processing, Volume 241, Home Informatics and Telematics: ICT for the Next Billion, eds. Venkatesh, A., Gonsalves, T., Monk, A., Buckner, K., (Boston: Springer), pp. 1-20.

1. Introduction

The term "rural women" refers to women living in an under-serviced or rural area. In these areas water, sanitation, drainage and electricity are scarce and rural women are afflicted with unemployment. The mortality rates are predominantly high amongst children. Although there are limited services offered by government fire station and police station to people living in rural areas, these places often lack public waste management system, public transport and people mostly depend on agriculture or fisheries for a living.

The way information and communication technologies are accessed by rural women is widely debated. "Gender is an issue because access to and use of ICTs are influenced by the cultural and institutional contexts in which they are applied" [1]. ICTs have the potential to alleviate the constraints that rural women currently face. Although rural women's indigenous knowledge should not be underestimated they experience a less equitable environment in accessing ICTs. Internet, e-mail and telephony remain the most widely used form of communication devices for women empowerment in developing countries. As internet and telephony top the list of tools that can empower rural women, this paper gives special focus on these sectors.

The authors look at how various NGOs use ICTs for content generation and capacity building using the internet. The authors have selected a few NGOs and companies in South Africa and India for field study taking into account how rural women benefit by using internet, telephony (both cellular and land lines) and video cameras. Other community projects specifically highlighting women's use of internet and mobile phones from different countries are also included. There are three reasons why authors focused on these countries.

Firstly it is due to the increasing deployment of mobile and rural telecommunications infrastructure in India in recent years. Secondly it is due to the innovative ways of South African women's organizations, various companies and NGOs bring communications via internet and cellular phones to rural women. The third reason why we focused on these countries for research is due to its unique way of empowering rural women through 3G and internet.

71.8% of the almost 1 billion Indian people still reside in villages (rural areas) and most of rural people did not have telephone connection. ICT penetration and teledensity in rural India and rural areas of South Africa is very low. For the above-mentioned population, India has 16 million Internet connection and 74 million telephone connections - most of which are confined in and around cities. Table 1 and Table 2 give a clear picture of internet penetration and mobile penetration in India and South Africa. The Indian government forecast that by 2010 India will have more than 500 million mobile subscribers [2].

Women are more likely to be involved in agriculture-related activity than men. India's 66% of the workforce are still employed in agricultural sector. But research has indicated they have found a means for living through other sectors as well.

Table 1: Comparison of internet and mobile penetration in India [3]

2003 Life expectancy at birth (years)	63.3
2005 Population	1.1 Billion
2005 GDP per capita	US $685
2005 Internet penetration	4.3%
2006 Mobile penetration	11%

Table 2: Comparison of internet and mobile penetration in South Africa [3]

2003 Life expectancy at birth (years)	48.4
2005 Population	44.8 Million
2005 GDP per capita	US $5,290
2005 Internet penetration	10.7%
2006 Mobile penetration	61%

The objectives of this paper are:

1. To raise awareness of gendered digital divide.
2. To learn more about the ICTs like mobile technology and internet and video that can benefit rural women.
3. To find out the critical factors for the successful empowerment of women through internet and telecommunications (including mobile phones).
4. To find out the bottlenecks and factors that hinder rural women from using ICTs and innovative ways by which they can be motivated.

Field study could be conducted only in a few organizations in South Africa for data gathering. Relevant information about various community projects especially in the Indian context was collected from databases such as Engineering Village and other peer-reviewed journals. In addition various publications and reports from World Bank and United Nations provided a good source of information.

Conceptual literature survey conducted from books and peer-reviewed articles by experts where they expressed opinions, experiences, theories and ideas about a problem area. It helped the authors to understand the validity or correctness of data and illuminated strong points which they could follow up.

Research literature conducted included reporting in respect of research that had been undertaken previously in the specific field and gave the authors a good indication of bottlenecks in respect of research, design and techniques in connection with the field.

Semi-structured interviews were conducted with various people in women's organizations in India and South Africa, to find out more on how rural women access ICTs. Some oral sources were organized interviews that were conducted with managers working in South African NGOs and other companies in India. Some of these organizations were kind enough to provide a brief description of their community projects.

2. Gender-related imbalances in the use of ICT- Is technology making things better?

According to a speech by Indian President Mr. APJ Abdul Kalam to SEWA (Self Employed Women's Association) members in India, "Children are the most precious properties. Male and female children are to be given equal importance in providing education and rights for growth of our society. Girl child education is the most important need to empower families"[4].

As the 2002 Rural Poverty Report of the International Fund for Agricultural Development indicates, in rural areas of developing countries there is no question that women are more likely to be resource poor, isolated, and less educated relative to men. "People lack many things: jobs, shelter, food, healthcare and drinkable water. Today, being cut off from basic telecommunications services is a hardship almost as acute as these other deprivations, and may indeed reduce the chances of finding remedies to them"[5]. Gender roles are society specific because there are socially constructed relations between men and women in society. In Cajamarca, Peru, when women undertook information technology training with men, the men mocked them saying that computers are for men, not women [6].

2.1. Convergence opportunities: Second Generation (2G) to Third generation (3G) mobile phones

One of the main objectives of the ICT companies today for service delivery is convergence. Convergence will allow customers to access multiple services via multiple interfaces which are translated into convenient services that are easy to use and access. Telecommunication companies like Vodacom, Telkom and Siemens Communications have realized the need for converged communication and ICT skills in rural community and established a Convergence Lab at University of Witwatersrand, South Africa.

The 2G technologies like GSM (Global System for Mobile communications) are still the most popular for mobile communications. It allows mobile phones to connect to it by searching for cells in the immediate vicinity. But research has shown third generation (3G) technology is slowly taking over 2G even for rural broadband connectivity.

3G is based on an International Telecommunication Union (ITU) initiative for a single global wireless standard called International Mobile Telecommunications-2000 (IMT-2000). This concept of a single standard evolved into a family of five 3G wireless standards. 3G is an appropriate technology to provide affordable voice and data access to people in rural areas. These areas have limited landline access. So 3G is a way to provide high-speed internet connectivity, education, public safety, healthcare, governance and environmental conservation in a sustainable, efficient and cost effective manner.

Code Division Multiple Access (CDMA) is a digital wireless technology that works by converting analog information, such as speech, into digital information, which is then transmitted as a radio signal over a wireless network. CDMA uses spread-spectrum technology, decreasing potential interference while achieving privacy. CDMA technology is the basis for 3G wireless, which offers increased voice capacity and provides higher data rates than 2G and 2.5G. Development of cell phones based on this technology was dominated by QUALCOMM Inc.

WCDMA is (Wideband Code Division Multiple Access), developed by NTTDoCoMo is a 3G cellular network whose key feature is radio channels that are 5MHz wide. High-Speed Downlink Packet Access (HSDPA) is a 3G technology that would bridge the gap between 3G and internet. High-Speed Uplink Packet Access (HSUPA) provides packet based uplink data transmission to WCDMA (Universal Mobile Telecommunication System). HSUPA and HSDPA can support an entire range of broadband applications that would deliver a complete wireless system. Other than using it for downloading graphics heavy website one may use it for viewing television and for video telephony.

Of the five wireless standards evolved, the most widely adopted are CDMA2000 and WCDMA (UMTS). CDMA2000 (also known as CDMA2000 1X) is a family of 3G standards that offers enhanced voice and data capacity and higher data rates than previous, second generation wireless standards. The CDMA2000 family of standards include CDMA2000 1X and CDMA2000 1xEV-DO (CDMA2000 1X Evolution Data Optimized).CDMA2000 is a direct evolution of the cdmaOne® standard. CDMA2000 enables both voice and data and is best suited to provide comprehensive connectivity to rural India and will enable inclusive growth and development for the benefit of these underserved citizens.

3G has accelerated the convergence of mobile communication devices with consumer electronic devices. 3G mobile phones will offer rural women facilities like video telephony, television viewing, digital camera, MP3 music players. It can provide high-speed broadband data connectivity (upto 14 Mbps) compared to DSL internet and /or cable modem internet in a mobile setting.

Both internet and latest telephony techniques have provided various forms of communication for rural women to e-mail, chat, and keep abreast with global market for trading. The authors have focused on internet and mobile phones and telephone usage by various NGOs and multi-national companies due to the convergence opportunities provided by them for women empowerment.

3. Current ICT initiatives for rural women empowerment

Women are actively learning about ICT through community telecentres and women's groups. But illiteracy and language barriers remain the grave concern for women while accessing ICT. Women's organizations aims to empower rural women by providing gender-sensitive training to use ICTs, by facilitating the dissemination of information in formats accessible to women, making technology accessible to historically disadvantaged, and creating a platform for women's voices.

Southern African NGO network (SANGONet) is one of the few NGOs involved in customising its ICT services to the specific needs of the NGO sector, improving its interaction, relationship and response to the needs of current and potential NGO clients. SANGONet is an information portal that allows community based organizations (mainly NGOs) to communicate with each other.

SANGONet (http://www.sangonet.org.za) is responsible for co-ordinating the collection and collation of inputs on rural women and development projects to the Dimitra database. The Southern African countries targeted by SANGONet include Angola, Botswana, Lesotho, Namibia, South Africa and Swaziland. Dimitra database showcases the profiles, development trends and description of various projects and programmes involving rural women and development in Africa, Europe and the Near East. This database aimed at empowering rural women, is updated every three years. Dimitra networks' goals include dissemination of information regarding achievements, contributions and challenges of rural women.

SANGONet's Dimitra Project shares information about the NGOs activities through PRODDER Directory. PRODDER is an online directory. It is the most comprehensive free on-line database of NGO and development organizations in South Africa. The participant organizations will receive bi-annual newsletters that provide more information on activities of the projects and will be given an opportunity to participate in local and regional networking opportunities.

Women'sNet was born out of a desire to develop a network that would facilitate the promotion of gender equality in South Africa by using various Information and Communication Technologies (ICTs). Women'sNet is an independent Non-Govermental Organisation that was initiated as a joint initiative of South African Non-Governmental Organization Network (SANGONeT) and the Commission on Gender Equality (CGE) was launched in 1998. Women'sNet is a member of the Association for Progressive Communications (APC) and the APC Women's Networking Support Programme (WNSP). Women'sNet aims to empower South African women by providing gender-sensitive training to use ICTs, by facilitating the dissemination of information in formats accessible to women, making technology accessible to historically disadvantaged, and creating a platform for women's voices.

Women'sNet uses ICT as a gendered tool and works to address gender imbalances in access by providing ICT training, gender awareness programmes and facilitating content dissemination. The contents created supports girls, women and women's organization to manage content and use ICT. It helps builds women's organizational capacity to use technology to find the people, resources, tools and content they need for social action. There are various networking support programmes designed to enable to use the Internet and other relevant ICTs to find the people, issues, resources and tools needed for women's social activism and empowerment.

The Women'sNet model which rests on, information/content generation linked to networking and capacity building ensures sustainability of South African women's organizations. Women'sNet has maintained its authenticity and uniqueness by facilitating participation in content generation of various women's organizations. It promotes use of ICT for social development and gender participation and its profile rests on capacity development through networking and ICT advocacy through its membership with APC Africa Women. The other projects include the work done in preparation of the Violence Against Women site, the human rights site, the governance site and work done for gender sensitive areas for information society in African context.

Women'sNet strategic priorities : Women'sNet's objectives include making ICT accessible to disadvantaged women, providing gender-sensitive training, creating a platform for women's voices through contents in Women'sNet website, disseminating information in formats accessible to women (not linked to net), facilitating in planning of website development for other women's networks, helps women to use Internet strategically to achieve goals, facilitating women empowerment through networking and special projects and raising awareness of FOSS.

Women's Net offers a number of services to NGOs and other institutions on using ICTs strategically to achieve their goals which include services like:

- Technology Planning: Many Women's organizations' very important work is undermined by their lack of information, structures and support with regard to ICTs. They are unable to communicate with each other, with policy makers and with global movements as well as their constituencies. Women'sNet advises NGOs to assist them in making strategic technology decisions to support their goals and activities. This includes activities to create awareness of free and open source software solutions (FOSS).
- Training: Women'sNet facilitators have conducted training on producing audio files for community radio and the internet, on using the internet and email effectively, on advocacy and lobbying online and other tailor made courses. Its first workshop on Free and Open Source Software (FOSS solutions) was on 2004. Its Women's Technology Training Center in Newtown, Johannesburg has 18 computers using FOSS.
- Website Planning and Development: Women'sNet assists other NGOs to design and maintain their websites, with regards to content and maintenance, making the website work. They also help organizations to revive older websites.
- Communication and Networking Support: Women'sNet's quarterly newsletter - Intersections has emphasized women's organizations should engage in ICT planning. Women'sNet helps organization's to make the best use of technology by advising on managing and facilitating email lists, buying technology tools, which software is most appropriate for your needs, using internet tools for advocacy and much more.
- (S)he-bytes project: (S)he-bytes project website helped training girls to record radio content about gender issues that impact their lives. It was funded by Open Society Foundation, called Recording Women's Voices. Although this

project came to an end in 2005, (S)he-bytes continue to facilitate the production of topical, thought-provoking audio content by amplifying the issues of women/girls and poor marginalized communities in the form of "sound portraits". It will continue to dissemminate women empowerment issues through radio magazines and discussion programs.

- Digital stories: Women's Net held two Digital Story Telling Workshops at Technical Training Center in NewTown, Johannesburg. The inexperienced women produced a movie with their own words, text using computers and other devices like scanners, digital cameras and audio recorders. They talked about their survival strategies, gender discrimifation, poverty, violence, HIV/AIDS illness, etc. Women'sNet will provide CD that will be shared by other NGOs for training in collecting, capturing and dissemination of local knowledge.

QUALCOMM Incorporated [3] is a leader in developing and delivering innovative digital wireless communications products and services based on CDMA and other advanced technologies. QUALCOMM launched the Wireless Reach™ [3] initiative to empower rural communities across the world through the use of 3G wireless technologies to strengthen economic and social development with a focus on education, governance, healthcare, the environment and emergency response services. Wireless Reach™ initiative achieves this by creating sustainable 3G projects through partnerships with non-government organizations, universities, government institutions, development agencies and other private sector companies.

Due to a huge disparity between urban and rural connectivity the government of India and several state governments, civil society organizations, industry partners and donor agencies have created an initiative, named Mission 2007. Its objective was to facilitate and accelerate through multi-stakeholder collaborations, the provision of Village Resource Centers in each of India's 600,000 villages by August 15, 2007 when it celebrates its 60 years of independence.

Village Resource Centers provide a central meeting point for knowledge-based livelihoods and income-generating opportunities for farming communities and all poor rural men and women. QUALCOMM has formed an alliance (on 28th July 2006) with the NASSCOM Foundation and Tata Teleservices to support of India's Mission 2007 initiative. This alliance launched QUALCOMM's first Wireless Reach™ initiative in India to provide CDMA2000 wireless connectivity solutions to 65 Village Resource Centers in India. This initiative was under NASSCOM's Rural Knowledge Network Program.

The initiative aims to empower communities that have limited or no telecommunications access through the use of 3G technologies, which will help contribute to long-term socio-economic development. Under the scope of this alliance, NASSCOM and QUALCOMM will provide connectivity and content to Village Resource Centres in the states of West Bengal; Orissa; Maharashtra; Andhra Pradesh; Karnataka; Tamil Nadu; Goa; Gujarat; and Kerala. QUALCOMM, as NASSCOM's

Convergence opportunities and factors influencing the use of internet and telephony
by rural women in South Africa and India towards empowerment

9

technology supporter, will provide Internet connectivity through CDMA2000 fixed wireless terminals to the Centres.

QUALCOMM's Wireless Reach™ initiative has partnered with wireless operator MTN to provide 3G high-speed Internet connectivity to entrepreneur-run centers in the township of Alexandra, north of Johannesburg, South Africa. This township is an under-serviced area which lacks affordable fixedline connections. QUALCOMM donated HSDPA data cards and laptops to this MTN-led pilot project, called MTN@ccess, providing Internet connectivity using the latest 3G standard, HSDPA, to payphone shops in Alexandra, South Africa.

The primary MTN@ccess initiative is to provide opportunities within communities for education, enterprise, economic empowerment, governance, Internet connectivity, and business development through connectivity to data and business tools such as the Internet, email, payphones and fax services. These pay phone shops are the world's first Internet cafes to use HSDPA.With MTN's HSDPA technology, which currently provides data rates of up to 1.8 megabits per second, users connect to the Internet via a specially designed MTN portal. This portal features direct links to recruitment services, email services, universities, government departments and many more useful web sites.

The Biamba Marie Mutombo Hospital and Research Center is the first hospital built in the Congo in nearly 40 years and an integral part of achieving the goals of the Dikembe Mutombo Foundation. QUALCOMM has made a commitment to provide a cash donation, 3G devices and medical software to this hospital and research center located in Kinshasa. 3G will allow doctors to have instant access to patient information, such as X-rays and CAT scans, and enable doctors to be notified immediately in case of an emergency. In addition, 3G offers the ability to diagnose patients remotely and instantly through electronic access to patient information.

On 13 Nov 2006 QUALCOMM Incorporated (Nasdaq: QCOM), announced an expansion to its QUALCOMM Single Chip™ (QSC™) family to include support for UMTS. This is the world's first solution to integrate a monolithic die - with integrated radio transceiver, baseband modem and multimedia processor - together with power management functionality into a single chip for WCDMA (UMTS) and HSDPA handsets. The cost and time-to-market advantages of the single-chip solutions will help drive wireless broadband and 3G adoption in mass markets around the world.

SEWA [7], founded in 1972 in Gujarat (India), is an organization for poor self-employed women workers. With 700000 members (includes 530000 women members) its goal is every family gets full employment. Almost 70% of these women are illiterate. The other objectives include capacity building, collaborating with government rural programme, increasing bargaining power of women, make women self-reliant and providing food and social security.

It has technology information centers based on satellite-based communication networks and distance learning classrooms. It's various IT- programs and rural Community Learning Centers presents poor self-employed women with ways to improve lives and apply those experiences in business related to village enterprises. "Anasooya" (means without hatred) is a fortnightly e-newsletter from SEWA which includes articles on dowry, working women problems, problems of children and their rights and on child labour.

SEWA Trade Facilitation Centre (STFC) uses innovative ways to empower women through traditional skills. The STFC, promoted by the Kutch Craft, The Banaskantha DWCRA Mahila SEWA Association has a planned turnover of USD 27,000 million. The 15000 women artisans are the shareholders/owners and suppliers of hand embriodred products. The types of work done by women include patch-work, jat, suf, tie and dye, mutava and mochi embroidery.

STFC has ensured a wage of Rs. 1500 (1USD = Rs. 46) to each artisan. STFC goals include capacity building of artisans, product development and increased access to local, regional and global markets. In fact most of the Indian homes in urban and rural areas have bags, cushion covers, bedspreads or wall hangings made by SEWA women. SEWA uses a website to market its products in global market.

Video SEWA had head-loaders and vegetable vendors who were given video equipment training to produce informative programmes on self-employed women's existence and contribution to society. These video tapes have reached policy makers in Washington and Delhi and the slum dwellers in Gujarat. SEWA has recognized the need for communication amongst groups of self employed women on issues like health, legal, existing government and non-government programmes and policies. SEWA Academy's trainers provide income-generating training on salt farming, crafts and diary farming. It also facilitates Advanced Leadership (Kadam) Training and research training and healthcare training

N-Logue Communications (P) Ltd. (India) [8] has used a franchise based business model to provide connectivity to rural people in India. This project has benefited both rural men and women in remote villages. With n-Logue and a Local Service Provider and Information Kiosk Operator, it has essentially provided rural internet cafes and pay phone booths in rural villages. N-Logue a pilot project (better known as SARI (Sustainable Access to Rural India) started in 2001, with an aim to provide communication services at low cost. The n-Logue uses Wireless Local Loop (WLL) to provide voice and data. This is a CorDect Technology (based on European Telecommunication Standards Institute Dect air interface) that uses radio frequency instead of wires.

CorDect provides voice, voice band FAX/DATA transfer and internet connectivity at 35-70 kbps to 1gbps when digitized. CorDect air interface can support to a maximum of 25kms of line-of sight connectivity. The internet connectivity is provided at a per-line access cost of Rs. 8000.Services offered by village information kiosk provided by N-Logue include giving online agricultural query, providing marketing prices, giving computer education and training, astrology, e-governance, online appointment with doctor, online registration for eye checkups and operation, movie shows for villagers, DTP work and to provide cartoon shows for village kiosks.

Vodacom [9] is a market leader in cellular communications providing GSM service to 21.5 million customers in Pan-African countries (South Africa, DRC, Tanzania, Mozambique and Lesotho). It launched its first 3G network in South Africa in 2004 and 3G HSDPA (offers internet connectivity at 1.8 Mbps) network in March 2006.The post-apartheid government under the President Nelson Mandela revised terms of license to provide under-serviced areas with cellular communications at low cost. With its unique community services and other activities Vodacom has served over 8 million subscribers and 4300 employees in urban and rural areas.

Vodacom Community Services phone franchise concept provides services in under-serviced, disadvantaged community. At a very low cost the prospective owner can start a franchise to operate multiple cellular lines in a pre-approved location. Most owners only operate one or two shops located in shipping containers. The consumer can make a phone call for 90 cents per minute. Although phone shops cannot receive calls due to the logistics of calculating pre-payments, individuals use it to pay bills, to call doctor, seek medical advice, to report service (electricity and water) outages, empowerment of women in townships by increasing the number of individuals who use cell phones and rely on phone shops to conduct business.

Another initiative in South Africa, UmNyango Project [10] has enabled rural women to report incidences of violence against women and children by using text messaging. This ongoing project will also allow women to produce their own radio programmes and allow them to distribute it via community radio. The other option is to distribute over the net as 'podcasts'. UmNyano project was established by Fahamu, an organization that supports the struggle of human rights and social justice in Africa. Fahamu publishes its prize-winning e-newsletter Pambazuka News (Pambazuka means arise or awaken in Kiswahili).

It is a tool for progressive social change in Africa. Its website www.pambazuka.org is updated every Thursday and consists of the latest news, commentary and analysis relevant to human rights and social justice organizations in Africa. Fahamu South Africa is one of the 10 winners of the Gender and Agriculture in the Information Society (GenARDIS) 2005 Award.

GrameenPhone [11] is a phone programme of Bangladesh's largest non-governmental organization, Grameen Bank. Low cost loans are only given to women to set up mobile phone exchanges in villages. Grameenphone ladies have set up these exchanges in locations where there are very few landines. It allows villagers to talk to their relatives abroad and provide vital link to hospitals.

GrameenPhone(GP) is a successful phone programme that introduces mobile technology to the rural women. Villagers flock to make calls at these exchanges and calls are charged per minute. It has helped rural women to alleviate poverty by earning US$1000 a year. GP's HealthLine service won the GSM Association's Global Mobile Award for Best use of Mobile for Social and Economic development. It is an interactive teleconference between the GP caller and a local physician. Health related information and medical advice are exchanged through out the day.

PEOPlink [12] is a non-profit organization that provides training and help to artisans to market their handmade items over the Internet. It equips grassroots artisan organizations and its talented producers in 22 developing countries to market their products online.

"CatGen.com" is a PEOPLink initiative that allows artisans and small and medium enterprises to use digital cameras and internet to market their products and showcase the services. Internet has enabled artisans mostly women to raise their sales, earning USD1-2 per day. The UNDP report "indicated that since 2004, 6756 artisans-jobs have been created through the use of CatGen in Nepal out of which 74% are women"[12]. Nepal's artisan's are currently marketing and selling their products online. Other countries using PEOPLink are Bangladesh, Kenya and other Asian and African countries.

Based on the various ICT initiatives discussed in this paper, for rural women in developing countries, the authors have derived Table 3. It gives insight on various opportunities that mobile technology and internet provide for successful empowerment of rural women.

The community projects discussed here shows that rural women may use mobile phone to increase local ties and for networking. Mobile phones would give them an opportunity to share their views and increase physical security. Sharing mobile phones with other community members helps to create a bond amongst rural women.

Table 3: Comparison of internet and mobile phones opportunities for rural women

General Opportunities for rural women	Internet	Mobile phone	Opportunities to improve social and community skills
Set reminder	*	x	
Appointment management	*	x	
Calendaring and scheduling	*	x	
Receive alerts	*	x	
Electronic document delivery	x	*	
Make long distance calls or local calls	*	x	
SMS and MMS (Multimedia message service)	*	x	
Spreadsheets	x	x	
Web content generation and surfing the net	x	*	
Access weather report or any agricultural information	x	x	
Exchange Email	x	x	
News update	x	x	
Provide ICT training	x	x	
Telemedicine	x	x	
For small business development	x	x	
Marketing products	x	x	
Web, video and audio conferencing	x	x	
Data Entry	x	x	
Instant messaging	x	x	

Table 3 (continued): Comparison of internet and mobile phones opportunities for rural women

General Opportunities for rural women	Internet	Mobile phone	Opportunities to improve social and community skills
Web discussions	x	*	
To exchange multimedia and graphics	x	x	
To report violence against women	x	x	
MP3 player	x	x	
Presentation applications	x	x	
Advertising products	x	x	
	x	x	Access community radio
	x	x	Improve participatory learning and communication
	x	x	Market Rural sports events
	*	x	Improve community bonds
	*	x	Increase physical security
	*	x	Improve speaker's confidence
	x	x	Rural appraisal
	x	*	Improve community trading

A '' in column "internet" and "x" in column "mobile phone" denotes with current technology limitations, rural women could use internet for the specific purpose only to a certain extent.. The "x" in both columns - "internet" and "mobile phone", denotes it is possible to use both internet and mobile phone for the given purpose.*

Table 3 further illustrates the possible social skills that rural women can improve by means of mobile phones and internet. 3G camera phones and internet will enable rural women to share and show pictures, access internet and exchange mails. Research has indicated how project team members in South Africa "successfully tested the use of SMS technology for rural women farmers in KwaZulu Natal to access agricultural extension information" [10]. Electronic communication via internet or mobile phones allows rural women to share their problems and enhance relationship with other community members. Mobile phones have helped them to be anonymous while reporting violence against women.

Rural population is scattered in wide geographical locations. So mobile phones would help their family to maintain contact with them while away at work in farms or while fetching water. Apart from providing physical security mobile technology has helped to improve rural women's confidence while speaking. Apart from this it allows them to conduct business more efficiently even with their international counterparts.

Telemedicine is the transmission of health related information. Infant mortality is relatively high in rural areas. This could be reduced by further knowledge on child bearing and health assistance during delivery. Telemedicine provides rural women support sessions that provide assistance to detect breast cancer, psychiatry assessment and treatment, to treat skin diseases etc.

For the successful empowerment of rural women using ICTs one needs to take into account how the ICT services are marketed amongst the women community, what kind of training is provided to rural women, affordability of services offered, competitiveness, relevance to rural women and service availability.

4. Critical factors for successful empowerment of rural women through internet and mobile phones

Critical analyses of various community projects discussed in this paper gives further insight on factors motivating and de-motivating rural women to use internet and mobile phones and possible solutions. These factors are explained below.

Marketing practices to promote ICT awareness: Good marketing practices are crucial for the growth of any business and to make ICT services popular amongst rural women. Product promotions and remuneration for using services are required to make women aware of services and benefits of ICTs. For example N-logue gives a gift for the winner of the lucky draw involving rural people who used their village information kiosk for a fixed duration. Other forms of advertising by N-logue include conducting autoshows about the kiosks in the village, door to door campaign, providing T-shirts to students with Chirag (N-logue's logo).

Training: It is very important to train the trainers. The trainer (women prefer women trainers) for an internet kiosk or community center must be trained so that they can provide further assistance. SEWA has its unique Training of Trainers (ToT) programmes that train the women trainers on practical experiences on role of trainers and in leading and training work groups. Another example is how company trainers from Vodacom travel nation wide and provide business, financial and HR training to the people who own phone shops.

Choupal: The concept of a community gathering (choupal) is very significant for any rural community's socio-economic development. GrameenPhone has reached the rural women community through the local champion in the community who encourages and influences other members (during choupal) of the community to access ICT.

Relevance to the community: Any ICT initiative provided by government or NGOs should focus on empowerment of community and target group (women) in particular. Installation of phone shops by Vodacom, Women'sNet Digital Story Telling Workshop, SEWA'S salt training and embroidery training and marketing craft products online – all these were successful due to the fact that they targeted on how relevant the ICT services provided benefited the community.

Use of global language for content generation: Language would not be a barrier while using internet for surfing, to a certain extent. Although English is one of the medium for on-line communication (especially via net), when it comes to training how to use the web-site, the trainers often communicate in local language. In most cases only the trainer would know this global language used for international communication. One needs to note how rural women were able to overcome the language barrier and use internet for surfing on artisan information and marketing products via PEOPLink website. Nowadays the web content is also generated in local languages for effective use of web portal by rural community. The manufacturers of mobile phones have included facilities to access contents in local languages. The other option would be 'local language to English' translation software. This would cater for communication via a global language and international trading. Anusaraka (www.iiit.net/anu/anu_home.html) is a machine translation project that allows users to translate web resources between various Indian languages and also access English language resources.

Low cost ICT: ICTs provided to rural women should be of low cost. Affordability is an issue when it comes to accessing internet and telephony. Most of the organizations discussed here have gone the low cost route. Lessons from Women'sNet's technology planning programmes shows how women's organizations make use of FOSS and hence provide low cost training. Linux is free and open source software and is the popular one used amongst women's organizations in South Africa for training. With the help of SANGONet, about 50 South African NGOs signed a petition to Minister for Public Service and Administration to encourage government to proactively drive change toward adoption of an open source policy. FOSS is free and open and if used, makes it is easy to create a local support capacity. N-logue used low investment low cost technology to cover communication needs of rural people.

Encouraging competitive market: The ease to which the business enters and exits the rural community should be taken into account. MTN another cell phone provider in South Africa has its yellow shipping containers with phone shops as close as possible to Vodacom's green shipping containers. Both cell phone providers target on the same under-serviced community and provide the same facility in phone shops. Women's organizations should help in buying and selling some of the products made by rural women and give a higher price based on quality.

Written Communication: SEWA's Anasooya, Vodacom's Ringer, SANGONet's NGO-Pulse and Women'sNet's Intersections e-newsletter all share experiences of the way rural women and women's organizations empower themselves by accessing ICTs. These newsletters are periodicals which provides useful information for other women and women's organisations to learn how to empower themselves using ICTs.

Connectivity: Internet connectivity should be provided in village information kiosk or a community center, for rural women to communicate with the world. Research shows all the organizations discussed here have a web portal and most of them have e-newletter. N-Logue's WLL systems are running across rural using radio link installations India operating on the 802.11 wireless protocol. SEWA has all its embroidered products online to compete with the global market. Women'sNet has conducted its Digital Story Telling Workshop to help women to talk about their survival strategies, gender discrimination, poverty, violence, HIV/AIDS illness.

Creativity: Video and still photography would be a creative medium to allow women to be vocal about their issues. Creativity is necessary for any form of communication. Note how SEWA members used video cameras to show their protest to municipal Commissioner for not allowing the use of market places for selling vegetables. This tape was a turning point for constructive negotiations. Another initiative is Women's Voices Kenya (Practical Action project) that used video camera to show unrest in settlements, HIV Aids issues etc.

Service availability and reliability: When the services are unavailable for a long time women may loose interest in ICT adoption. It is important to keep track of frequency of usage of the service provided for rural women. For example women would not want to waste their time trying to get connected. Although, at this stage it is something to dream about for under-serviced communities in most developing countries, mobile phones with HSDPA data cards (offers internet connectivity at 1.8 Mbps) would be an advantage to rural connectivity in near future. QUALCOMM Inc.'s Wireless Reach initiative discussed in this paper shows how it partnered with MTN to provide 3G high-speed internet connectivity to pay-phone shops in Alexandra (an under-serviced township in South Africa).

Human Computer Interaction: The physical user interfaces for outputting and inputting information using a mobile phone should be taken into consideration when designing interfaces for mobile phones. These graphical user interfaces should vary for urban and their rural counterparts, depending on their needs, interest and cultural values. Nowadays mobile phone companies pay more attention on the design of the hardware than the physical user interfaces for targeted group. The internet should be a tool for assisting rural women to communicate with their international counterparts and the interfaces created should cater for hand gestures and facial expressions.

Participatory technical development: Experts and researchers should brief local people about the specific technology to be developed for rural women. Rural women's participation in research and technical development is crucial for their empowerment and would take their needs into consideration. Participatory learning and action research allow mutual learning between rural people and researcher. It would also cater to decentralize and transfer the decision making power to rural women.

Documenting rural women's achievements while using ICT: We need to document the wonderful stories on how rural women use innovative ways for empowerment using ICTs despite all odds. For example not many people are aware that rural women use SMS technology to report violence against them, or to market their small business. Apart from creating avenues for sharing own experiences, these reports and documentation would make other rural women in community aware, how powerful internet and mobile phones are for their empowerment.

4.1 Bottlenecks, factors de-motivating rural women to use ICTs and solutions

Electronic communication via SMS or internet and e-mail often lack the aspect of face-to-face communication. This is one of important bottlenecks while introducing rural women to mobile technology. Rural women are so used to face-to-face conversations in community gatherings. To an extent video-conferencing would allow such conversations with other community members.

Electronic relationships hinder people's ability to show their emotions. Somehow rural women tend to be more emotional and loud than their urban counterparts. The use of mobile phones inhibits rural women to show emotions more freely. To an extent being anonymous would help rural women to report violence or incidents of unrest in settlements. Another important threat of electronic communication is deception, especially while exchanging ideas over the net.

Another de-motivating factor that hinders use of mobile phones is the prevalent health threats related to its usage. The use of mobile phones will expose the person using it to heat generated when radio frequency (RF) energy is absorbed into the body. Studies are underway to find whether exposure to such low RF fields will cause diseases. The "speaker phone" option allows people to hold handset a little away from body, and thus reducing the RF exposure to a bare minimum.

Prolonged use of computers and mobile phones may affect sleeping patterns, and reaction times. Using mobile phones while driving may cause accidents. This can be avoided by using hands-free device. The prolonged use of computers may cause backache and headache. Proximity to medical devices while using mobile phones may cause electromagnetic interference as well.

African women have the lowest participation rates in use of Information and communication technologies. Some of the challenges faced by rural women in ICT adoption are:

- Lack of internet access other than through local institutions, governments and some health centers or even churches.
- Lack of effective dissemination medium (street theatre / radio) which demonstrates full potential of internet and mobile phones.
- Not focusing on the sectors in which ICTs will be of most use to women.
- Language barrier (not always)
- Geographical location of the internet kiosk
- Social and cultural norms
- Lack of access to resources like computer
- Lack of education and computer literacy among rural women
- Lack of telecenters in some local communities
- Lack of interest in technology adoption
- Lack of participation in meetings or themes which focus on ICT for development

As James mentions about the information on internet there is very little that "..*rural people in developing countries can understand and use*" [13]. If the gendered digital divide is to be closed the countervailing ICT policies should incorporate ICT services at low cost and take into account the needs of rural women.

Robert Chambers amongst others has criticized that the knowledge of rural poor often is quite advanced and innovative, more so than most professionals would think [14]. So the ICT projects or initiatives in developing world should take into account the needs and the knowledge of rural men and women. Women targeted programs to create ICT awareness will give females full realization of the opportunities ICT can present for women. There is a need to integrate ICTs' into girls' education and expose them to new technologies, as women are less confident in their skills.

Some of the projects done by SEWA and Women'sNet have become role models in providing ICT training to meet the needs of rural women.There should be a provision to create and encourage business friendly environment for women while using technologies. The rural women should be given local training in ICT skills through women's organizations which reduces high cost of expatriate skills. Internet access should be affordable to rural women.

5. Conclusion

Information and communication technology is highly fragmented and difficult to access especially for rural women. The purpose of this paper is to attract attention of NGO's, policy makers and researchers to categorize the priority areas for gender equity and to find the success factors influencing use of internet and mobile phones by rural women for empowerment.

In future affordable wireless service will reach under-serviced market and the rural women in these areas will use mobile solutions for broadband connectivity.

Research has found a technical mix of telecommunications systems will benefit rural women for empowerment. Community projects described in this paper gives a clear indication of how rural women were able to overcome language barrier, lack of mobility, social and cultural norms and used internet and mobile phones for empowerment. It was clear that if NGO's and women's organizations used a low-cost innovative ICT it would motivate women to use it. A lack of interest in ICT adoption and location of internet kiosks sometimes de-motivated them to use internet.

A full understanding of gendered digital divide requires more qualitative and participatory action research. There is a scope for future research on participatory learning and technical development and find out innovative ways of rural women appraisal. Rural women's participation in research and development is very important to develop any ICT that they might use. They play an important role in producing much of the subsistence food crops. ICTs play an important role in food production and natural resource management. There is scope for future research on how rural women use mobile technology and internet for accessing agricultural information.

The deployment of Information and Communication Technologies (ICTs) in developing countries has become a key strategy of the international development community to support poverty reduction strategies [15].The ICT awareness and ICT project handling skills of rural women in developing countries - one of the factors affecting gender equity need to be monitored. There is a need to monitor and evaluate ICT policies for women in the least developed countries.

6. Acknowledgements

The authors are grateful to the reviewers for their insightful comments. We express sincere gratitude to Mr. Patrick Burnett, Pambazuka News/Fahamu, Ms. Sibil Jhaveri, The PRactice Contact: QUALCOMM India Pvt. Ltd., Ms. Shubhram Tripati, SEWA, India, Ms. Kwena Moyo, Vodacom, South Africa, Ms. Janine Moolman, Information and Media Manager, Women's Net, South Africa, Ms. Aadila Molale, Database Manager, Fazila Farouk Deputy Director/Editor and Butjwana Seokoma, Information Coordinator working in SANGONeT's Civil Society Information team, South Africa for providing valuable information during interviews.

7. References

[1] M. Carr, (September 16 2006); Gender and technology: Is there a problem?" Paper for TOOL Consult Conference on Technology and Development: Strategies for the Integration of Gender, Amsterdam; www.unifem.undp.org/ g&tech.htm.

[2] India Telecom News (March 7 2007); http://www.indiatelecomnews.com/newdetails.asp?newsid=534

[3] Wireless reach (March 7 2007); http://www.qualcomm.com/press/PDF/WirelessReach_Overview.pdf

[4] A.P.J.A. Kalam, (August 21 2006); Speech by Honorable President of India to SEWA members (2003); http://www.sewa.org/events/index.asp#

[5] K. Annan, Secretary General, United Nations, Announcing the need for a Summit onInformation and Communications Technology (ICT), World Summit on the InformationSociety (1999).

[6] N.Puican, Gender review in the InfoDev project *Information Systems for Rural Development: A Demonstration Project*. (2002).

[7] SEWA (Nov 28 2006); http://www.sewa.org/aboutus/index.asp

[8] N-logue (Nov 12 2006); http://www.n-logue.com/

[9] Vodacom (Mar 7 2007); http://www.vodacom.co.za/welcome.do

[10]   UmNyango   Project   (Mar   7   2007); http://www.pambazuka.org/en/category/advocacy/38739

[11] Grameenphone (February 12 2007); http://www.grameenphone.com

[12] PEOPLink (Mar 7 2006); www.peoplelink.org

[13] J. James, Pro-Poor Modes of Technical Integration into the Global Economy, *Development and Change*, Vol. 31, pp 765-783 (2000).

[14] R. Chambers, *Rural Development. Putting the Last First* (Pearson Education Limited, England, 1983).

[15] C. Jauering, Review of Telecentre Sustainability Criteria for the Establishment of Sustainable Rural Business Resource Centers for SMMEs in Developing Countries, (United Nations Industrial Development Organization, Vienna, 2003).

Untapped Resources! Amazing Potential! TeNeT's Rural BPO Initiative

Saloni Malhotra[1], P.Rathi[2], Timothy A. Gonsalves[2], Ashok Jhunjhunwala[2], Thejus Giri[3]

1 DesiCrew Solutions(P) Ltd. ,
2 TeNeT Group of IIT Madras,
3 Nilgiri Networks(P) Ltd. , Ooty

Abstract: DesiCrew is a unique Business Process Outsourcing (BPO) initiative that provides high volume data related services at an affordable cost from rural areas across India. The model provides cost cutting alternatives to urban clients and new sources of income and employment to the villagers, by leveraging Internet technology. The DesiCrew central team in Chennai manages training of rural workforce, distribution and monitoring of work, quality control and client interaction all remotely. In this paper, we describe the Rural BPO model and one specific application, data entry of forms. We describe the software, Pegasus, developed for this purpose and explain the management of the distributed workforce.

1 Introduction

In a village in South India, with a population of six thousand, where the primary occupation is weaving, Thenmozhi, a young graduate, runs an Internet kiosk business. With a single internet-connected computer, she provides a variety of services to the community that includes browsing, games, photography, education, and Desk Top Publishing among other BPO services. Over a period of a year, her income has grown and she has added two more computers to the kiosk. Today, with three PCs, she provides Business Process Outsourcing (BPO) services such as data entry and data conversion to clients located in distant urban centres.

In another village, Rosy, a young mother, runs a kiosk where she employs four people and provides BPO services such as Localization of content and Computer Aided Design (CAD). While these stories are undoubtedly incongruent with our

Please use the following format when citing this chapter:

Malhotra, S., Rathi, P., Gonsalves, T. A., Jhunjhunwala, A., Giri, T., 2007, in IFIP International Federation for Information Processing, Volume 241, Home Informatics and Telematics: ICT for the Next Billion, eds. Venkatesh, A., Gonsalves, T., Monk, A., Buckner, K., (Boston: Springer), pp. 21-33.

predominant perceptions of rural India, indeed today BPO operations are making their way to the most remote and unlikely parts in the country.

As celebrated New York Times columnist, Thomas Friedman, observes in his latest book *The World Is Flat* [1], "all you need now is a global, web-enabled platform for multiple forms of sharing knowledge and work, irrespective of time, distance, geography and increasingly, language". As rural India increasingly becomes more connected, there is no reason that jobs cannot move - as they have from London to Bangalore – further to Vadalur, an unheard of village in the southern state of Tamil Nadu. Today there are approximately 15,000 Internet-enabled villages in India. With various efforts underway toward enabling rural connectivity, such as Mission 2007 and the Common Service Centre [2] scheme of the Government of India, this number is projected to reach 100,000 by 2008. In this scenario, the potential for the rural BPO industry can only be expected to grow.

In this paper, this unique initiative of the TeNeT [3] of IIT Madras is described. First the business model is discussed in Section 2. This is followed by a description of the software used for one aspect of BPO in Section 4. The paper is concluded with our future vision in Section 6.

2 The Rural BPO Business Model [4]

The TeNeT at IIT-Madras has worked over the past 26 months on a Rural BPO initiative that links urban clients with a rural workforce through the Internet kiosk network. This is now spun off as the company DesiCrew [5]. The team identifies and trains workers in rural areas in various skills relevant to the BPO industry. It liaises with urban clients and takes complete responsibility for the outsourcing and timely delivery of the projects undertaken, and ensures that quality standards are met. As a coordinating agency, the team protects the interests of both the clients and the kiosks. At the village-end it filters out unproductive kiosks from the system, and at the city-end it runs due diligence checks on the client to guard against fraudulent BPO activity.

This unique initiative has a portfolio of services that includes
1.   Typing in English and regional languages,
2.   Data entry operations, web and multimedia development and
3.   Regional language translation.

More recently, engineering services such as 2D drafting and conversion of 2D to 3D for the manufacturing sector have also been introduced.

The model today runs on a smaller scale, with 3-4 seats in each center and an entrepreneur is responsible for hiring and managing the staff, ensuring that timelines and quality standards are adhered to, and managing daily operations. However a typical rural BPO center envisaged in the future would consist of 10 PCs running in two shifts. Each center would employ between 10-20 individuals.

2.1   Impacts and Benefits

BPO activity in India is clustered around 5 main hubs today. These centers will continue to remain important in the future, but the industry is looking to expand to other locations for several reasons:

1. Newer locations would imply access to a larger workforce

2. Provide an opportunity to further reduce costs of operation

3. Acquire language-specific skills for the domestic industry

4. Mitigate overall business risk and ensure business continuity

5. Reduce the pressure on infrastructure being faced in the current locations

Rural areas can be attractive outsourcing destinations for the BPO industry due to the following reasons:

Access to available infrastructure: Currently 15,000 rural internet kiosks have been set up across the country. Even at a modest 10%, 1,500 such centers could be utilized for the purpose of Rural BPOs.

Access to untapped and well trained work force: The model employs 10-20 individuals in each village. At 1500 villages with 20 employees, the rural BPO has the potential of bringing 30,000 youth into the workforce, considering the existing infrastructure.

Lower costs of operation: A reduction of 50-60% in costs can be achieved using this model owing to the lower cost of living, real estate and overheads in a rural area.

Bench strength at a lower cost: Leverage low cost resources to maintain mandatory bench size.

Improve skill levels at lower training costs: About 70% of Indian youth remain under/ unemployed in the first 3 years after graduation. Such resources can be trained at a lower cost in the rural BPO settings.

Scalability: Significant amount of time at DesiCrew is spent at how to leverage a workforce distributed across different villages. Tools, applications, processes and policy have been laid down to ensure rapid scalability.

Strong regional language skills can be leveraged for domestic outsourcing work including regional language call centers.

Presence of a entrepreneur: The existence of an entrepreneur running a rural BPO center ensures local knowledge of the location and culture. The entrepreneur is also a trusted entry point into the village.

DesiCrew's rural BPO model offers significant benefits to the rural population. With IT training, the youth in rural areas are exposed to skills that are highly valued in today's economy. As a result their productivity and incomes increase, and so also their personal confidence. The entire rural economy begins to thrive as more money flows into villages, allowing for more equitable economic growth at the national level.

While the concept described above has been executed with encouraging results, the challenge is to scale it to thousands of villages.

3 Network Architecture

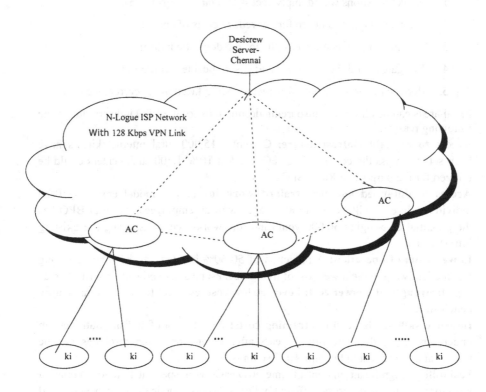

 VPN Link 128 Kbps

―――――   LAN 35-70 Kbps

AC   Access Centre

Fig 1: Internet Connectivity used by DesiCrew for Rural BPO

DesiCrew works closely with a partner, N-Logue communications [6], a rural ISP to reach the connected population in rural areas. N-Logue provides the internet connectivity for the rural BPO centres through the Access Centres located at the district level. Kiosks are internet centres at villages. The Access Centres are connected across in a VPN link provided by the N-Logue. The kiosks at each village are connected to their respective Access Centres through a LAN of 35-70 Kbps bandwidth. DesiCrew uses this infrastructure.

4   Need for Pegasus

DesiCrew Solutions have taken up the challenge of distributing work from the city to the rural areas where the available skills are seldom utilised. For DesiCrew to do such work requires appropriate processes to distribute work, manage and monitor work, make quality checks, collect work and redistribute to clients.

Given the scenario of a distributed workforce, DesiCrew requires a web-based application to do all of the above. One such application built is Pegasus, a web-based application that supports remote distribution and supervision of work.

Pegasus is an online data entry software where the image of the to-be digitized data appear on the upper half of the browser and the lower half has the form for data entry. The entered data are stored on a central server from where the data is consolidated and sent to the client. The data can also be used for various supervisory reports.

As seen in the image, Pegasus consists of a split screen interface with a digital replica of the image to be entered. The operator is required to look at the image above and enter the data in the HTML replica below. The images and the data entered are stored on a central server for the purpose of security.

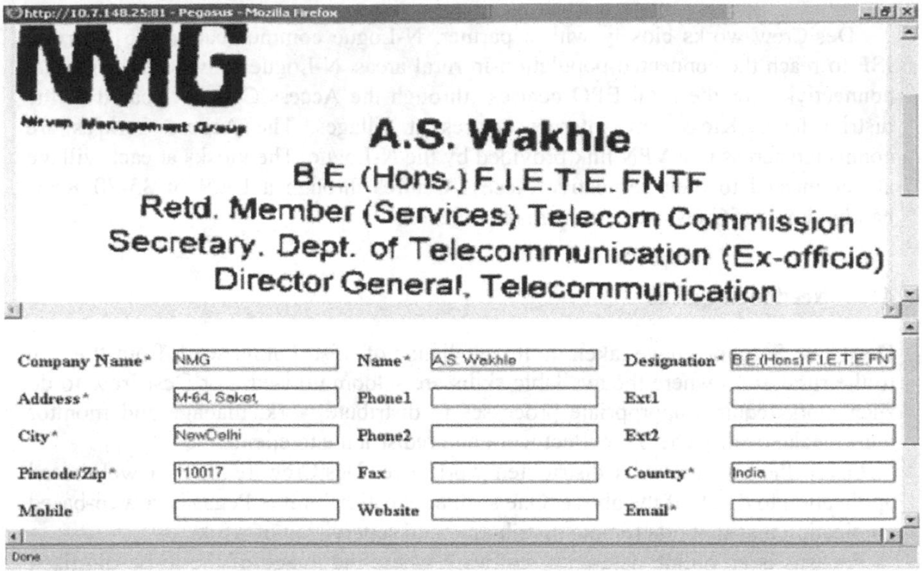

Fig 2: Screenshot of Image (Top half) and DataEntry Form (Bottom half)

4.1   Features of Pegasus

1. **Productivity:**
   (i) Tracks number of forms entered
   (ii) No of errors
   (iii) Time per form
2. **Validation:** Field validations such as date, email, phone number, etc.
3. Report Generation

Table 1. Users of the Application, their roles and responsiblities

S.No.	User	Rights	Roles & Responsibilities
1	First Entry Operator	Enter data, View Performance Reports	Enters Data
2	Second Entry Operator	Enter data, View Performance Reports	Enters Data
3	Coordinator	View mismatches between First and Second Entry Data, View His own Performance Reports	Verifies mismatches, Corrects Data, Specifies error comments

S.No.	User	Rights	Roles & Responsibilities
4	Admin	Views all Operator and Activity Reports, Add/Delete Activity, Add/Delete Operator	Adds Activity, Adds operators to Activity, Manages and supervises the whole process

4.2   Process Flow Diagram

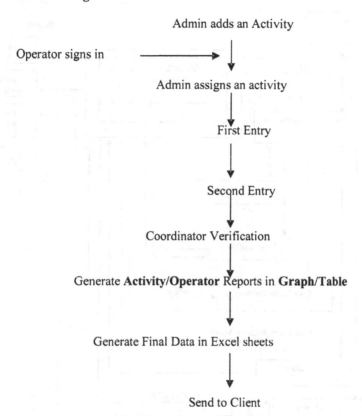

Admin adds an Activity

Operator signs in

Admin assigns an activity

First Entry

Second Entry

Coordinator Verification

Generate **Activity/Operator** Reports in **Graph/Table**

Generate Final Data in Excel sheets

Send to Client

Fig 3: Process Flow of Data Entry Outsourcing

Activity: The work related to each client is defined as an activity. Adding an activity to Pegasus involves specifying duration of the activity, number of operators required,number of forms to be filled, tariff to be followed for payments, uploading of images, etc. Pegasus supports two types of Activities-Regular and Training.

Administrator adds an activity to the Pegasus system. Whenever a new operator signs up, the administrator assigns him to an activity after which the operator is allowed to do dataentry. First, Second and Coordinator entries are done in sequence by the three types of operators. The Final data is now available in the system for generation of reports and the consolidated data is sent to the client.

4.3 Design of Pegasus

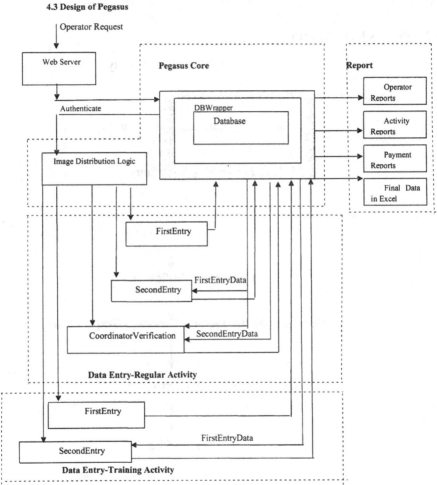

Fig 4: Block Diagram of Pegasus

Pegasus has a light-weight web services design [7] using fully open-source software. The core is written in PHP and runs on Linux with data stored in Postgresql RDBMS. The user interface runs in a browser on the kiosk PC. It uses AJAX technology [8] for fast response over slow rural connections.

4.4   Pegasus Core

The Pegasus Core comprises of the database which is accessed and manipulated by the APIs through the DBWrapper classes. The Pegasus Core logic handles any user requests for authentication. It also handles expiry of sessions in case of idle time.

ImageDistributionLogic
Based on the type of operator and the status of an image the Image Distribution Logic fetches the same in the browser. Once the image is accessed it's status is changed such that the same image does not reappear. The Image distribution logic determines which type of operator gets what images based on the image status. An image which has been idle on the browser without being entered is checked and reverted to it's original status.

Download of images is optimized for low bandwidth situations such as 35 kbps by AJAX. The image is also provided with zooming option for clarity on browser.

An additional training module is incorporated in Pegasus wherein the same set of images are distributed across to all authenticated trainees.

The Image distribution logic works in such a way that the same image never appears for another user for a regular activity whereas for a training activity the same set of images appear for all users.

Image Downloading
The image size is reduced to about 20-40 KB/page. Over the 35 Kbps link to the kiosk the download time is about 20 seconds. Note that during this time the operator is idle. If the operator takes 30 sec/page to enter the data, she is idle for about 40% of the time. This affects productivity. We are exploring techniques to reduce this idle time by overlapping the fetching of the next image with the dataentry of one image. Another alternative is is distribution of images on CD. This would require special precaution to preserve the security of data.

4.5   Data Entry

Pegasus supports triple data Entry for greater accuracy and reliability of data. The process of Data Entry requires a person to view the image on the browser and type the data in the form provided below. DataEntry Component allows DataEntry in three steps by three different types of operators-FirstEntry, SecondEntry and CoordinatorEntry. This has the

First Entry: An operator in this phase enters the data with reference to the image on the screen. The data is transferred to the database. Additionally the DataEntry component records the number of keystrokes, time and duration of updation.

SecondEntry: A second entry operator is allowed to enter the data in the same way as a first entry operator. Additionally this component retrieves the first entry data for this image for the second entry operator for correction incase of mismatches.

Co ordinator Verification: To add to the accuracy of the entered data, the Data Entry Logic also supports a verification by the co ordinator. He is provided with the data entered by the first and second entry operators for each image which has mismatches. The approval/rejection of the data of first and second entry operators by the coordinator results in computation of error percentage which in turn affects the Payout.

Trainee Entry: The first entry for a training activity is done by the administrator. The trainee does the second entry. Pegasus gives the trainee his error reports based on the mismatches from the administrator's entry.

4.6   Report Generation

Graphical and Tabular reports are generated for Activity,Operator and Payments Reports.

Operator Reports: Performance reports of each operator can be generated giving information about the number of forms filled, keystrokes and error percentage.

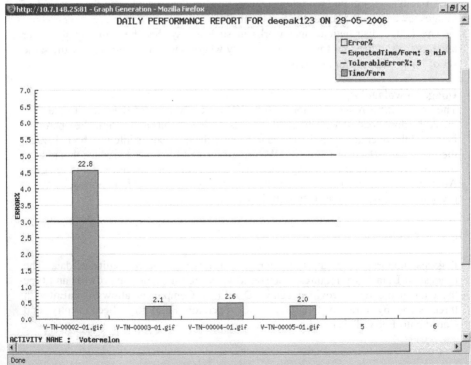

Fig 5: Sample Daily Report of an operator

Pegasus core does the computation of the error percentage and speed of each operator based on the number of keystrokes.

- Daily Performance Reports
- Weekly Performance Reports
- Overall Performance Reports
- Performance Comparison

Each bar (See Fig 5) corresponds to each form filled by the operator. For each form filled by the operator the time taken/form and the number of errors are tracked Error % is calculated and compared with the Tolerable Error% and time/form with Expected Time/Form.

Activity Reports: Activity Reports (See Fig 6) contain all possible information about the activity such as start and End dates of activity, name of Activity Manager, number of operators working in the activity, status of the activity at any point of time, etc. At every stage the reports provide information about the scheduled activity and the actual status of it.

Payment Reports: Based on the tariff chosen for the activity, number of forms filled by each operator and error percentage payment reports are generated. Payout Module handles two types of payouts-Based on Keystrokes, Based on Forms Filled. It also generates periodic reports about the payments made and to-be made for each operator.

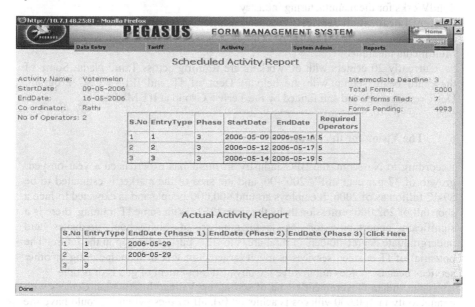

Fig 6: Screenshot of Activity Report

Session Management: Session management is used to keep track of the user logged in to the application. This is helpful to keep track of the operator activity internally

Pegasus is a secure web-based data entry software due to

Login: Each user is provided with a login account which helps the administrator to keep track of who accessed the images and when.

VPN: The data transfer is in VPN and cannot be accessed by any intruder/hacker on the Internet.

Restricted Access: The images reside at the server and are not available for downloading /editing those images from any client.

The images are not cached in the browsers and hence a copy of an image at the local machine is not available.

Cut/Copy/Paste/SaveAs options are prevented by disabling the right click on the image.

5   About DesiCrew

DesiCrew acts as a one point contact for the client and takes responsibility for assuring quality and delivery within the timeline. DesiCrew offers the following services:

Administrative Services: Includes services like digitization and data entry, data collection from secondary sources, data validation

Engineering Services: Covers 2D drafting in AutoCAD and 2D to 3D modeling in SolidWorks for the manufacturing industry

Content Localization Services: Entails translation of text and voice from English to regional languages (eg Tamil) by schoolteachers and integration with Web and Multimedia mediums

Currently 20 centers with 60 workers are running across Tamil Nadu. Some of these are being set up with the help of Dept of IT and ILFS's CSC Program. DesiCrew is supported and funded by the TeNeT Group at IIT Madras.

6   The Vision for the Future

According to Nasscom, the BPO industry in India has experienced a year-on-year growth of 37 per cent in FY 2005-06, and the size of the market is estimated to be $9-12 billion as of 2006. It employs around 400,000 people and is expected to face a shortfall of 262,000 professionals by the year 2012. With some IT training, there is a significant opportunity for the large number of high-school graduates and undergraduate degree-holders in rural areas to fill a part of this gap in the future. The potential of IT-enabled services is much larger than that of manufacturing or other services because it does not involve the physical movement of goods or people.

If the Indian Government's goal of setting up Village Information Centers with connectivity in 100,000 villages is achieved [9], all of these villages would have the potential to act as BPO centers. Consider 10% of these villages employing 20 people at an average salary of $65 per month. This would directly add $1.56 billion to the rural economy per annum and create 200,000 jobs. The demand for several allied industries such as hardware servicing and software development would also grow.

The Rural BPO team envisions playing a significant role in this IT revolution, by leveraging the power of computing and connectivity to create wealth in rural areas.

The team intends to build capacity in villages, create the right systems and networks for remote business operations and ensure the highest level of professionalism and quality standards. The group believes that this is not just a significant business opportunity, but also a means to catapult the pace of rural development in the country under a wholly different paradigm.

6   References

1.   Thomas Friedman, *The World is Flat*, Farrar, Straus and Giroux, April 2005.
2.   http://www.ocac.in/csc/Default.asp
3.   http://tenet.res.in/
4.   http://ites.tenet.res.in/
5.   http://desicrew.in/
6.   http://www.n-logue.com/
7.   T.A. Gonsalves, "Web Services For Rural India", *CSI Communications*, Vol 29, No 9, March 2006, PP 21-23.
8.   http://www.modernmethod.com/*sajax, http://en.wikipedia.org/wiki/AJAX
9.   Source For VIC – 1,00,000 – Mission 2007
10.   *Rural BPOs 14D*, Leading International magazine on ICT for Development, September 2006 issue on ICTs and Small Medium Business

A Set of Heuristic Measurements for Evaluating the Inclusiveness of a Technology

K. Pitula and T. Radhakrishnan
Department of Computer Science and Software Engineering
Concordia University, Montreal, Canada

Abstract. At a high level of abstraction, 'social inclusion' can be defined as the extent to which an individual or community can fully participate in society and control their own collective destiny. There are large disparities in this, particularly in underdeveloped rural areas of the world. Information and communication technologies designed to address this disparity must take into account the many barriers in the use of technology that these communities face. We define an 'inclusive technology' as a technology which overcomes the barriers to using technology inherent within a given community and increases the opportunities available to that community. We propose a conceptual model and a set of heuristic measurements for examining the 'inclusiveness' of a technology with respect to a given community, and illustrate their use by applying them to two real-world projects. By proposing this model and set of measurements, we hope to achieve a better understanding of 'development projects' and create a systematic process and a framework to assist software engineers in designing and evaluating software based services intended to reduce the Digital Divide.

1 Introduction

In this information age, the ability to access and understand the right information in a timely fashion has become essential. There are significant disparities in the socio-economic opportunities available to people in rural versus urban areas throughout the world, contributing to inequities in the ability to use *Information and Communication Technologies* (ICT) to access information and services [1]. New low cost technologies such as inexpensive computers, wireless connected hand-held devices, and open source software tools, offer possibilities for reducing this gap. However, experience has shown that simply providing access to technology is insufficient. What people need is the ability to make use of technology in order to engage in meaningful and gainful social activities in a sustainable manner [2]. We introduce the term 'inclusive technology' to emphasise this dual aspect of technology and its sustainable use for benefit.

Please use the following format when citing this chapter:

Pitula, K., Radhakrishnan, T., 2007, in IFIP International Federation for Information Processing, Volume 241, Home Informatics and Telematics: ICT for the Next Billion, eds. Venkatesh, A., Gonsalves, T., Monk, A., Buckner, K., (Boston: Springer), pp. 35-48.

In recent years, numerous ICT projects have attempted to bring the benefits of technology to marginalised communities. While the literature is full of case studies describing the launch of pilot projects in optimistic terms, the lack of rigour in evaluating and monitoring many of these projects raises questions about their long term success and sustainability [3]. Experience indicates that technology designed for marginalized communities poses unique design challenges and requires a multidisciplinary approach [4]. Current efforts to develop a systematic framework for assessing such projects, such as the *Digital Opportunity Index* defined by the WSIS [5] or the IDRC guidelines [6], largely focus on measuring technology use in the population or the impact of technology on society at a macroscopic level.

In this paper, we tackle the design challenge by applying a software engineering approach to designing technology to bring sustainable, measurable benefits to a community. By the term 'technology' we refer to the complex combination of hardware, software, content, information accessibility and the social infrastructure that allows people to benefit from it. Drawing on theoretical frameworks and empirical results from sociology, rural development, and technology adoption, we investigate how a given community can 'appropriate' a technology and put it to its own beneficial use. We propose a parameterised, conceptual model and a preliminary set of heuristic measurements to assess a technology's 'inclusiveness', where 'inclusiveness' characterises to what extent a given community can use a specific technology to achieve its goals. We then apply this model to some actual, real-life projects described in the literature.

We believe that such a model would be useful to software engineers when designing a targeted software project to address issues pertaining to the Digital Divide. With our model we hope to achieve the following:

1. Develop a better understanding of the Digital Divide problem domain on a project by project basis by modeling the key concepts and their relationships and attributes.
2. Provide the basis for a theoretical model that can be used to share the positive and negative experiences of the ICT4D community.
3. Augment the software design process with a systematic sub-process for 'situation based analysis' of technology inclusiveness, and develop a framework to assist software engineers in designing technology for projects in the Digital Divide domain.

Inclusive technology. At a high level of abstraction, social inclusion can be defined as the extent to which an individual or community can fully participate in society and control their own destinies. Among the many motives for social interaction, our focus is on the need for information at the individual level, by people who live in and are influenced by a community. The ability to use the appropriate technology plays a critical role in this regard, and there are several recognised barriers to achieving it. These barriers consist of access to (a) the physical resources such as devices and infrastructure, (b) the digital information resources such as software and content, (c) the human resources which correspond to the skills people need to extract and apply knowledge, and (d) the social resources which refers to the broader social context in which the technology is applied [2]. However, simply addressing these barriers does not guarantee that a technology will be used by its intended users. According to the *Unified Theory of Acceptance and Use of Technology* (UTAUT) model, a technology must be perceived as beneficial, easy to use, and socially endorsed, with an adequate infrastructure in place to support its use [7]. To meet these objectives a technology must be relevant to the needs of the community, it must expand on existing knowledge and skills, and it must be affordable and sustainable. To be part of a sustainable cycle, the benefits that can be derived from using the technology must balance the costs. Such a technology that fits into and is compatible with its environment is considered 'appropriate' [1]. All of these factors must be taken into account for a software project to be successful.

Based on the above, we define an 'inclusive technology' as a technology which empowers community members to more fully participate in benefiting from the information services provided so as to make a difference in their decisions and their lives. What changes are beneficial will be specific to a community's needs and values, but in general will increase the opportunities available to the advantage of the entire community. The ability to use and benefit from the information services will vary depending on several factors. To give some examples of factors that would contribute to making a technology inclusive with respect to some community, if a device is affordable, if the infrastructure on which it relies is available, if the software and content are in the local language, if people have or can develop the skills to use it, and if it addresses a local need, then all of these factors would contribute to enabling that community to benefit from using that technology.

2 Conceptual model of inclusive technology

Our conceptual model of inclusive technology is based on Maslow's Theory whereby needs motivate human behaviour. Here we briefly describe the key concepts of our model. A more detailed description is provided in [8]. Based on the literature on rural development, we characterise the rural communities in which we are interested as follows [9, 10]:

- They are remote, making transportation and communications costs prohibitive
- Livelihoods of community members are largely based on subsistence activities
- Household incomes are low, at or below the poverty level
- Many communities have limited or no public services and utilities such as schools, health clinics, banks, government services, electricity, phone lines, etc.
- Most community members speak primarily local languages
- Schooling is limited, leading to low reading and writing skills
- Most community members have limited or no exposure to computer technology

According to our model, the rural environment in which a community is embedded largely shapes that community's socio-economic activity. This in turn largely determines that community's needs. A community is composed of individuals who are connected in one way or the other. Needs motivate an individual to identify goals whose achievement will result in a quantifiable or qualifiable gain, which is the motivating factor for undertaking that activity. Achieving these goals requires both knowledge and action. Acquiring that knowledge and acting upon it, both require a set of skills, resources and tools. We divide these latter into two disjoint subsets: ICT specific and *non* ICT specific. This is depicted in the Entity-Relationship diagram presented in Fig. 1.

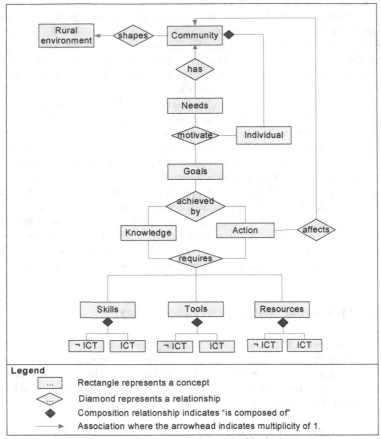

Fig. 1. ER diagram of a conceptual model of inclusive technology

Within this model, a sustainable cycle is achieved by selecting goals which result in a balance between social and economic benefits. This cycle can be described as follows: 'needs' stimulate the discovery of relevant 'knowledge' which leads to 'actions' resulting in 'benefits'. As the community's situation improves, its needs evolve creating more 'wants' stimulating the discovery of more relevant knowledge, and so forth. This process is illustrated in Fig. 2.

Our focus is on evaluating the ICT specific skills, resources, and tools to determine to what degree they support a community in developing the skills it needs to achieve its goals and improve its situation. Towards this end we associate certain attributes with each of the nodes in Fig. 1, based on our characterisation of the rural environment and the barriers to the use and acceptance of technology identified in [2]. These attributes are listed in the tables that follow.

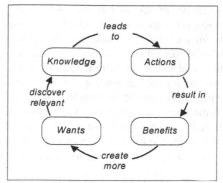

Fig. 2. Sustainable cycle

Table 1. Attributes of the environment and community

Rural environment	Community
<ul><li>population density</li><li>transportation and communications networks</li><li>distances to other communities and urban centres</li><li>climatic conditions affecting technology</li></ul>	<ul><li>cost of transportation and communications</li><li>availability and cost of electricity, phone lines, high-speed internet connections</li><li>current economic and social activities</li><li>organisations (political, community, social, non-governmental, private sector)</li><li>services (schools, health clinics, banking, government, etc.)</li><li>sources of funding</li></ul>
Individual	
<ul><li>household income</li><li>livelihood</li><li>reading and writing skills</li><li>languages</li><li>computer skills</li></ul>	
Need	**Goal**
<ul><li>determined by the community and the individual</li></ul>	<ul><li>defined by the community and the individual to fulfill a need</li></ul>

Table 2. Attributes of the ICT tools, resources and skills

ICT tools	ICT resources	ICT skills
<ul><li>device</li><li>I/O and peripherals</li><li>power sources</li><li>connectivity</li><li>parts, maintenance & upgrades</li></ul>	<ul><li>content</li><li>applications</li><li>training</li><li>peer support</li><li>maintenance and updates</li><li>consultation</li></ul>	<ul><li>operate ICT tools</li><li>access and create content</li><li>run applications</li><li>technical and administrative support</li></ul>

3   ICT heuristic measurements

The set of measurements we propose here was developed and tested by applying them to a number of actual, real-life projects described in the literature [11-19]. To evaluate a given application of the underlying technology and the information services provided with respect to some community, the key questions to ask are:

- *Is it feasible to deploy within the community's environment?* This measures how practical it is to satisfy or adapt a technology's project requirements to the prevailing conditions and constraints within a given community.
- *Is it affordable, cost-wise to the community?* This measures the cost/benefit of the technology with respect to the community. It reflects to what extent the community and its members can afford to pay any costs and fees associated with the technology based services. Here, we only consider those costs that the community will be responsible for, either on an individual basis or as a group, in terms of acquiring, operating, maintaining, using and otherwise benefiting from the technology.
- *Is it usable by the community?* This measures both the standard usability metrics (effective, efficient, error-tolerant, easy to use, and engaging) and the physical accessibility of the software system with respect to the community of users. Accessibility looks at whether access is open to a critical mass of people in the community, including groups that might otherwise be marginalised for political, economic or social reasons.
- *Is it relevant to the community's needs and goals?* These measures how appropriate or significant the technology is to the community, given the community's needs and goals.
- *Is it trustworthy?* This measures how much trust the community can place in the technology. In other words, it measures if the community can rely on the tools, can trust the resources and can have confidence in the skills.
- *Does it have the potential to improve and provide benefits to the community?* These measures to what extent the technology can contribute to a positive and measurable outcome in line with the goals that the community has defined for itself.
- *Does it advance the knowledge available within the community?* These measures to what extent the technology adds to the body of knowledge that will enable the community and its members to act in the future.

These measurements are interrelated. A technology must be feasible, affordable, usable, relevant, and trustworthy for it to be able to lead to improvements or advances in knowledge. And any actual improvements can only be discovered after people have put the new knowledge they have acquired to beneficial action. In addition, for the technology to be sustainable, the improvements must balance the costs. A technology might be feasible, but at a cost that the community cannot afford. For example, although generator powered satellite connectivity can bring internet connections almost anywhere; few communities can afford this type of investment on their own. A technology might be feasible and affordable, but might be unusable by the community for many reasons; e.g. the community might lack the skills or language to use it. And even if it is usable, if it is not relevant to the community's needs and can not make a change, then there is little motivation to use it. On the other hand, if the technology is not trustworthy people will abandon it for a more reliable alternative. The following tables describe how each of these measurements is applied with respect to three dimensions: the tools, resources and required skills.

Table 3. Measurements with respect to the ICT tools

ICT tools	Factors Considered
feasible	• Can the required equipment and infrastructure be transported to the site? • How will climatic conditions affect the operation of tools? • Can parts, maintenance and upgrades be obtained in a timely fashion? • Is there a location to house equipment? • Is the infrastructure required to operate the tools available? • Is there an organisation that can assume responsibility for managing and maintaining the tools on-site? • Are the tools appropriate or can they be adapted to the local language and skill set?
affordable	• Given available funding, can the community afford all start-up and on-going costs associated with obtaining and using the tools at the community level? • Given household incomes, can people afford all costs and fees associated with using the tools at the individual level?
usable	• Are there any climatic conditions which might restrict the use of the tools, given their intended context of use? • Are the tools usable, given their operating characteristics under the available infrastructure? • Does the intended context of use fit current economic and social practices? • Does a critical mass of people have access to the tools? Is anyone excluded? • Does the use of the tools require any special skills or languages beyond current or potential capabilities? • Are the tools usable (i.e. effective, efficient, error-tolerant, easy to learn and to use, and engaging)?
relevant	• Do the tools support applications and content that are relevant to the community as a whole, to individual members?
trustworthy	• Are the tools reliable?
improvement	• Does the use of the tools contribute to a positive and meaningful outcome for the community as a whole, for individual members?
advancement	• Does the use of the tools advance the knowledge available to the community as a whole, to individual members?

Table 4. Measurements with respect to the ICT resources

ICT resources	Factors Considered
feasible	• Can the resources be made available on-site either physically or electronically? • Will climatic conditions affect the availability of resources? • How will the resources be administered, maintained and updated? • How will distance affect maintenance and updates? Will distance affect the ability of people to use the resources? • Is there a place where people can congregate to get training and share their experiences and ideas? • Are the applications, content and training program appropriate for or adaptable to the local language and skill set?

affordable	• Can the community afford the start-up and on-going costs for resources? (i.e. software licenses, subscriptions, training materials, programs, etc.) • Can individuals afford any costs associated with accessing the resources? • Can people afford to take the time away from their other activities?
usable	• Does a critical mass of the population have access to the resources? Is any group excluded? • Are the resources available in the local language? • Does the use of the resources require any special skills beyond current or potential capabilities? • Are the applications and content usable (i.e. effective, efficient, error-tolerant, easy to learn and to use, and engaging)?
relevant	• Are the resources relevant to the community as a whole and its individual members given current activities, practices, needs and goals?
trustworthy	• Can the resources be trusted to operate in a dependable and fail safe manner?
improvement	• Do the resources contribute to a positive and meaningful outcome for the community as a whole? For individual members?
advancement	• Do the resources advance the knowledge available to the community? To its individual members?

Table 5. Measurements with respect to the ICT skills

ICT skills	Factors Considered
feasible	• If specialised skills are required, is it feasible to make them available in the community? • Is it reasonable to expect people to have or develop the required skills, given their background?
affordable	• Can the community afford the costs to develop or pay for the skills? • Can individuals afford the costs to develop or pay for the skills ?
usable	• Does everyone have access to someone with the necessary skills? • Does everyone have access to the means of developing these skills? • Can these skills be developed in an easy, effective, efficient, error-tolerant and engaging way?
relevant	• Are these skills relevant to the community as a whole and individual members, given current activities, practices, needs and goals?
trustworthy	• Does the community have confidence in the usefulness of the services provided by the technology?
improvement	• Do these skills contribute to a positive and meaningful outcome for the community as a whole? for individual members?
advancement	• Do these skills advance the knowledge available to the community? To individual members?

Use of the Proposed Model: Our intentions in building this model are two fold: (a) to arrive at a set of measurable parameters in terms of which a technology's inclusiveness can be studied and then, (b) to study how the model can be used in both cases, namely in evaluating an existing project (technology) or in developing a new one. If a project is already operational, the metrics can be obtained based on experience and measurements; or if a new project is embarked upon, they can be estimated based on a 'situation based analysis' or from experience with similar projects.

When estimating, we believe that three different parameter values of low, medium, or high would be adequate. If a given measure is dependent upon unpredictable, external factors we assign it a "neutral" value. To give an example of value assignment, if the use of a certain technology requires face-to-face training of users, however the community in question is very distant with high transport costs, this will impact the feasibility and affordability of training for that technology, which will be reflected by a low rating for those measures on the skills dimension.

The measurements for a given dimension are combined by applying a MIN function. We infer that if an operational technology scores "high" on all measures, then it could be considered as highly inclusive. On the other hand, a technology which scores "low" on one or more measures will have potential sources of deficiency , and those aspects of the technology should be reworked. In the case of a proposed new project these high and low values could be treated as signals to decide what aspects of the design need to be improved before embarking on the project implementation so as to make the project a success. In this context, it is interesting to note from the literature that many funding agencies and other stakeholders involved in such projects find projects related to "ICT for rural Development" are either not evaluated or have no funds for evaluation, even though they all wish these projects to be successful [3].

4 Examples of applying the measurements

In this section we illustrate these measurements by applying them to two real-life projects described in the literature. In our first example, we look at a project to provide internet access in the Peruvian Amazon. The second is a project providing broadband access to remote communities in Canada. The evaluations we propose here are neither definitive nor absolute, but simply an outcome of our exercise based on the information available in the literature we accessed.

4.1 Internet access in the Peruvian Amazon

This was a telecentre project launched in 2000, to bring internet access to a remote community in the Peruvian Amazon [13]. The community in question, Marakiri Bajo, is extremely poor, with a subsistence economy, no electricity and very limited basic social services. The program had strong supporters and many people had high expectations about the potential benefits. In the words of a local leader and project champion, "through the help of the internet indigenous peoples have the opportunity to overcome their exclusion and to have improved access to education, markets and political participation". Others were sceptical about the program's utility from the start. With external support, a technical solution was found to provide telephone and internet connectivity. As one of the key objectives was youth education, along with the telecentre, a state-of-the-art video-conferencing centre via a generator operated satellite system was installed.

At first the project appeared very successful. Many people, including youth and women, began to explore the new technologies, and ICT training programs were launched. The youth quickly picked up skills, and several set up websites and made contact with other groups within the country and beyond. The program was hailed as a success and presented internationally. However, the project also ran into serious difficulties. For one, the centre was controlled by a small group and not open to the general public. As a result, many people within the community and neighbouring areas felt excluded from its potential benefits, aggravating tensions between different social groups. Secondly, many people had hoped that the centre would enable them to better sell their local produce. They were unable to realise this due to a lack of experience in e-commerce and the absence of on-line markets in Peru. Third, many people became disinterested because content was not available in the local language, and there was no information or services they could use in their daily lives. Finally, little benefit was drawn from the videoconference equipment due to the unavailability of educational programs and low demand.

A year after the centre was launched it mysteriously burnt down. After some serious reflection, the community relaunched its ICT program by opening a local radio station to broadcast programs of local interest in the local language. The closest internet access is now available in a telecentre located in a city at 2 hours distance. Our evaluation of the initial project is presented below.

Table 6. Evaluation of the Marikiri Bajo project

	Score	Explanation
ICT tools	low	Overall score low based on low affordability, restricted access and low relevance of the videoconference equipment.
feasible	*high*	Generators and satellite connections are standard technologies.
affordable	*low*	Even if initial start-up costs are externally funded, on-going costs to run generators and satellite connections are high when compared to incomes in a subsistence economy.
usable	*low*	Access to tools restricted to a small group.
relevant	*low*	The videoconference equipment has low relevance with respect to the goals that community members would have liked to achieve.
trustworthy	*neutral*	The tools will be reliable as long as the equipment is maintained and fuel to run the generator is available.
improvement	*neutral*	Potential to contribute to community improvement is neutral.
advancement	*neutral*	Potential to contribute to community knowledge is neutral.
ICT resources	low	Overall score low based on unavailability of resources, restricted access, and the lack of relevant content in the local language.
feasible	*low*	The unavailability of educational programs, of an on-line market, of content in the local language, and of local information and services are very real and practical barriers.
affordable	*low*	Access to resources restricted to a small group.
usable	*low*	Lack of content in local language
relevant	*low*	The resources available did not support community expectations i.e. information and services of local interest; better sales of

		local products, education in topics of interest
trustworthy	*neutral*	Validity depends on the content consulted.
improvement	*low*	Low relevance results in low potential for improvement.
advancement	*low*	Low relevance results in low potential for increasing knowledge.
ICT skills	**medium**	Overall score of medium based on the benefit some individuals were able to obtain by developing ICT skills.
feasible	*high*	The project showed that it was both feasible and possible for members of the community to develop the necessary skills.
affordable	*high*	We assume no costs were associated with developing the skills
usable	*low*	We assume access was also restricted.
relevant	*medium*	Although the skills developed were not relevant to the community as a whole, they were relevant to certain individuals.
trustworthy	*neutral*	Confidence in the skills depends upon the individual.
improvement	*medium*	Although it did not apply to the whole community, certain individuals did benefit from the skills they developed.
advancement	*medium*	Although not applicable to the whole community, certain individuals were able to increase their knowledge.

Based on this evaluation we conclude that overall the technology in the initial project had low inclusiveness. Although it was feasible, the on-going costs to run a generator and satellite connection would have been unaffordable over the long term. The lack of relevant content in the local language as well as the inability to meet community expectations with the available resources gave it a low likelihood of resulting in any tangible improvements. The restricted access contributed to tensions within the community. On the other hand, although the technology in itself did not advance the available knowledge, the community's experience with the technology did, as reflected in the new priorities of the subsequent project.

4.2   K-Net Services in Canada

K-Net is a community network providing broadband service to 60 First Nation communities in northern Canada. Launched in the mid-90s, it has been the subject of many well documented studies [11, 12, 16, 19, 18]. The communities served are remote, small and in sparsely populated areas, with limited or no road access. Although most people speak English, Oji-Cree and Cree are the primary languages. For decades these communities experienced high unemployment, high suicide rates, and low school completion rates. In addition, most communities lacked basic health and school services, obliging members to fly great distances for medical treatment and schooling. In 1994, a council of Northern Chiefs in partnership with the government launched a regional broadband network called K-Net Services with the goal of promoting "economic development, social capital and civic participation". In the words of one of the founders, "if the internet is the information highway of the future, then our youth should be the drivers and not passengers".

The K-Net has a decentralised structure. K-Net Services negotiates with the different service providers to provide broadband services to the communities at wholesale prices. In turn each community owns, manages and maintains its own local network, buying services from K-Net according to community priorities, and offering them locally at an affordable price. Each community covers its connection costs by aggregating demand from band offices, schools, constabulary, nursing stations, businesses and subsidised on-line services along with individual use. A "champion" from the community represents local interests and is locally accountable. Champions are responsible for engaging the community in planning potential ICT projects and are involved in building support for projects at all levels in the community, government and with potential partners.

The initial service offering based on extensive consultation in the communities focused on telehealth and high school education. Since then a wide range of training and capacity building programs have been developed and delivered. Current services include video conferencing, telephony, VOIP, web and email services. Telehealth services in local nursing stations remain the most used and generate the most revenue, while VOIP provides 40% savings over standard long distance. There are currently over 38,000 email accounts and 18,000 group and hosting sites with free registration for First Nations and members of remote communities. In addition to broadband services, K-Net also provides technical training for local network managers and technicians, on-line support and a toll free help desk. It also runs workshops for youth in web page development and content management, and hosts various community and cultural web sites and discussion forums.

Table 7. Evaluation of the K-Net project

	Score	Explanation
ICT tools	high	Overall score high based on high feasibility, affordability, usability and trustworthiness.
feasible	*high*	The equipment and infrastructure are standard technologies.
affordable	*high*	By prioritising goals and aggregating demand, can provide service at an affordable price.
usable	*high*	Training of local management ensures that the tools are usable. Access to tools does not appear restricted.
relevant	*neutral*	Communities can select services according to their priorities.
trustworthy	*high*	The network and tools are well supported through training programs and assistance.
improvement	*neutral*	Communities can select services according to their priorities.
advancement	*neutral*	Communities can select services according to their priorities.
ICT resources	high	Overall score high based on high score for all measurements.
feasible	*high*	Resources are designed for and made available to the communities.
affordable	*high*	By prioritising goals and aggregating demand, resources are offered at affordable prices.
usable	*high*	As the services are chosen by the community and designed for these communities we assume that they are usable.
relevant	*high*	Communities select services according to their priorities. Resources are designed based on consultation with the communities and by community members themselves.
trustworthy	*high*	Local management and accountability provide a basis for trust.
improvement	*high*	Resources provided address community needs.

advancement	*high*	Resources provided with intent to increase the available knowledge.
ICT skills	**high**	Overall score high based on high score for all measurements.
feasible	*high*	Training and workshops are provided at no additional cost to the community.
affordable	*high*	Training and workshops are provided at no additional cost to the community.
usable	*high*	Training does not appear restricted, and the required skills are available locally.
relevant	*high*	Training addresses local needs.
trustworthy	*high*	Local management and accountability provide a basis for confidence in the skills.
improvement	*high*	Training addresses local needs.
advancement	*high*	Training increases knowledge available to the community.

Based on the above we conclude that the technology is highly inclusive. The tools are highly feasible, affordable, usable and reliable. Training is provided to develop the required skills locally. The resources are designed with the intent to address the community's goals and increase the knowledge available at a local level.

5   Conclusions

In recent years, a growing number of software based projects have attempted to address the disparity in opportunities available to people in urban versus rural and underdeveloped areas of the world through technology. Some of these projects have been successful while others have failed. In this paper, we proposed a conceptual model that lays out the key factors involved in making an ICT based project inclusive with respect to some community, and a set of heuristic measurements for evaluating that technology's inclusiveness. We then apply this model to two projects that were already deployed and reported in the literature; and found that the model fits the findings reported. Our ultimate intention is to make this model useful to software engineers in different stages of the development cycle: requirements gathering, design, testing, deployment, and in on-going maintenance.

Acknowledgement: We thank the anonymous reviewers for their criticism and helpful references to the various ICT4D literatures relevant to our efforts. The preliminary model reported in this paper will be refined further for its future use.

References

1.   Schumaker E.F. *Small is Beautiful. Economics as if people mattered ... 25 years later with commentaries*, Hartley & Marks (1999).
2.   Warschauer Marc. *Technology and Social Inclusion*, MIT Press (2003).

3. Unwin, T. (ed.) *ICT4D, Information and Communication Technology for Development.* Draft retrieved 2007-02-24 from http://www.ict4d.org.uk/. To be published 2008 by Cambridge University Press.

4. Brewer E. Demmer M., Du B., Ho M., Kam M., Nedevschi S., Pal J., Patra R., Surana S. The Case for Technology in Developing Regions. *IEEE Computer*, Vol. 38, No. 6, 25-38. (June 2005).

5. *World Information Society Report 2006.* International Telecommunication Union (ITU). Retrieved 2007-02-23 http://www.itu.int/osg/spu/publications/worldinformationsociety /2006/report.html (2006).

6. Whyte, Anne Assessing Community Telecentres: Guidelines for Researchers, IDRC Books (International Development Research Centre). Retrieved 2007-02-21 http://www.idrc.ca/en/ev-9415-201-1-DO_TOPIC.html#begining. (2000).

7. Venkatesh, Viswanath; Morris, Michael G.; Davis, Gordon B.; Davis, Fred D. User Acceptance Of Information Technology: Toward A Unified View. *MIS Quarterly*, Vol. 27 No. 3, pp. 425-478 (September 2003).

8. Pitula, Kristina; Radhakrishnan, T. A conceptual model of inclusive technology for information access by the rural sector. To appear in *HCI International 2007 Conference Proceedings*, Springer-Verlag. (2007)

9. Ashley, Caroline; Maxwell, Simon (principal authors). Rethinking Rural Development. Overseas Development Institute briefing paper reprinted in *Current Issues in Rural Development*, Swedish University of Agricultural Sciences, No. 31/32 (October 2003).

10. Reimer, Bill. Rural and Urban: Differences and Common Ground, in *Urban Canada: Sociological Perspectives*, ed. Harry H. Hiller, Oxford University Press (2005).

11. Beaton, B. The K-Net story: community ICT development work. *The Journal of Community Informatics*, Vol. 1, Issue 1 (2004).

12. Canadian Research Alliance For Community Innovation And Networking. *K-Net Case Study Profile.* Retrieved 2006-11-20 http://www3.fis.utoronto.ca/research/iprp/cracin/ research/K-Net%20Case%20study%20Profile_2005.pdf (2005).

13. Gigler, Björn-Sörn. Including the excluded – Can ICT empower communities? Towards an alternative evaluation framework based on the capability approach. *4th International Conference on the Capability Approach*, University of Pavia, Italy. (2004).

14. Cecchini, Simone; Raina, Monica. Electronic government and the rural poor: the case of Gyandoot. MIT, *Information Technologies and International Development*, Vol. 2, No. 2, Winter (2004).

15. Garai, Atanu; Shadrach, B. *Taking ICT to every Indian village: opportunities and challenges.* One World South Asia, New Delhi (2006).

16. Longford, Graham. Community Networking and Civic Participation in Canada: A Background Paper. CRACIN report prepared for The Department of Canadian Heritage. Retrieved 2006-11-20 http://www3.fis.utoronto.ca/research/iprp/cracin/publications/ pdfs/wips/CRACIN_CNCP_webversion.pdf. (2005)

17. Shaik. N. Meera, Anita Jhamtani, and D.U.M. Rao. Information and communications technology in agricultural development: a comparative analysis of three projects in India. *Agricultural Research and Extension Network* Paper No. 135 (2004).

18. Walmark, B., O'Donnell, S., and Beaton, B. *Research on ICT with Aboriginal Communities: Report from RICTA*, National Research Council Canada (2005).

19. Ramirez, R. A model for rural and remote information and communication technologies: a Canadian exploration. *Telecommunications Policy* No. 25, 315-330 (2001).

The Tech-Enabled Neighborhood: Findings from an experience in Tecámac, Mexico

Victor M. Gonzalez[1], Kenneth Kraemer[2], Luis A. Castro[1] and Alladi Venkatesh[2]

1 Manchester Business School
University of Manchester, United Kingdom

2 Paul Merage School of Business
University of California, Irvine, USA

Abstract. .Following worldwide tendencies, the patterns of usage of Information and Communication Technologies (ICT) in Mexico are being influenced by increasing affordability. In this work we present the results of a study on the use and adoption of ICTs to support daily life in residential communities conducted in Tecamac, Mexico. There, neighbors were provided with computers and broadband internet access as part of the facilities. The study consists of analysis of interviews conducted in situ with members of the community. We mainly discuss incidents and situations beyond and around the use of technology such as the services neighbors need when moving in. This study provides some insights for the design and deployment of technology in real communities on a large scale.

1 Introduction

Following worldwide tendencies, the patterns of usage of Information and Communication Technologies (ICT) in Mexico are being influenced by increasing affordability. The usage of personal computers at home is now more common as a result of cheaper technologies and credit plans. Related to this is the increased connectivity of family homes through dial-up lines and high-speed broadband. According to the Mexican Association of Internet, in 2005 about 20 million people have internet access, from which 43% is from home [1]. In 2005, the number of computer with Internet access at home increased about 20% with respect the previous year [2].

In parallel, in Mexico there is a huge investment to build housing infrastructure and make it affordable, especially for low and middle-income people. After years of housing scarcity, now in Mexico more and more people are able to purchase their

Please use the following format when citing this chapter:

Gonzalez, V. M., Kraemer, K., Castro, L. A., Venkatesh, A., 2007, in IFIP International Federation for Information Processing, Volume 241, Home Informatics and Telematics: ICT for the Next Billion, eds. Venkatesh, A., Gonsalves, T., Monk, A., Buckner, K., (Boston: Springer), pp. 49-63.

own household. These two aspects do not necessarily reflect an idealistic scenario where digital and housing divides have been eliminated; Mexico is far from that. Instead, they reflect a set of conditions where technologies are likely to impact the very conceptual bases of what we understand for homes and more generally neighborhoods; a vision that we refer here as Habitat Computing.

This paper presents the results of a study conducted to understand the practicalities of implementing a feasible vision of Habitat Computing in a Mexican neighborhood. At the beginning of 2005, in the city of Tecámac, in Mexico, Real Paraiso Residencial, a housing company, in partnership with Conectha, an Internet Service Provider, had the vision to develop a residential complex (Real del Sol) consisting of about 2000 houses all equipped with a computer and broadband internet access. Neighbors were also provided with a community portal through which they access to a variety of neighborhood-oriented online services such as message board, online shopping, ordering taxis, access to educational content and access to security video cameras around the neighborhood.

Using semi-structured interviews, we explored the factors motivating the purchase of the house, the experience of moving in, the relationships with the neighbors and the community, their use of the technology to support domestic practices as well as perspectives on how to make the technology more useful.

Our analysis reveals challenges and opportunities for the deployment of current ICT to allow residents to better integrate themselves into their community and contribute to its wellbeing. Our results also indicated that the implementation of ICTs to support daily life in residential communities might not support the, to some extent, idealistic perspective explored in previous research [3]. Social problems are very likely to arise such as disagreement among neighbors on quotidian tasks or division of labor. However, in contrast, there are other challenges faced by the neighbors and they act as sources for community integration. Our results indicate that looking for solutions for these problems could make the community more cohesive and increase their likeliness of self-organization.

2   Some Characteristics of the Mexican Housing Context

In recent years, housing developments for low income people have been blooming in masse all over Mexico, thanks to a federal government initiative that provides grants and mortgages. These urban settlements are usually located in the outskirts of the main Mexican cities, and they all share the same characteristics: affordable mortgages (i.e., requiring a payment of around 200 dollars a month, for over 20 years), reduced in-house areas, reduced build areas per home (usually consisting in two bedrooms at most, a bathroom, living-dining room, small patio, one parking space, and a garden), architecturally similar constructions, and heavy concentrations of houses, altogether.

Whilst this initiative is helping to solve the shortage of housing for low-income Mexican citizens, it is creating a new set of problems, previously unheard of. First, the distance between the cities main working facilities and the housing developments are considerable, often involving an hour plus commute time. Since these housing developments are generally built on less expensive city locations, supermarkets, hospitals, universities and the like are usually far from these projects. In some cases, the availability of phone lines may even be scarce.

Security is other main concern for the inhabitants of these housing developments. Many houses remain empty during the day, because both husband and wife often work in the city, which makes the houses susceptible to burglary. Statistics from the Mexican NGOs such as "Mexico Unido Contra la Delincuencia" point out that in Mexico City twenty percent (20%) of all burglaries are committed in households and one in eight is reported to the authorities [4]. Facing insecurity, many Mexican housing developments have opted to create some sort of isolation for the community with the external world in order to increase the safety of the properties. Similar to other parts of the world, a common solution has been to create what is called "gated communities" in which the access to the community is controlled and physical barriers are erected to avoid intrusions [5].

Beyond physical barriers that might created just a sense (but not real) security, many authors argue that the foundations for safer and better places to live lies on the community of neighbors. The perception of living in a safe and secure housing environment can increase if the residents are unfamiliar with their neighbors [5, 6]. Consequently, people have a lot to gain from organizing with their neighbors not just to protect each other against crime but because they can act together to improve their neighborhoods and respond with more power to shared challenges. However to achieve such organization is not easy as people lack the time to meet, discuss, plan and organize with their neighbors.

Within this context, it is possible to argue that the use of information and communication technologies (ICTs) can facilitate the creation of communities and increase with this the quality of living. This follows in spirit the work of others which aim to use ICTs to create the conditions to support the local and social interaction in urban or rural neighborhoods [3, 6-8]. For instance, in Foth's approach a socially strong community will be the result of neighbors finding out about common interests and becoming involved in door-to-door interactions. In our the characteristics of Mexican urban household with long commute distances, elevated safety concerns and particular ways to approach community life bring particular characteristics to the phenomenon of technology as community communication mediator.

3   Characteristics of the Study and Methodology

At the end of February 2006, we conducted a set of ethnographic interviews with families living in or about to move to Real del Sol. The housing development is located in the city of Tecámac, in the State of Mexico[1]. Although Tecámac is not part of the metropolitan area of Mexico City, it is close enough as to allow a reasonable

---

[1] The State of Mexico is located in central Mexico, and it almost completely encapsulates Mexico City. Some of the most populated counties in Mexico are in the State of Mexico, particularly those that comprise the Metropolitan Area of Mexico City.

commute to the city (approximately an hour long trip, with good traffic conditions). The vast majority of inhabitants in Real del Sol work in Mexico City itself.

A total of 34 individuals were interviewed covering 27 households averaging 3 members per family (87 individuals in total). Interviewees have a variety of occupations, from journalists to primary school teacher, from house keepers to tourist agents. The interviews were semi-structured and covered a set of topics including the factors motivating the purchase of the houses, the experience of moving in, the relationships with the neighbors and the rest of the community, their use of the technology to support domestic practices as well as perspectives on how to make the technology more useful. Each interview lasted an average of 45 minutes and was conducted at the home of the resident. Just in two cases interviews were conducted at Conectha's offices, as the informants had not yet moved to their properties by the time of the interviews.

The interviews were complemented with a number of observations of the community and informal interviews with staff from both Conectha and Real Paraiso Residencial, as well as with people from the Ojo de Agua community (not living at Real del Sol), including taxi drivers, shop owners and security staff.

Data were analyzed using a comparative approach (inspired in Grounded Theory [9]) to identify patterns among the informant's responses and produce a coherent and integrated set of findings from where the points and conclusions of this work are derived.

4   Real del Sol: the Habitat of the Seventh Generation (G7 Habitat)

At the beginning of 2005 started the construction of a housing development guided by a concept called "Habitat of Seventh Generation" o G7 Habitat. The developers, designers and architects from Real Paraíso Residencial and Conectha, an ISP provider, defined G7 Habitat as a household concept that emerges from sixth previous generations experienced by the domestic household. With the G7 Habitat concept, the designers aimed at the Information and Communications Technologies (ICTs) playing not just a strategic role, but one where they are intrinsically linked and embedded to the basic idea of what a household is. Figure 1 shows a picture of a house in Real del Sol.

Figure 1. A typical house in Real del Sol. Privada Ananke.

The concept G7 Habitat includes access to high-speed Internet as part of the basic house infrastructure together with water, electricity and sewage drain. Each unit is connected thorough a wireless network that allows speeds up to 340 Kbps. Some of the houses also include a personal computer for free or it is offered by Conectha at preferential prices. Through the computer the neighbors have access to a set of services in the neighborhood intranet designed by Conectha. Figure 2 shows a screen shot of the Intranet. The services of the Intranet include: access to security cameras, community information, e-mail, educational content, on-line ordering of grocery and other products.

Figure 2. Community Intranet in Real del Sol.

G7 Habitat aims to go beyond providing Internet access to neighbors and provides services that are shaped to the community. For instance, access to the security cameras is only allowed to neighbors and just to those cameras of their *privadas* and common areas. Similarly, the online shopping service links neighbors to small local businesses from Tecamac and Ojo de Agua communities. The Intranet also includes a section where neighbors can get discount coupons from local businesses. Interestingly, the way that online shopping is operating respond to the actual needs of the community. As opposed to other scenarios with transactions are done with credit or debit cards, the transactions in Tecamac are in cash. People order their products online and then the shop delivers the goods by bike or motorbike and charges the costumer in cash at their door.

G7 Habitat was conceived as a concept that encourages community integration. The development counts with two small parks, basketball courts, a primary school, a kindergarten, and other communal areas. To facilitate organization, the development is organized in *privadas*, groups of ten or twenty houses that are separated of the rest with gates. People in the *privadas* share some green areas and services (trash bins sections).

5   Implementing the idea of Habitat Computing: Results and Findings

In this section we present some of the results emerging from the analysis of data. We analyze the materialization of the idea of Habitat computing through the concept G7 habitat as implemented and proposed by Real Paraiso Residencial. The results are organized in three main areas: (1) the role of Habitat computing as a point of entry when buying a property, (2) the role of Habitat computing to settle in, (3) the role of Habitat computing to support neighborhood coexistence.

Figure 3. One of the common areas at Real del Sol.

5.1   Finding about Real del Sol and deciding about buying a property

From the beginning of our field work at Tecamac, it was possible to notice how potential buyers of houses in Real del Sol were attracted to visit the demo houses by an extensive advertising campaign which clearly served to portrait the properties as going beyond the typical house of social interest. Phrases such "G7 Habitat", "Concepto G7" or "Tu casa conectada al mundo[2]" were placed on advertising together with images of Californian style houses linked to images of computer and internet-related symbols. Because this emphasis was present throughout the sale and post-sale process, it was not a surprise that people interviewed were well aware of the concepts and used them as part of their vocabulary to talk about their properties. Perhaps more important is the fact that those concepts were instrumental for neighbors setting their expectations about their property and the life in general at Real del Sol.

As indicated by our interviewees, the concept G7 Habitat certainly served as a marketing tool to attract visitors to the demo houses, but we also noticed that the concept was interpreted in a different way once the decision to make a purchase had to be made. At that stage, the G7 concept seemed to be linked to architectural design, style of the property, rather than to images of a technology-enabled home. We asked the informants to identify the three most persuading reasons to buy a property at Real del Sol. Figure 5 shows a consolidated of mentions of the three reasons to buy. As it can be seen, the most two important aspects were the peace of mind and the G7 habitat concept, followed by the cost of the dwelling.

Figure 4. A spectacular with advertising for Real del Sol with the phrase "Tu Casa Conectada al Mundo"

Peace of mind basically refers to the quietness and perceived safety resulting from the zone where Real del Sol is located. Many interviewees commented that the

---

[2] Your home connected to the world

zone is a not so populated area, thus it has lower pollution levels, less traffic, etc. Some of them, contrasting the zone with their old neighborhoods in Mexico City, defining connections between low populated areas and safer contexts, "... *the zone is not very populated and consequently not very affected by gangs*". Furthermore, informants made clear that in order to assess the level of a security of a property, what counts is not just the household itself, but the area where it is located, as the following informant commented with regard to living in Mexico City "*the apartment where I lived was very safe, I mean, the building, but the zone was definitely awful, horrible place, one of the most dangerous areas in the city.*" To what extent zone takes precedence over individual household characteristics with regards evaluating safety it is not completely clear, but our understanding is that most of our informants considered the area of Tecamac as being safer that Mexico City and this was their starting criteria to evaluate the property.

With similar relevance, when taking a decision in regards of acquiring a property at Real del Sol, was the fact that informants perceived that they were buying a house within distinctive characteristics. Many of them mentioned that they bought "el concepto que me ofrecieron" (the offered concept). However, we found that the actual meaning of the G7 Habitat concept moved from the integrated vision of seven basic services to a more practical meaning. When we asked informants about what they meant by the G7 concept, they often refer and limit their descriptions to aesthetic values. For instance, some of them mentioned that they found the houses very attractive when comparing them to other nearby complexes or properties available through credit programs (e.g., Infonavit): "*I actually liked the... the kind of façade... I liked... the finishes... [You see,] I studied Architecture so I was more or less watching [for those aspects]...*" commented one of the informants.

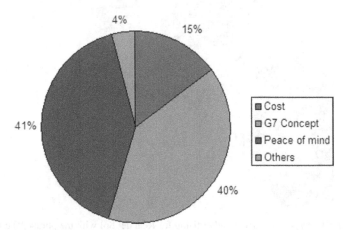

Figure 5. Pie chart with the main reasons to move in

Finally, but less relevant, cost was indicated as a factor influencing the purchase of the property. Neighbors reported that they obtained better value for their money and more pleasant households. One informant, a young housewife, commented "*the facades are really nice and the houses are not really expensive...*" Similarly, other informant pointed out "*after I visited some other complexes in the area and even in the DF, I decided that this one was the best deal as offered so many benefits such as construction, finishes and ways of access...*" The Californian style of the properties and the individual touch of each one were aspects that were often emphasized by our informants.

The fact that cost was not mentioned as being as relevant as peace of mind or aesthetic design, can be explained by understanding how the properties were purchased. According to data provided by Real Paraiso Residencial, all the informants bought their properties using either government-sponsored or commercial credit schemes. Many of them knew that because they were planning to get a mortgage to pay for the household anyway and because there were many housing complexes offering properties within similar range of price, they had to focus not just on price but other factors.

Considering the great effort to promote the idea of a tech-enabled home connected to the world, we found very relevant that this meaning of the G7 concept was not mentioned as a relevant factor on persuading people to buy the property. Our conclusion is that despite the fact that having a computer and temporal free internet access was attractive for potential buyers, the benefits were not clear at the beginning. Many neighbors were not able to perceive how the vision of "your house connected to the world" would mean for them in practice. Their expectations were based on what they knew about computers and what they were able to do before moving to Real del Sol. Many families already had a computer before coming to Real del Sol and many accessed the Internet regularly. Among the 27 families interviewed, 25 of them owned a computer before moving in. They foresaw that the benefit was that they would be able to access the Internet for free, at least during some period, but they didn't mention other major benefits.

Figure 6. An image from one of the cameras connected to the Internet

We noticed that one of the benefits derived from the technological infrastructure was the possibility for residents to watch their properties while away and mainly before moving in. Because many of the future residents were provided with access to surveillance video cameras, which they could be accessed from any computer connected to Internet, they were enabled to follow up the erection of the house as the construction moved on. Some of them, after moving in, were using the cameras not only to keep an eye on their home but also for showing their homes off to their relatives and friends. This benefit indicated that for some neighbors at the early stages after the purchase, the catchy phrase was not "Tu casa conectada al Mundo", but "Tu casa a la vista del Mundo".[3]

5.2   The experience of moving in

One of the main challenges when moving to a new residential zone is the fact that the area is very unfamiliar and quotidian activities such as shopping or getting services can turn to be cumbersome. Usually people try to identify shops and services before moving in, but that process can be time-consuming and neighbors end up with just a limited picture of the kind of shops or services in the area. It is generally throughout a process of trial and error that eventually people are able to re-establish their trusted sources. Many of the informants prioritized this identification of services and, particularly for families and for obvious reasons, schools were one of the main things to secure before moving in. However, other services such as auto repair shops, general doctors, and dentist were also mentioned. Going down in terms of priorities, people mentioned services such as electricians, plumbers, carpenters, or gardeners.

Our analysis indicates that by far one of the most successful services provided by the G7 Habitat concept was the online commercial link. Through the commercial link informants reported to have access to a local pharmacy, butchery and a small convenience store. According to people interviewed, this service was particularly relevant and useful during the initial stage when families were settling in. When asked about the usage of the commercial link, informants mentioned that they only used the service when they just moved in and mainly because they did not know what other alternatives were around and did not have time to look for them.

Once neighbors established, people were encouraged to start using the online services provided by Conectha to shop at local stores, but it seems indeed that the usage declined and in most cases simply vanished. When many of the informants who bought at least once using the service were asked about whether they would continue using the service or not, they were not even aware if it was still working. For instance, as part of the conversation about the use of Conectha's services, this is what one neighbor remarked *"...and basically, I don't do this every day, but once in a while, for example [what I do is] shopping some meat...but [now] I don't know what happened... it is temporally... I don't know, maybe the service was too expensive,.... paying to be in the web site, right now it says is temporally out of service..."* Furthermore, when we asked them if they would continue using the service (assuming it was working), many of them expressed that they preferred to see the groceries they shop and many times they just find the whole experience of going out and shopping more enjoyable.

---

[3] Your house to be seen by the world.

5.3   Getting to know neighbors and community organizations

As part of the post-sale service including in the G7 Habitat concept, Real Paraiso Residencial organized and led an initial meeting where neighbors met each other and participated in group exercises aimed to *break the ice* and incentive social integration. Such meetings were organized once a number of neighbors moved to each *privada*. The perception of the meetings organized by Real Paraiso was, in general, very positive among the people interviewed. Most of the informants agreed that this was a good way to bring out all the problems, concerns and disquiets. From those meetings people were able to define an organizational structure naming a committee with president, treasurer and secretary, as well as operation rules with regards the monthly maintenance fees and operative schemes.

We found that the fact that post-sale people from Real Paraiso Residencial organized the initial meetings caused the neighbors to develop some sense of dependence on them. For neighbors, it was clear that their organization and operation of their *privada* committee was independent from the post-sale team. However, at the same time, they expressed that sometimes there were some issues, formerly managed by Real Paraiso Residencial, that they wouldn't have the capacity (or authority) to deal with. Thus, they expressed that the future of the community meetings was uncertain as they feared a dramatic decrease on attendees and even disorganization. A couple commented "...*my husband and me were talking about that, I asked him if Real del Sol was always going to be there, if there was always going to be a post-sale department and if they will be always taking care of us or what?*" This uncertainty resulted from the lack of information with regards the duration of the post-sale cycle and the level of involvement of Real Paraiso Residencial in the life of the community. Neighbors just speculated about for how long the post-sale service would stay and how the whole community could be governed afterwards.

The main concern from neighbors was about the preservation of the G7 Habitat concept. Again, here the concept was meant to be the architectonic and style characteristics of the household. Informants were worried about the aspect of the complex once Real del Sol leaves and whether or not they would be able to maintain the regulations with regards facades, styles, etc. One of the interviewees commented: "*What are we going to do when Real del sol is not there? Who's going to decide what is allowed and what is not?*".

Our findings indicate people had crossed feelings with regard to the idea of living in a *privada*. For many informants the idea of living in a *privada* resulted attractive initially, but then it turned out to be disruptive in practice. People knew they were moving to a privada-style setting where many of the facilities would be shared (e.g., trash bins areas, gardens). However, the perception of residents is that they were not aware that the *privada* style of life would require them not just to share some facilities, but to interact with others to achieve collective goals (e.g., paint the common areas). This caused some discomfort among those not used to establish cooperative relationship with neighbors or those stating that their neighbors were not as friendly as they expected.

Other issue concerning the communication and coexistence among neighbors is the fact that many people do not feel engaged at all in a community in terms of their responsibilities to achieve a general well being. For instance, we were informed that many people were not so willing to pay the monthly maintenance fees. This caused annoyance for those paying regularly and raised initial signs of conflict among neighbors. Similarly, no all residents were happy with the idea of maintaining the design guidelines for their properties which would preserve their market price. For instance, one of our interviewees expressed some discomfort as he wanted their front door to be different since he had bought already some supplies for a house: *"...when I came here, the model houses had these doors, the finishes... and I asked May I change our door? And they said No, because everything has to be in harmony, everything has to be respected... They even told me that I could change the front door as long as I changed its color to white"*. The interviewee did not see the point of conforming to the rest even that he knew that in the long term the houses could be depreciated as a result of it.

Other incidents reflected the natural challenges of living together such as noisy neighbors or lack of respect for other properties. For instance other interviewee commented that his neighbor was washing her car and all the water went straight to his yard causing a flood. Definitely, these situations cause some distress in the community, but are part of what one can expect from people living together.

On the positive side, we noticed that even at the early stage many informants were concerned about community problems identified as likely community integrators to procure the well-being of all people. These concerns were identified as critical problems by many of the informants. Among them, two have major relevance: the water supply problem and the cow stable located next to Real del Sol.

The stable, as remarked by our informants, is not a minor issue and indeed has already upset some of them. Actually, a woman commented *"... We never were told about the stable, perhaps people already told you about, didn't they? ... Yes, it's then... disgusting because there are a lot of flies... and the smell. The smell at the beginning was like... I had headaches, and I didn't know about that! And then I said... 'I was supposed to be running away from pollution' and I came here and it's a stable! The stable is what is dislike more... and the smell is really strong down here, and that actually is a disadvantage and that was precisely what I was telling them 'the thing is that you gave us a stable as a gift without asking for it and you didn't even tell us, that's the problem!'"* Actually people were really concerned about health-related issues because of the flies, mosquitoes and dung.

In regards to the water supply problem, a neighbor was concerned about the fact the well was going to be managed by the municipal government and commented *"How can I be sure that the water is going to be enough for us once the government takes the control of the well? What if the adjacent complexes need water?"* Such problems and others of that magnitude could be a trigger to make this community a very cohesive and organized group and start working together for the wellbeing of the community.

4   Discussion of challenges and revealed opportunities

Of major importance is the connection between Conectha's Intranet as a point of access and the potential that neighbors would be likely to receive information from this channel. Although many of them had email accounts provided by Conectha's none of the informants (except one) used them as their main account. That was clear when we talked about the services and when we asked them for their email addresses. The fact that they did not use their account is an indication that they are less likely to visit the Intranet and therefore defeats the purpose of posting relevant information there as neighbors would not read it. It is likely that an scheme that either, presents the Intranet as a gateway to access the Internet when using Conectha's network or promotes the use of Conectha's email addresses by providing larger inbox spaces and better functionality would make more effective the communication through this mean.

As part of the technologically-enabled offer of the G7 Habitat concept is the safety of the complex as well as the wellbeing of their inhabitants. This was a palpable challenge faced by the informants, perhaps the most important. Peace of mind, as remarked by our informants, is a priority, and that was one of the main reasons of why they moved to Real del Sol. Thus, adequate, sophisticated equipment should be then provided to security services in order to accomplish their work appropriately since one of the main worries of the neighbors has to do indeed with safety and security. The G7 Habitat concept aimed to address this issue by providing security video cameras in the *privadas* and in some public areas of the complex. However, neighbors soon became aware of some issues regarding the video cameras. Firstly, the security staff did not monitor the security cameras. Secondly, even if they decided to monitor them by themselves, the level of detail and quality of the image was not optimal, and finally, perhaps the most important, no video-recording was done, thus eliminating the possibility of analysis in case of robberies.

Finally, another challenge we found for the fully implementation of the G7 concept is that many neighbors feel that the absence of Real Paraiso Residencial, as mentioned before, will dishearten others and they were very concerned about this as they have already faced confrontations and disagreements among them because of the regulations and the lack of an entity as a moderator.

As the study moved on, some insights emerged as opportunities to improve current and future developments. The information gained from the interviews with regards to the services offered to neighbors should be classified in 1) moving-in services and 2) daily-living services. The former refers to the services offered when the residents are moving in such as a set of basic domestic products. On the other hand, the latter refers to the services needed when the residents are already settled in, such as medical services, stationery stores and an eBay-like Web site to enable neighbors to sale used items among them.

Figure 7. A public notice on one of the privada's entrances giving instructions about the use of trash bins

Finally, we found that the needs of communication among neighbors could be fulfilled in a better way. We found that Conectha e-mail account is not very popular among the residents. Moreover, not everybody even owns a computer. The residents have fulfilled this need of communication with pieces of paper posted on the houses' front doors and public places such as the school. Regarding this, one resident commented *"... we use little pieces of paper glued on the walls, this because I know that not all the 100% of the inhabitants either has a computer or visits the Conectha website"*. One solution that might encourage the use of the Web site is an electronic posting service together with a public display such as the ones used in most banks (e.g., led-based displays).

5   Conclusions

This paper presented the results of an initial analysis of data gathered through a set of interviews conducted with families from a suburban area of Mexico City by the end of February, 2006, where neighbors were provided with computers and internet as part of the facilities.

From a technological standpoint, our results indicated that the implementation of ICTs to support daily life in residential communities experienced radical and unpredictable adaptations. Our findings confirm that the full adoption of any technology should be in terms of the relative usefulness perceived by users, but this perception of usefulness can change with time or just be supported by undiscovered needs which become evident once people interact with the technology. The case of the online commercial link illustrate the former point and the security cameras the latter point. Moreover, even when the technological scenario presented in this paper can be somewhat simplistic, our findings revealed that a lot of social issues might arise thus hampering the proper adoption and use of the services provided. This experience suggest that the implementation of fully tech-enabled houses such as efforts made by MIT [10] and Georgia Tech [11] may be still far away from now thus leaving them somewhat futuristic. Although these latter projects are aimed at other purposes rather than facilitating the interactions and coexistence between neighbors, results from our study suggest that social implications are often left aside when designing, developing and implementing technology that is intended to alter the 'natural' manner people carry out quotidian things.

On the other hand, the experience itself at Tecamac indicate that the proposal of the G7 Habitat concept as a technology-enabled household served well as a marketing tool and promoted the first contact with the housing development. However, as people moved to the step of taking a decision with regards of buying the property, the most important criteria is to have peace of mind by living in a safe, secure environment. As we continue our study, collection and analysis of our data, we expect to consolidate a solid understanding of some of the issues expressed here and the way people at Real del Sol are experiencing a home connected to the world. Finally, we believe that studies such us this one are of paramount importance as they provide valuable insights and implications for the design and deployment of technology in real communities on a large scale.

References

[1]   AMIPCI, "Hábitos de los Usuarios de Internet en México 2005." Oct, 2005.

[2]   INEGI, "Encuesta Nacional sobre Disponibilidad y Uso de Tecnologías de la Información en los Hogares.," 2005.

[3]   M. Foth and M.Brereton, "Enabling local interaction and personalized networking in residential communities through action research and participatory design," in *OZCHI 2004: Supporting community interaction*, P. Hyland and L. Vrazilic, Eds. Wollongong, NSW: University of Wollongong, 2004, pp. 20-24.

[4]   MexicoUnido.org, "Mexico Unido por la Democracia," in *http://www.mexicounido.org/*, 2006.

[5]   S. Low, "Behind the Gates," *New York and London: Routledge*, 2003.

[6]   M. Foth, "Analyzing the Factors Influencing the Successful Design and Uptake of Interactive Systems to Support Social Networks in Urban Neighborhoods," *International Journal of Technology and Human Interaction*, vol. 2, pp. 65-82, 2006.

[7]   J. M. Carroll and M. B. Rosson, "A Trajectory for Community Networks," *The Information Society*, vol. 19, pp. 381-393, 2003.

[8]   M. Gurstein, "Community informatics, community networks and strategies for flexible networking," *Community informatics: Shaping computer-mediated social relations*, pp. 263-283, 2001.

[9]   J. Corbin and A. Strauss, "Basics of Qualitative Research," *Thousand Oaks (CA): Sage Publications*, 1998.

[10]   S. Intille, K. Larson, and C. Kukla, "House_n: The MIT Home of the Future Project," MIT Dept. of Architecture. http://architecture.mit.edu/house_n, 2000.

[11]   X. Bian, G. D. Abowd, and J. M. Rehg, "Using Sound Source Localization to Monitor and Infer Activities in the Home," Georgia Institute of Technology Report Number: GIT-GVU-04-20, 2004.

Intelligent Tutoring Systems using Reinforcement Learning to teach Autistic Students

B. H. Sreenivasa Sarma and B. Ravindran
Department of Computer Science and Engineering,
Indian Institute of Technology Madras, India.

Abstract. Many Intelligent Tutoring Systems have been developed using different Artificial Intelligence techniques. In this paper we propose to use Reinforcement Learning for building an intelligent tutoring system to teach autistic students, who can't communicate well with others. In reinforcement learning, a policy is updated for taking appropriate action to teach the student. The main advantage of using reinforcement learning is that, it eliminates the need for encoding pedagogical rules. Various issues in using reinforcement learning for intelligent tutoring systems are discussed in this paper.

1 Introduction

A student learns better through one-to-one teaching than through class room teaching. Intelligent Tutoring System (ITS) is one of the best ways of one-to-one teaching. ITS instructs about the topic to a student, who is using it. The student has to learn the topic from an ITS by solving problems. The system gives a problem and compares the solution it has with that of the student and then it evaluates the student based on the differences. The system keeps on updating the student model by interacting with the student. As the system keeps updating the student's knowledge, it considers what the student needs to know, which part of the topic is to be taught next, and how to present the topic. It then selects the problems accordingly.

There are three modules in ITS, namely domain, pedagogical and student modules as shown in Fig.1. The domain module or knowledge base is the set of questions being taught. The pedagogical module contains the methods of instruction and how the knowledge should be presented to the student. The student module contains the knowledge about the student.

Please use the following format when citing this chapter:

Sarma, B. H. S., Ravindran, B., 2007, in IFIP International Federation for Information Processing, Volume 241, Home Informatics and Telematics: ICT for the Next Billion, eds. Venkatesh, A., Gonsalves, T., Monk, A., Buckner, K., (Boston: Springer), pp. 65-78.

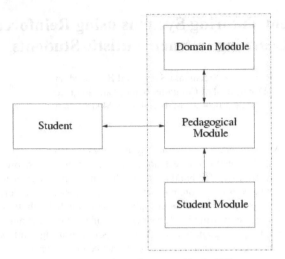

Fig. 1. Block diagram of basic ITS

1.1   Need of an ITS for autistic students

Autism is a semantic pragmatic disorder, characterized by deficits in *socialization, communication and imagination*. Along with the deficits, autistic children may have exceptional learning skills of unknown origin. Many children with autism do make eye contact, especially with familiar people. However, often it is observed that the eye contact is less frequent than would be expected, or it is not used effectively to communicate with others. Our approach mainly focuses on developing an ITS to teach such students.

1.2   Motivation for using Reinforcement Learning

Usually, ITS uses artificial intelligence techniques [5] to customize their instructions according to the student's need. For this purpose the system should have the knowledge of the student (student model) and the set of pedagogical rules. Pedagogical rules are usually in the rule-based form. For example, "if-then" where the "if" part is student model dependent and the "then" part is the teaching action taken. There are some disadvantages with this method. First, there are many rules which a system can use to teach efficiently, but which are very difficult to encode. Secondly, it is difficult to incorporate the knowledge that human teachers use, but cannot express. The machine tutors have a different set of data available than the human tutors, so the knowledge that could improve the tutor's performance is ignored. Third, rule-based systems are not adaptive to new student's behavior.

The organization of this paper is as follows: Section 2 gives a brief description of reinforcement learning (RL). Section 3 presents the basic idea of using RL for ITS. In Sections 4 and 5, experimental results have been discussed. Some issues in the designing ITS and future work have been discussed in Section 6.

2   Reinforcement learning

RL [9] is learning what to do, how to map situations to actions, so as to maximize a numerical reward signal. The learner is not told which actions to take, as in most forms of machine learning, but instead must discover which actions yield the most reward by trying them. To obtain high reward, an RL agent must prefer actions that it has tried in the past and found to be effective in producing reward. But to discover such actions, it has to try actions that it has not selected before.

An RL system consists of a *policy*, a *reward function*, a *value function*, and, optionally, a *model* of the environment. A *policy* defines the learning agent's way of behaving at a given time, it is a mapping from perceived states of the environment to the actions to be taken when in those states. A *reward function* defines the goal in an RL problem, it maps each perceived state of the environment to a single number, a *reward*, indicating the intrinsic desirability of that state. The *value* of a state is the total amount of reward an agent can expect to accumulate over the future, starting from that state.

In an ITS, the RL agent acts as the pedagogical module. The RL agent learns a policy for presenting the examples and the hints to the student. In [1, 5], the authors have proposed theoretically, the idea that RL can be efficiently used for learning to teach in an ITS. In [8], the authors used basic RL algorithms like softmax and ε - greedy for evaluating the effects of hints on the student. They used the method of clustering students into different levels according to their knowledge. The RL agent then uses this cluster information to take teaching actions. But in our case we have taken the information of individual students, which we expect to provide efficient information to the ITS about a student. In [4], RL is used for modeling a student. They proposed different ways of selecting state variables for an RL agent.

2.1   Mathematical background

This section gives definitions and a brief description of the concepts used in RL. In RL framework, the agent makes its decisions as a function of a signal from the environment's *state, s*. A state signal summarizes past sensations compactly, in such a way that all relevant information is retained. This normally requires more than the immediate sensations, but never more than the complete history of all past sensations. A state signal that succeeds in retaining all relevant information is said to be *Markov*, or to have the *Markov property*.

2.2   Markov Decision Process

An RL task that satisfies the Markov property is called a *Markov decision process* or MDP. If the state and action spaces are finite, then it is called a finite *Markov decision process (finite* MDP). Finite MDPs are particularly important to the theory of RL.

It is relevant to think that a state signal is Markov even when the state signal is non-Markov. A state should predict subsequent states, where the environment model is learned. Markov states are efficient to do these things. If the state is designed as Markov then RL systems perform better than with a non-Markov state. For these reason, it is better to think of the state at each time step as an approximation to a Markov state, though it is not fully Markov. Theory that applies to Markov cases can also be applied to many tasks that are not fully Markov.

2.3   Value Functions

The *value function* is the future reward that can be expected or the expected return. The value functions are defined with respect to particular policies. Let S be the set of possible states and $A(s)$ be the set of actions taken in state s, then the *policy*, π, is a mapping from each state, $s \in S$ and action, $a \in A(s)$, to the probability, $\pi(s, a)$, of taking an action, a, when in state, s. The *value* of a state, s, under a policy, π, defined $V^{\pi}(s)$, is the expected return when starting in s and following π thereafter. For MDPs, we can define $V^{\pi}(s)$ formally as

$$V^{\pi}(s) = E_{\pi}\{R_t \mid s_t = s\}$$

$$= E_{\pi}\left\{\sum_{k=0}^{x} \gamma^k r_{t+k+1} \mid s_t = s\right\} \tag{1}$$

Where $E_{\pi}\{\}$ denotes the expected value given that the agent follows policy, π, r_{t+k+1} is the reward for $(t + k + 1)^{th}$ time step and γ is the *discount factor*. Note that the value of the terminal state, if any, is always zero. We call the function $V^{\pi}(s)$, the *state-value function* for policy, π. Similarly, the value of taking action a in state s under a policy, π, denoted $Q_{\pi}(s, a)$, as the expected return starting from s, taking the action a, and thereafter following policy π :

$$Q^{\pi}(s, a) = E_{\pi}\{R_t \mid s_t = s, a_t = a\}$$

$$= E_{\pi}\left\{\sum_{k=0}^{x} \gamma^k r_{t+k+1} \mid s_t = s, a_t = a\right\} \tag{2}$$

Where $Q_{\pi}(s, a)$ is the *action-value function* for policy, π.

Finding an optimal policy that gives a high reward over long run is the goal of an RL task. For finite MDPs, an optimal policy is a policy, π, that is better than or equal to a policy π', if its expected return is greater than or equal to that of π' for all states. There would be at least one policy, that is better than or equal to other policies, which is called an optimal policy. All the optimal policies are denoted by π^*, and their value functions are denoted by V^* and Q^*.

2.4   Q-learning

Q-learning [10] is a popular RL algorithm that does not need a model of its environment and can be used on-line. Q-learning algorithm works by estimating the values of state-action pairs. Once these values have been learned, the optimal action from any state is the one with the highest Q-value. Q-values are estimated on the basis of experience as in Eq. (3).

$$Q(s,a) \leftarrow Q(s,a) + \alpha[r + \gamma \max_{a'} Q(s',a') - Q(s,a)] \quad (3)$$

This algorithm is guaranteed to converge to the correct Q-values with probability one if the environment is stationary and depends on the current state and the action taken in it.

3   ITS using RL

In this case, RL acts as a pedagogical module which selects appropriate action to teach student by updating Q-values. The RL agent has a function approximator and an RL algorithm, as show in Fig. 2. The state of the student is the summary of a few past training questions asked and the response of the student for those questions. As we are not considering the entire history of questions and answers, this problem is a non-Markov problem. So, to make it more Markov we considered the responses of some of the past questions for the state of the student.

Initially, a random state of the student is considered and a reward for RL agent is obtained. The RL agent takes an action according to the state and reward. The action of the RL agent is to select appropriate question or hint for the student. Each question has its own target. Student is tested with this question as shown in Fig. 2. By following a strategy, a reward for the RL is calculated from the student's response. Then the student is trained with same question as shown in Fig. 3 and state of the student is obtained from the trained output. This process is continued for some number of questions, which is called an *episode*.

A function approximator is used for generalization of states in a large state space. Most states encountered will never have been experienced exactly before. The only way to learn anything at all is to generalize from previously experienced states to one that have never been seen. Many RL algorithms [9] are available which updates Q-values and selects an action accordingly. The knowledge base consists of the questions from a topic, which are represented according to that needed for a student to learn.

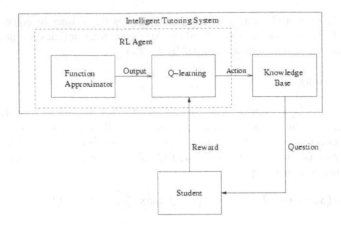

Fig.2. Block diagram of testing phase of the student using ITS with RL.

3.1 Simulated Students

Cohen [6] has shown that Artificial Neural Networks (ANN) trained with backpropogation can appropriately model the selective attention and generalization abilities of autistic students. The model is based on neuropathological studies which suggest that affected individuals have either too few or too many neuronal connections in various regions of the brain. In simulations, where the model was taught to discriminate children with autism from children with mental retardation, having too few simulated neuronal connections led to relatively inferior discrimination of the input train patterns, consequently, relatively inferior generalization of the discrimination to a novel train patterns. Too many connections produced excellent discrimination but inferior generalization because of overemphasis on details unique to the training set.

By using simulated-student, teachers can keep checking the simulated student's knowledge base. If the teachers don't like the recently taken action, they can reset the student's knowledge and try again. Teachers can teach as many times as they can to the simulated student to study the effect of the instructions on the student. Teachers can experiment their tactics with simulated student without fear of failing, which can give negative results with human student. We have used appropriately chosen ANNs to simulate students in our work.

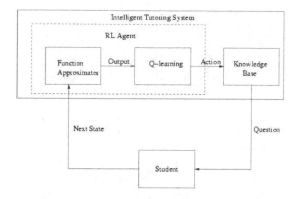

Fig. 3. Block diagram of training phase of the student using ITS with RL.

4 Experiments

We have developed an ITS to teach pattern classification problem. In our case, pattern classification problem is that the student has to classify the pattern (question) given to him. This problem is selected for validating the approach using ANNs, though this is not directly relevant to teaching children. Appropriate question banks should be developed to teach human students.

In pattern classification problem, the knowledge base contains two dimensional patterns from four classes, A, B, C and D, as shown in Fig. 4. The classes are selected in such a way that if a random action is selected, the probability of selecting the pattern from class A is more than from the other classes. The target output for ANN is a four dimensional vector, for example, [1 0 0 0] is the target for class A, [0 1 0 0] is for class B, and so on.

On-line training and testing have been performed on the ANN. The response (output) of ANN is classified into correct (1) and wrong (0) answers. For example, if the target of training question is [0 0 1 0] and if the third output of the ANN is higher than all other outputs then the response is considered as correct, else wrong. The summary of the ANN's response for past 300 questions and the history of responses for past 50 questions are considered for a state of the ANN.

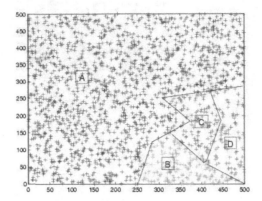

Fig.4. Knowledge base of pattern classes

Among the past 300 questions, let N_A be the number of questions asked from class A. Let N_{AC} and N_{AW} be the number of correct answers and wrong answers for N_A , respectively. Similarly, let $N_B, N_{BC}, N_{BW}, N_C, N_{CC}, N_{CW}, N_D, N_{DC}$ and N_{DW} be the number of questions asked, correct answers and wrong answers from classes B, C and D, respectively. Let x_i be the ith question in an episode. Let z_{i-j}, $1 \le j \le 50$, be the answer for x_{i-j} question. Then the state of the ANN is   classes $[N_A N_{AC} N_{AW} N_B N_{BC} N_{BW} N_C N_{CC} N_{CW} N_D N_{DC} N_{DW} x_{i-50} z_{i-50} x_{i-49} z_{i-49} ... x_{i-1} z_{i-1}]$ These four form an action set, $A(s)$, for the RL agent. It selects a question from the knowledge base, through policy and ANN is tested with that question. The negative of the Mean Square Error (MSE) of the output of ANN is given as a reward for the RL agent. The same question is used to train the ANN, and the output is used to find the next state of the ANN. This procedure is repeated for 25 episodes, each episode containing 2000 questions. These experiments are done on normal ANN and on ANN model of autistic student.

4.1   RL algorithm

For training of the RL agent, a slightly modified version of Watkin's Q-learning with backpropagation [2] is used. An ANN with single hidden layer is used to learn the $Q(s, a)$ function. The number of input neurons is equal to the dimension of the state, hidden layer contains number of neurons required for feature extraction and number of output neurons equal to the number of actions taken. In this case, we have 72 dimension states, feature size is 80 and 4 actions to be taken.

Activation function for the hidden units is the approximate Gaussian function. Let d_i be the squared distance between the current input vector, s, and the weights in the hidden unit, j. Then,

$$d_j = \sum_{i=1}^{72} (s_i - w_{ji}\alpha)^2 \tag{4}$$

Where, s_i is the ith component of s at current time and w_{ji} are the weights of hidden layer. The output, y_i, of hidden unit j is

$$y_j = \begin{cases} \left(1-\frac{d_j}{\rho}\right)^2, & if \ \ d_j < \rho \\ 0, & otherwise \end{cases} \tag{5}$$

Where ρ controls the radius of the region in which the unit's output is nonzero and α controls the position of the RBFs in the state space.

Actions are selected ε-greedily, to explore the effect of each action. To update all weights, error back-propagation is applied at each step using the following temporal-difference error

$$e_t = r_{t+1} + \gamma \max_{a_{t+1}}[Q(s_{t+1}, a_{t+1})] - Q(s_t, a_t) \tag{6}$$

Let v_{jl} be the weights of the lth output neuron. Then weights are updated by the following equations, assuming unit k is the output unit corresponding to the action taken, and all variables are for the current time t.

$$\Delta w_{ji} = \frac{\beta_h}{\rho} e_t y_j v_{j,k} (s_i - w_{j,i}) \tag{7}$$

$$\Delta v_{j,k} = \beta e_t y_i \tag{8}$$

$Q(s_{t+1}, a')$, $\forall a' \in A(s)$, is the product of updated $v_{j,k}$ and the output of function approximator, y_i.

5 Results

The results in Fig. 5 and 6 are obtained for $\varepsilon = 0.2$, $\beta_h = 0.09$ which means the exploration is done for 20% of the questions. The other parameters are, $\beta = 1.0$ and $\alpha = 200$.

Fig. 5(a) shows the average percentage classification for first 500 questions selected for the normal ANN with 5 hidden layer neurons, without ITS and with ITS. Classification of ANN without ITS is around 26%, which is much less than that compared to the classification of ANN with ITS, which is around 70%. Fig. 5(b) shows the histogram of actions taken by ITS. The uniform distribution of the actions shows that the ITS is not stuck in the local optima. ITS selects an action depending on the present state of the student, to increase the future classification rate of the ANN.

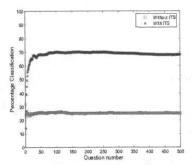 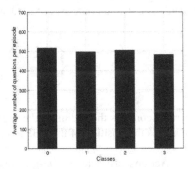

Fig. 5. (a) Percentage classification (left figure) by ANN model of normal student (learning rate 0.2). (b) Histogram (right figure) of actions taken by RL agent, averaged over episodes. (0, 1, 2 and 3 represent classes A, B, C, and D respectively).

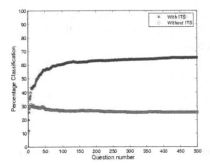 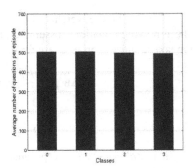

Fig. 6. (a) Percentage classification (left figure) by ANN model of an autistic child (learning rate 0.2). (b) Histogram (right figure) of actions taken by RL agent (0, 1, 2 and 3 represent classes A, B, C, and D respectively)

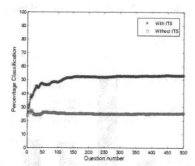
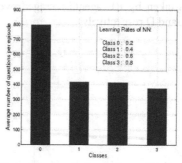

Fig. 7. (a) Percentage classification by ANN model of autistic student with learning rates 0.2, 0.4, 0.6 and 0.8 for classes 0, 1, 2, and 3, respectively. (b) Histogram of actions taken by RL agent, averaged over episodes (0, 1, 2 and 3 represent classes A,B,C, and D respectively)

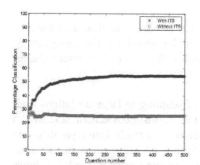
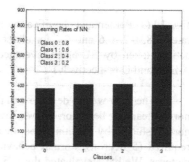

Fig. 8. (a) Percentage classification by ANN model of normal student with learning rates 0.8, 0.6, 0.4 and 0.2 for classes 0,1,2 and 3 respectively (b) Histogram of actions taken by RL agent, averaged over episodes (0,1,2 and 3 represent classes A,B,C, and D respectively)

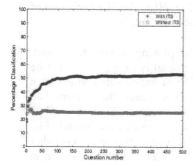
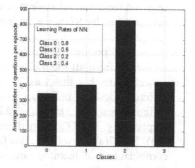

Fig. 9 (a) Percentage classification by ANN model of normal student with learning rates 0.8, 0.6, 0.2 and 0.4 for classes 0, 1, 2, and 3 respectively (b) Histogram of

actions taken by RL agent, averaged over episodes (0,1,2 and 3 represent classes A,B,C, and D respectively)

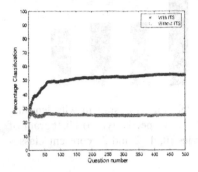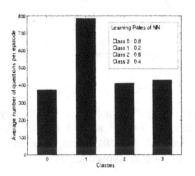

Fig. 10 (a) Percentage classification by ANN model of normal student with learning rates 0.8, 0.2, 0.6 and 0.4 for classes 0, 1, 2, and 3 respectively (b) Histogram of actions taken by RL agent, averaged over episodes (0,1,2 and 3 represent classes A,B,C, and D respectively)

The goal was to develop an ITS capable of adapting to large deviations from normal learning behavior. So, we have simulated models of both autistic student and normal student by selecting more neurons (15 neurons) in the hidden layer than that required (5 neurons, normal behavior) for capturing the information in the input patterns. We have evaluated the ITS using these simulated models. Fig. 6(a) shows the classification rate for ANN model for autistic student, with ITS and without ITS. Classification rate of autistic model can be compared with that of the normal ANN. In both cases, the percentage classification is approaching the same value (70%), indicating the autistic student can be taught effectively using ITS. But autistic student needs more number of questions (around 175 questions) to learn, than that required for a normal student (around 50 questions). Fig. 6(b) gives the histogram of actions taken by RL agent for the ANN model of autistic student.

The policy learned by the ITS seemed to be picking actions at random, uniformly from all the 4 classes. Though this is the desired behavior, we cannot be entirely sure that this was learned. So we tried different experiments which have different desired behaviors. For example, experiments where the student had different learning rates like 0.2, 0.4, 0.6 and 0.8 for classes A, B, C, and D respectively. The ITS learned the appropriate mix of actions to take, as shown in Fig. 7(b). Fig. 7(a) shows the classification performance of such combination. For other combinations of learning rate, similar learned behavior was observed as shown in Fig. 8, 9 and 10.

6   Conclusions and Future Work

Sections 4 and 5 presented the experiments performed to test the application of RL for ITS to teach an autistic student. We conclude that, by considering the history and summary of past few questions as state variables, an autistic student can be taught as effectively as a normal student.

We are now concentrating on improving the present ITS using the hierarchical framework [3]. In a hierarchical framework, entire knowledge base is divided into lessons and each lesson is divided into different categories. The RL agent has to learn two policies, one for picking a lesson and the other for picking a categories within the lesson, which is expected to improve the performance of the ITS.

This can be extended to real world problems like teaching mathematics, where selection of state variables and action variables is much more difficult task. In this paper, we used the history of past 50 questions and summary of past 300 questions as state variables. But in real world situation, we can consider the variables like the amount of time taken by the student to answer a question, history of hints the student requested. More work can be done in selecting state variables, which can improve, not only the percentage classification but also the learning rate. In this case, we have to consider which type of questions form a group, for example, easy questions form a group and tough questions form another group.

Other applications of our work include pattern synthesis and active learning. Pattern synthesis is the process of generating patterns for training and testing a machine. In our case, the two dimensional data generated as a question can be considered as the pattern synthesis problem. Active learning is the "learning with examples" [7]. This is a closed-loop phenomenon of a learner asking questions that can influence the data added to its training examples. In the case of ITS, the student has the facility to ask for hints for improving his knowledge on the topic, this can be considered as active learning. Active learning provides greatest reward in situations where data are expensive or difficult to obtain.

References

1. B. Abdellah, D. Theo and M. Bernard. An approach of reinforcement learning use in tutoring systems. In *Proceedings of International Conference on Machine learning and Applications, ICMLA '02*, 2002.
2. C. W. Anderson. Q-learning with hidden-unit restarting. In *Proceedings of Fifth International Conference on Neural Information Processing Systems*, pages 81-88, 1992.
3. A. Barto and S. Mahadevan. Recent advances in hierarchical reinforcement learning. *Discrete Event Dynamics Systems: Theory and Applications*, 13: 343-379, 2003.

4. J. E. Beck. Modeling the student with reinforcement learning. *Machine learning for User Modeling Workshop at the Sixth International Conference on User Modeling*, 1997.
5. J. E. Beck. Learning to teach with a reinforcement learning agent. *American Association for Artificial Intelligence (AAAI)*, 1998.
6. I. L. Cohen. An artificial neural network analogue of learning in autism. *Biological Psychiatry*, **36**(1):5-20, 1994.
7. D. A. Cohn, Z. Ghahramani, and M. I. Jordan. Active learning with statistical models. *Journal of Artificial Intelligence Research*, **4**: 129-145, 1996.
8. K. N. Martin and I. Arroya. AgentX: Using reinforcement learning to improve the effectiveness of intelligent tutoring systems.
9. R. S. Sutton and A. G. Barto. *Reinforcement learning: An Introduction*. MIT Press, Cambridge, MA, 1998.
10. Watkins, C. J. C. H. (1989). Learning from delayed rewards. Ph.D. thesis, Cambridge University.

Teaching - Learning Strategies in Interactive Education – A Case Study

V Bharathi Harishankar[1], Archana Ghode[3], Alankar Bandyopadhayay[2], Maryma Scotlin[3], and Hema A Murthy[3], Timothy A Gonsalves[3], Ashok Jhunjhunwala[3]

1   Department of English, Institute of Distance Education, University of Madras

2   University of Maryland

3   TeNeT Group, IIT Madras

Abstract. . This paper discusses active teaching and learning strategies that have been used in the TeNeT Online tutorials [1]. The focus of these tutorials is to enable rural students to pass the Standard X examination. The highlight of the tutorial is the use of the Question and Answer format. This problem-solving approach is evident in its three-pronged format: Learn, Practice and Test. Every module is based on questions and answers. In the learn mode, students learn the steps to answer a question and thus the concepts behind it. In the practice and evaluation modes, students can test their knowledge and understanding. This approach enhances the element of interactivity in these tutorials. Combined together, the elements of interactivity and problem-solving have made the tutorials a healthy supplement to conventional class rooms.

Keywords: web-based, interactivity, learn, practice, test, problem-solving

1   Introduction

The dynamics of teaching and learning usually involves three entities: teacher, domain of knowledge and student. The Internet has today become the fourth entity. The Internet has made available information at the click of a mouse. It is being increasingly used as an important resource in distance learning [2–6]. What is key in these initiatives is the inclusion of interactivity. In fact, feedback on MIT's [2] initiative has been that most youngsters would like more interactivity.

The TeNeT Online tutorials correspond to a similar experiment at the high school level. Since the target audience are high school students, the emphasis in material has been to keep the interactivity as high as possible. This is achieved by using a problem-solving approach to learning. The paper is organized as follows: Section 2 briefly

Please use the following format when citing this chapter:

Harishankar, V. B., Ghode, A., Bandyopadhayay, A., Scotlin, M. Murthy, H. A., Gonsalves, T. A., Jhunjhunwala, A., 2007, in IFIP International Federation for Information Processing, Volume 241, Home Informatics and Telematics: ICT for the Next Billion, eds. Venkatesh, A., Gonsalves, T., Monk, A., Buckner, K., (Boston: Springer), pp. 79-89.

outlines the aims and goals of the tutorials. Section 3 analyses the overall design features of the tutorials. Section 4 elaborates the three main features of our tutorials namely Learn, Practice and Test sections. Section 5 examines the problem-solving approach that has been enhanced in this method. Section 6 gives details on field trials of the tutorials. Section 7 concludes on an optimistic note in terms of scalability of effort.

2 Background to TeNeT Online Project

The TeNeT online project was initiated with the express purpose of enabling rural students in Tamil Nadu to pass the Standard X examinations. A random survey revealed that the percentage of failures was very high in English followed by Maths, Science and Social Studies in that order. One possible reason is that for students of vernacular medium, English is a subject taught within the confines of the classroom and not a language used prevalently in day to day communication. This is compounded by the fact that most rural students are first generation learners and do not have a support system at home (parents/tuition teachers) to supplement the material taught at school. The inevitable fallout of this is that rural students are rarely encouraged by their parents to repeat the exams again. Very often, they go back to the family trades and professions. More importantly, this failure keeps them out of more lucrative jobs because even shop floor jobs require a minimum pass in Standard X.

TeNeT Online's first set of material was a solved question bank with ten question papers each for English papers 1 and 2 of the Tamil Nadu board. The small initial feedback showed a marked improvement in marks obtained in class room tests. It also showed that there was demand for similar materials in other subjects, namely, Maths, Science and Social Studies. The primary goal of the TeNeT Online Tutorial is to supplement class room teaching. Another goal of the tutorial is to reach uniform teaching material to a large number of rural students. This is the primary reason for making the material web-based. Further the tutorials are able to provide individual attention to a student as opposed to a teacher who has to cater to 120 children in a high school. The obvious caution we took is to avoid making the online course "an electronic page turning" or "an audio-visual aid to rote learning." A major shift in focus that we have effected through interactivity is to transform the approach from conceptual learning to one of problem solving.

3 Design Strategies in TeNeT Online

Against this background, our goal was to provide, an easy to use interface. The following criteria were kept in mind when we design the tutorials:

1. gaining the attention of the students
2. stimulating recall
3. providing learning guidance

4. providing instant feedback
5. assessing performance
6. enhancing retention and transfer

In our tutorials, we combined a variety of commonly known software. Our program combines HTML and Java script at the front end and MySQL at the backend with PHP providing the link between the two. Different features of our tutorials combine to achieve the various steps in the instruction process. These include voice-overs, visual pop ups, gifs, mouse-overs, highlighting of key phrases and division of the web page in to main and work areas. This has resulted in the on line tutorials becoming guided educational explorations. These features have been combined in different fashions in the three main divisions of our tutorials, namely learn, practice and Test.

4 Main Components of TeNeT Online

A typical module of our tutorial provides three options to the learner: learn, practice, test. Of these, learn and practice are presented simultaneously as 2 links on the same page so that students can easily switch between learning and self-testing mode.

4.1 Learn mode

In this mode, the student comes across a question and its answer, If it is a multiple choice question, the answer is highlighted in a different color. A click on the "Play" (Figure 1) button enables the student to listen to the teacher's voice guiding them through the different steps to solve a particular question.

In subjects like Maths, different steps carry marks in the final exam. Key words and phrases in each answer are highlighted. In common practice, we don't recall entire answers from a book in xerox fashion but remember phrases/ points (Figure 2) which become memory cues. (Eg. Science and Social Studies – especially, formulae, concepts, definitions, years, etc.)

In a subject like English, the learn mode offers a bilingual experience. The page that is viewed is in English whereas the voice overs are in the local language.

Apart from enabling understanding, it allows the students to relate words

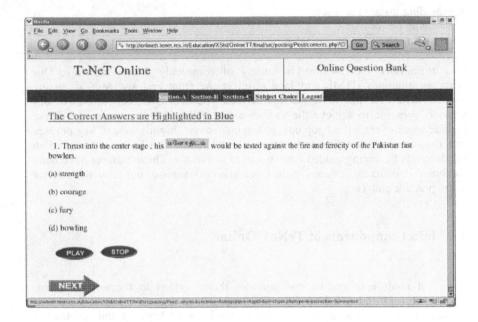

Figure 1: Multiple choice questions

to their meanings. Moreover, difficult words are highlighted and on mouse over, the meaning appears in the local language (Figure 1, 2)

Some picture gifs are also introduced to provide variety to the text. The underlying rationale for all these features is to maintain a high instructor profile as also to preempt possible queries and doubts.

4.2   Practice Mode

In this mode, students get an opportunity to assess themselves on what they have learnt. This apparently simple format is, in fact, the key to the interactivity of the module. For instance, once the student makes the choice, the voice over says 'correct' or 'wrong' (Figure 3)

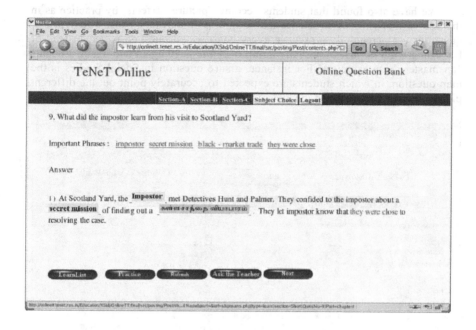

Figure 2: Keywords and phrases

Simultaneously, a picture gif projects a laughing face for the correct answer and a crying face for the wrong answer Figure 3). Apart from allowing students to know their mistakes, some modules, like our Social Science module, provide a clue as to where the correct answer may be found in the text book.

Since the online tutorial is almost always taken by a group of students (say 4 or 5), the practice module offers "collaborative or group learning" [7] by which an answer may be discussed, corrected or guessed without any penalty of marks or punishment and justified by the students themselves. This aspect is rarely encouraged in typical class room conditions and is therefore a highlight of our modules. The objective is to develop a testing environment with instant feedback to students.

Typically, every answer has key phrases. In the practice mode, the key phrases are given with several options in listboxes and the student makes a choice to click the correct answer. This mode teaches the students the step-by-step ordering of an answer. It is extremely useful in a subject like Maths, where every correct step is apportioned some marks.

By dividing the page into two halves, we follow an instant display of the correct and wrong options. This is done through the use of font colours. For instance, the 'red' display indicates a wrong choice and 'blue' indicates the correct choice. Moreover, it alerts the students to understand that in practice, if they go wrong in step 1, they cannot reach step 2 and so on. Indirectly, this weans them away from memorising the answers and to a minimal extent work on a cause and effect model.

We have also found that students become "picture perfect," by practice as in the use of maps in social science and diagrams in science. These two types of questions are perennially present in every board exam question paper. Instead of hazarding a guess, just by visually going over the page again and again, students can master these exercises. For instance, a sure question in Social Studies is the map question, in which students are expected to accurately point out the different places, regions and rivers on the given map (Figure 4).

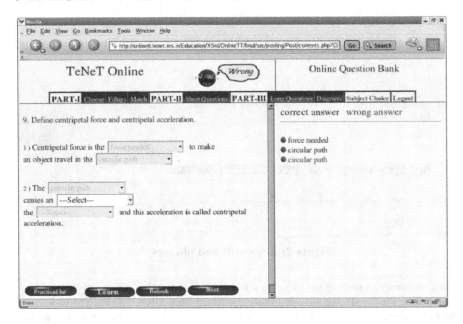

Figure 3: Practice Mode

In this mode, we provide a map with a lot of hot keys. After choosing the name of the place, students have to click on the correct location. This provides an interesting way of learning to mark the maps. Students also realize that it is not enough to know the location roughly and that a difference of even a millimeter will render their marking incorrect. In the present model, everything from specific places, to regions and rivers are isolated single points. In our future course of work, we hope to create a program by which students can actually draw the course of the river, for instance.

4.3 Test Mode

In the test mode, students are given the choice of attempting an entire question paper, thus simulating an exam hall situation. A further step in our tutorial is the concept of automatic generation of papers. This ensures that students receive a new question paper, every time they access it. It also simulates the pattern their final examination paper will take. For example, a typical computer generated question paper takes in to account the weightage given to each chapter, choices available, answer keys used by examiners to correct the answers and the like. Our final evaluation apportions marks for each section, by which a students can judge her/his own weaknesses and strengths. They will also be able to compare their earlier performances, overall and in individual sections (Figure 5).

Figure 4: Map marking

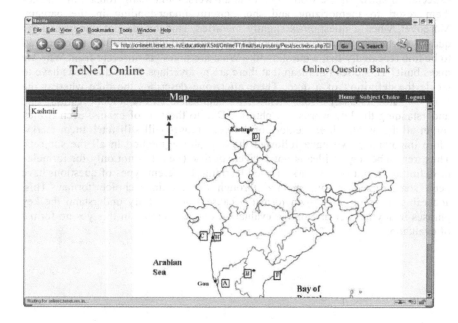

5   Problem Solving Approach in TeNeT Online

The focus of this paper and our online tutorial is to consider design aspects that can help improve the instructional effectiveness of teaching and learning. By designing an interactive instructional environment, the tutorials have taken into account two main factors, namely, the ways in which an information is processed and how learners perceive the process, store and recall information. Further, the interactivity is not achieved through tools like email, list servers, chat rooms or news groups, but through a dynamism worked in to the format of the web page itself. The effort here is to transform the student from being a"passive recipient of knowledge towards being a student involved in the learning process as an active, self- directed participant" [8].

The online tutorials reinforce a problem-solving approach to teaching and learning. For instance, there are certain common types of questions in each paper. These include: Fill in the blanks, Choose the best answer, Match the following, Short questions and Long questions. At a surface level, each of these questions seems to demand a different answer. However, they are all taken from the same lessons or chapters. Therefore, we don't necessarily have to learn the same chapter differently for different questions. Once we understand the key ideas, we use different combinations to tackle different questions.

For all practical purposes, we have made key words and phrases as important elements in an answer. While this makes the students word perfect in objective type of questions like Fill ups, Choose and Match, it also offers them hints to develop and answer the short and long questions. For example, a student cannot be expected to know all the words in all the answers. Quite dangerously, this makes them resort to memorizing and short circuit understanding in the bargain. Moreover, when a question is slightly modified, students do not understand the question, let alone know the answer. [In the English Online Tutorial, students had to be told repeatedly that a question like What are dikes? is different from Why are dikes built? This does not mean that there are no overlaps. Both questions have to tackle the definition of a dike! There after, one describes the dike whereas the other explains its use.] In our method, we emphasise on the student learning and understanding the key words and phrases. Due to the fear of exams, even if they forget all the words, their memory of the key phrases will still fetch them marks. More importantly, we have followed the key phrase method in all the subjects. Thus, remembering an idea is not subject specific (i.e., it is not only for formulae or definitions), but is the mark of good learning. Different types of questions have been standardized in our method through the multiple choice format. This, according to us, is a win-win format because students fully understand the key phrases in any answer and online evaluation is made simple in this yes-no format of evaluation.

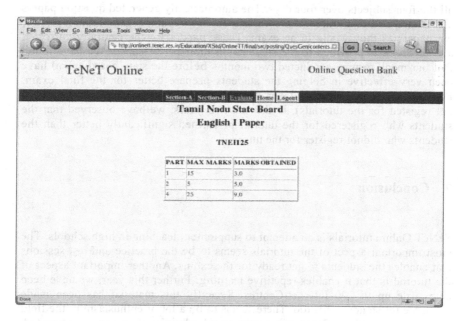

Figure 5: Test Results

6 Field Trials and Monitoring

The TeNeT online tutorials have been tested in the field for over two years now. The material was deployed in four centres in the first year, and in 18 centres in the second year. An NGO provided a scholarship for students to use this service. During the first year of deployment about 168 students went through the tutorials while during the second year about 800 students went through the tutorials. In both years, the performance in the final board exams has been complimentary. About 82% of the rural students passed the exam although the average for the entire state was about 75-77%. Internet centre wise, it was observed that centres that had good moderators to present the material performed well. This clearly indicates that the material can be only used to supplement instruction and not replace it. In many villages, the school teachers encouraged the students to take the tutorials as it helped them perform better in the school internal exams.

To test the effectiveness of the tutorial reports are automatically generated which detail the usage at every Internet-centre. This includes information namely, number of hours used, details of subjects that were used, details of questions attempted (Figure 6). We also have details of students that are registered for the program (photo-ids of the students registered are available). Ideally one would like to use technology to automatically take the attendance at every session. Further, we also use videoconferencing to interact with students and monitor progress. In addition to this we also conduct mock examinations in all the four subjects over four days. The automatically generated question papers are printed and distributed to the various Internet centres. The students answer the papers as they would in an exam. These papers are the centrally corrected and feedback is provided to the students on their performance. We have found that our mock exams (conducted two months before the state board exam) have been very effective in helping the students prepare better for the final exam. Further, the mock exams are taken by all students (includes students who have not registed for the tutorials). In the last two years, we have observed that the students who registered for the tutorial performed significantly better than the students who didnot register for the tutorial.

7   Conclusion

TeNeT Online tutorials is an attempt to supplement teaching in high schools. The most important aspect of the tutorials seems to be the practice and test sessions that enables the students to get ready for the exams. Another important aspect of the tutorial is that it enables repetitive learning. Further this year, we have been able scale up to 200 Internet-Centres. Recently this material has been made available for standard XII too. There seems to be a lot of enthusiasm in the field with a large number of students, teachers and administrators getting interested. An important aspect of the tutorials is that it provides a uniform teacher for all students irrespective of village, town, city or school that they are from. As the Internet is used as the medium for delivery of instruction, it was very easy to scale up from a mere 4 Internet-centres in the first year to 18 centres in the second year and to 200 centres this year. This year we have started reaching out to other states. We have started work on Standard X material for Karnataka and Gujarat.

8   Acknowledgement

This work was funded by the Intel Project: Driving Applications over Wireless in Rural India (ELE0304103INTIASHO/R430).

References
[1] http://onlinett.tenet.res.in
[2]http://www.ocw.mit.edu
[3]http://www.cmu.edu/oli
[4]http://ocw.usu.edu
[5[http://ocw.jhsph.edu
[6]   http://ocw.tufts.edu
[7] Le Jeune, Noel F, "Paper on Collaborative Learning in WBI",

http://www.ouray.cudenver.edu/nflejeun/doctoralweb/Courses/IT 5640.html
[8]Mathew, Norman and Maryanne Dobery-Poirier, "Using the WWW to Enhance Classroom Instruction" First Monday. Vol.5, number 3, March 2000
http://firstmonday.org/issues/issue53/mathew/index.html

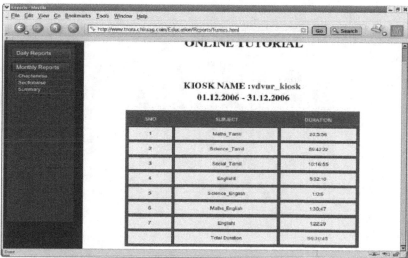

Figure 6: Usage Reports of an Internet Centre

On the role of awareness systems for supporting parent involvement in young children's schooling

Vassilis-Javed Khan, Panos Markopoulos and Berry Eggen
Eindhoven University of Technology, Eindhoven, The Netherlands

Abstract. This paper reports on an investigation of how Awareness Systems can support communication between busy parents and young children at school. The study involved the deployment and test of a rudimentary awareness system so that surveying opinions and wishes regarding this type of technology would be grounded upon concrete experiences. The prototype was installed in a classroom for two weeks and connected five families with their children. Overall, parents appreciated receiving awareness information and did not experience it as an undesirable distraction. Both they and their children did not experience privacy problems. They raised concerns about the possibility of children becoming more dependent upon their parents from such technology and stated they would not want to receive information that they would not be able to react upon.

1   Introduction

In recent years there has been an increasing interest in technologies that support sustained communication channels between individuals or groups that allow them to build up and maintain a mental model of the activities of each other. Often these technologies are discussed under the label of "awareness systems", in juxtaposition to solutions that support the efficient and goal directed exchange of information. Early research on Media Spaces examined the use of long-term video and audio-links supporting co-workers, [1] or in a domestic context [2], [3].

Awareness systems are usually conceived as requiring low effort: information is usually captured semi-autonomously and the display of it is usually designed to be non-disruptive. Often the terms 'peripheral display' and 'peripheral awareness' are used respectively to suggest that the information they present furnishes the periphery of someone's attention and is easily brought to the foreground when needed or that the person viewing it has to expend minimal effort and almost without noticing build up awareness of another person or group.

Please use the following format when citing this chapter:

Khan, V.-J., Markopoulos, P., Eggen, B., 2007, in IFIP International Federation for Information Processing, Volume 241, Home Informatics and Telematics: ICT for the Next Billion, eds. Venkatesh, A., Gonsalves, T., Monk, A., Buckner, K., (Boston: Springer), pp. 91-101.

The interest in awareness systems can be seen as symptomatic of an ever increasing availability of information and communication technology, in different contexts, for different user groups. The present research investigates the potential of awareness systems to support busy working families with children. We are especially interested in how to provide technological solutions that will stimulate and facilitate parental involvement in children's lives. Increased parental involvement is recognized by social scientists to provide benefits for the development of children socially and academically [4], [5].

There have been several attempts to support communication between parents and children and to inform parents of school activities. For example, [6] report the use of voice-mail to support communication between teachers and parents. A voice-mail-messaging application enabled parents and teachers exchange messages asynchronously. The experimental use of the system was reported to result in a steep increase of information exchange between them. School failure of students dropped and there was an increase in the number of students who became eligible for academic honor. This case suggests the potential benefits of the deployment of modern communication technologies.

While such a direct system such as a voice-mail has a lot of potential it only supports communication between teacher and parent and it requires an explicit effort by the teacher. This kind of effort may be hard to sustain over longer periods of time and to scale up for a large number of pupils. Awareness systems connecting parents to their children through the day could address this limitation, by supporting the semi-automatic capture of relevant information and its use as a complement to extant communication channels, including face-to-face communication or even voice-mail.

The auxiliary nature of awareness information has to be stressed here. Parents and children who are not separated by distance or other social problems (like a divorce) are most likely to get ample opportunity to communicate with each other. However, especially for younger children, parents may find it problematic to find out what is happening through the day, what are the problems their children are facing, what are their successes and joys. It is well known and confirmed by recent studies, e.g., Hoenderdos et al. [7], how difficult it is for parents to obtain answers to the question "how was your day?" beyond one-word descriptions such as 'fine', 'ok'. Hounderdos et al. proposed a sound capture device that children could use through the day to record sounds from their environment. The main concept (that was never realized and tested) was to play these sounds for parents later in the day, letting them provide triggers for their conversations. Another interesting project [8] examined the exchange of video clips between children and other family members to support them in feeling connected.

The main difference of our motivation with the aforementioned projects lies in the explicit/intentional nature of communication. We are interested in supporting automatic exchange of awareness information rather than have explicit communication. The advantages are obvious for the group of people we are focusing:

saving time and effort for parents and teachers while keeping informal communication channels open. However, challenges lie in what content should such systems exchange, how it will be used and what type of privacy concerns arise.

The present study builds on an earlier interview study regarding the communication needs of busy parents [9]. In that study semi-structured interviews were held with 20 parents and were analyzed qualitatively. The analysis inventorized communication needs that are not met sufficiently by current technology and explored the potential and drawbacks of awareness systems for this target user group. One of the main findings was that parents wish for more awareness of what happens at school. There were several questions left open; specifically some skepticism towards the potential role of awareness systems was expressed.

More specifically, parents were skeptical of an 'always-on' communication channel. For example, interviewees suggested that when at work they might prefer not to have information they cannot react to (e.g., if their child is missing them) or that the constant availability of information about their children might distract them from their work, disturbing the boundaries they try to maintain between their work and their private lives. Parental involvement in children's lives emerged as a category of particular importance, influencing the behavior, communication and awareness needs of the working parent throughout the day. Finally, the exchange of experiences especially during dinner, was found to be a valued ritual among our participants. The present study aimed to probe deeper in those issues and examine when awareness information is distracting or undesirable and what kind of information may be most valued.

While very informative, these interviews relied on self-reported beliefs and attitudes expressed outside a specific context and without reference to a specific technology. Interviewed parents found it hard to relate to the concept of awareness systems and as a result the related discussion was hypothetical and results not very reliable. We felt that exposing parents to using a system comparable to the class of systems we envision would provide richer and more reliable outcomes. In the remainder of this paper, we describe how we set up a simple awareness service for parents and their children and the reactions we obtained from a two week field trial. We do not suppose that this specific system is the solution they require yet it embodies some important characteristics of the type of systems we are interested in and as such serves to solicit relevant reactions and opinions from them.

2   Method

The study aimed to explore how busy parents and their children would experience a system providing awareness information about the children during school hours. A simple awareness system was built and parents were encouraged to use it for two weeks, after which they were interviewed regarding their experience. The study aimed to answer the following questions:

- Is there a need of parents having awareness information during the day about their children?
- Are such systems disruptive for the parents?
- Are such systems perceived privacy-threatening for children?

Accepting that the awareness information we provided was very basic and limited to what was easy to build in a short time, we set out to explore what kind of awareness information would be more valuable for our informants than what we could provide at this stage of our research.

2.1   Participants

We recruited five families from an international school. Our target group was "busy parents". More specifically we were looking for participants that:

- Are married or cohabiting,
- Have at least one dependent child,
- Both parents in the household work a minimum of 20 hours a week,
- Have children between the ages of 6 and 10.

We covered all of our requirements except the third one. Three of the couples we recruited had only one member who was working full time whereas the other was not working. We had in total five children and eight parents (three couples and two parents). The children were ten years old studying at the 7th class. They were fluent in English. It was a culturally mixed group consisting of one Korean, one Taiwanese, one American and two British. The average age of the participating parents was 43; they have been married on average 13,8 years and have on average of 2,2 children. Our participants were highly educated and hold higher than average positions in their employment.

2.2   Process

First, we held a briefing session at school. We handed the prototype PC application in a CD the week before the study was executed. One of the parents for each child involved in the study participated in the briefing session. During the session we presented background information to the research, introduced the study and answered questions they had.

By handing out the CD a week, we gave them the opportunity to install it and check whether everything was running properly prior to the actual study. Two participants had some technical problems but were promptly solved. One participant had several computers and decided not to install it at all, without informing us. We found this out only at the end. Another participant installed it but the connection was probably blocked by the firewall of his company. All this happened despite that we contacted the participants during the installation and at the first week through email about problems they might be experiencing.

We let parents experience the prototype for one week. At the end of the first week parents were asked to complete a web questionnaire. At the end of the second week we interviewed the parents. We analyzed those interviews qualitatively. As part of the interview we presented to parents four storyboards illustrating alternative concepts for an awareness system situated in a classroom. We asked the parents to rate each storyboard in scales of the ABC questionnaire [10] and then had a discussion about the system presented in the storyboard. The storyboards and their results cannot be described in the space of this article.

2.3   Materials

2.3.1   Prototype description

The prototype we used had three main components. First, was a small Bluetooth headset device. Participating children were asked to turn this on and keep it in their pocket every morning. They carried this device till the end of the school day and then turned it off and left it in the class so that they could turn it on and carry it again next morning.

Next, we installed a PC with an Internet connection and a USB Bluetooth dongle, at the classroom, running XP SP2 and our software[1] which queried every minute for the presence of the children's devices.

After querying, our prototype made a record in a database server at the University[2]. Along with the almost-real-time presence of children the database contained information regarding their day schedule.

The parents' client[3] was querying through http the database server at the University and was presenting the information to the parents' desktop. We also developed an alternative solution for the parents' in case they could not install our prototype. This was a dynamic web page presenting exactly the same information. We preferred parents to install our prototype in their desktop so that they would not associate this awareness service with a website or another web service. It actually turned out that one parent who had a Macintosh and could not install the software. This parent used the alternative web application.

---

[1] The prototype application running at the PC in the classroom was developed with C#. For querying the Bluetooth devices we used OpenNETCF. It was compiled for Windows XP.
[2] MySQL was used as the database server.
[3] The parent's program was developed with C# and compiled for Windows XP.

In our prototype, parents could view three possible images. These are shown in Figure 1. By moving the mouse over the image parents would see more detailed information about when was the last check by the PC in the classroom performed. It was developed to be always on top of other windows. Using two buttons parents could minimize or close it.

Child's device is detected   Child's device is not   There is a technical
                                          detected   problem

Fig. 1. Graphical presentation of awareness information

Fig. 2. Screenshot of a parent's desktop

2.3.2   Web questionnaire

The web questionnaire included five questions. Participants were asked about their experience till that moment, if they felt the system influenced their conversation with their child, what information was missing and how the child felt about it.

The purpose of having this questionnaire was twofold:

1. Get insight to the participants' experience halfway through the trial.
2. Anchor the final interview to the answers they provided.

2.3.3   Interview

The interview was scheduled after the period of two weeks. It lasted approximately 30 minutes and we began by discussing the answers from the web questionnaire. This was followed by an open discussion about the usage, the feelings and the overall experience of the system followed. Both participating parents and children were present. Children were asked about their experience of the system as well as if they felt their privacy was compromised.

3   Results

We must first clarify that we have two groups of users among the participating parents. The ones that used the system in the office (four) and the ones that used it at home (four). The four office users were fathers and the four home users were mothers.

3.1   On Disruptiveness

In our earlier interview study mentioned above participants expressed concerns about having a constant information flow. This did not turn out to be an issue for the participants we had. When participants were asked if it was disruptive they mentioned that this was not the case. In the words of a participant: "*it was no more demanding than a ping from an email or a PDA or another website, it wasn't sufficiently big*".

On the other hand, we must mention that office users complained about the space the image of Figure 1 occupied on their screens. Especially for laptop users; who were compelled to minimize it. Once minimized it was forgotten. The fact that screen space is important for work use denotes the need of having a separate device (e.g., a photo-frame, or a physical output device) for providing awareness information. Participants also mentioned that it did not create a feeling of involvement for them. That might be because when the system was minimized it was forgotten.

Home users reported also that the system was not disruptive. This we believe has to do with the general use of the home computer. It was not constantly used so having such an application running on the computer was a reason for the users to check it. For one participant this system became part of her routine, for the short time of the field study. When going to the kitchen she would also peak at what was going on at the class of her child.

3.2   On privacy threat

No privacy threat was reported by participants. When explicitly asked, both children and parents responded negatively. A child participant mentioned: *"it just felt normal"*. On the other hand, parents thought that if children were older it would have been different. This is consistent with literature on family communication suggesting that children have loose privacy concerns before the age of adolescence [11]. This may explain the different results of [12]; that study involved participants in their adolescence, who experienced serious privacy concerns.

When children were asked about carrying the device and if that created a feeling of being "looked over the shoulder" they unanimously said that this was not the case. Even three of them, in some occasions, forgot that the Bluetooth device was in their pocket and carried it back home. This shows that the device easily fitted their routine and was not something bothering them. In their words: *"I didn't even feel it was on me"*, *"I totally forgot about it"*.

3.2.1   The feeling of involvement versus the feeling of surveillance

Though not conclusive, the study was also positive regarding the feelings of involvement in children's lives. In the words of one participant who was a home user: *"it actually stirred the spirit of involvement rather than the spirit of surveillance and I didn't expect that"*. This particular participant liked the fact that the child felt that she was involved in her life.

Moreover this participant reported that the system helped in posing more precise questions to the child about her day. That was the effect of having schedule information. This participant's observation was that the child would easier respond to questions. In the participant's words:
"I always asks them about what happened at school but you sometimes get a word or nothing. If I would ask something like: "what was science like today" it kind of focuses them [referring to the child] cause otherwise the day becomes blur"

Another unexpected observation of the same couple was that they became more sensitized to their child's need to communicate with them. Their child would ask at the evening if they checked the system and asked them for more details about the way it was working.

3.3   Awareness information that could add value to AS in the context of a school

Higher precision information would be generally appreciated. Detail was required in the exact location of the children. One of our participants put it very eloquently: *"half the story is worse than no story at all"*. This was a common comment we received by all participants. Conversely, participants expressed a concern; they did not want to have information that would make them worry without the ability of reacting, e.g., if the system would show that there was a scheduled outdoor activity whereas the child was sitting in class. Such contradicting information might create a tension. On the one hand it would make the parent feel worried on the other hand the parent knows well that responsibility is handed over to the teacher. We think that this is an important observation that confirms our earlier interview study, reported in [9]. In light of these statements, we believe that an important acceptance factor for awareness systems used in this context is how they impact upon accountability of parents and teachers, and whether they create new concerns and responsibilities for parents who could be expected to react to awareness information shown to them.

An exception to not wanting to have to react to what is displayed to them concerned the safety of the child, e.g., they would want to be informed when the child leaves the school periphery unattended. This was expressed by several participants. One home-participant who was checking the prototype every day would welcome a "red icon" among the grey and green. That red icon would denote danger. Note though that the same participant added that such a system might be a solution for the school rather than the parents.

Another participant stressed the need of having richer information regarding "special occasions". These occasions would include school assemblies, happenings and generally social activities. One more participant wished to be able to observe the social dynamics between the participating children during the day. Another parent mentioned that she would check the prototype when there was a break scheduled because she wanted to be sure her child was out (presumably) playing with other children rather than sitting inside the class. It seems that observing social interactions between the children is a pronounced need for parents. This finding might map to the development phase the children are in.

4 Conclusions

Awareness Systems are still in their infancy particularly regarding their use outside collaborative work. The proposed benefits and costs they might bring are still very much hypothesized. Research studies such as the one presented here may help document what needs they can serve and what could be hindrances to their eventual acceptance and adoption.

An outcome of the previous interview study [9] was that busy parents might not want to have continuously available information about their children during their working day. The trial of the prototype suggests that this is not true. Parents valued the awareness information despite the fact that the simplicity of the prototype they experienced prevented it from offering substantial benefits and valuable information to the parents. This seems to be more pronounced for parents using the system from the office. Participants used the prototype more from home rather than the office and were more able to fit its use to their daily routine. However, the fact that participants expressed specific needs for awareness information suggests that such systems can bring added value to "busy parents" if appropriately designed and if higher quality information (in accuracy and relevance) would be provided.

The prototype we tested did not raise privacy concerns. A major reason for this was the age of the children concerned. We can expect more privacy concerns for children close to or during adolescence. Hence, more flexible and socially acceptable forms of information capture and communication need to be designed for that group.

Our main conclusion regarding our research aims concerns the need for more specific information from the school such as information about the social development of children.

Currently we are extending our system to be able to provide richer awareness information and to enable the survey of parents' opinions in situ. Such a contextual survey (using diary or experience sampling method) is necessary in order to explore the situatedness of the use of awareness information, that is largely unexplored when surveying the opinions of informants post-hoc. Further we are examining also the requirements of teachers and what their communication and privacy needs are that need to be addressed. Teachers tend to advocate parental involvement and wish to open up communication channels regarding the education of children. On the flip side they also need to protect themselves from excessive communication and excessive workload in providing the required information.

5   References

1.   S.A. Bly, S.R. Harrison, S. Irwin: Media Spaces: Bringing People Together in a Video, Audio and Computing Environment. Communications of the ACM, 36,1, 1993 p28-47.

2.   P. Markopoulos, N. Romero, J. van Baren, W. IJsselsteijn, B. de Ruyter, and B. Farshchian: Keeping in touch with the family: home and away with the ASTRA awareness system. In: Proceedings CHI '04, ACM Press, p. 1351-1354. 2004

3.   D. Hindus, S.D. Mainwaring, N. Leduc, A.E. Hagström, and O. Bayley: Casablanca: designing social communication devices for the home. In: Proceedings CHI '01, ACM Press, 2001 p. 325-223.

4.   J. Blanchard: The family-school connection and Technology. Paper presented at the Families, Technology, and Education Conference, Washington, DC. 1997

5.   K. Hoover-Dempsey, J. M. T. Walker, H. M. Sandler, D. Whetsel, C. L. Green, A. S. Wilkins, and K. E. Closson: Why do parents become involved? Research findings and implications. Elementary School Journal, 106(2); (2005) 105-130

6.   J.P. Bauch: Applications of technology to linking schools, families and students. Proceedings of the Families, Technology, and Education Conference. Retrieved Oct. 1, 2001

7.   R. Hoenderdos, A. Vermeen, M. Bekker, and A. Pierik: Design for experience: the "Look, mama!" experience, Proceedings of IDC, 2002, p. 4.

8.   O. Zuckerman, and P. Maes: CASY: Awareness System for Children in Distributed Families. In Proc. IDC'05, Conference on Interaction Design and Children. Boulder, Colorado, New York, NY, ACM Press. 2005

9.   V.J. Khan, P. Markopoulos, S. Mota, W. IJsselsteijn, B. de Ruyter: Intra-family communication needs; how can awareness systems provide support? Proceedings of the 2nd international conference on Intelligent Environments. 2006

10.   J. van Baren, W.A. IJsselsteijn, N. Romero, P. Markopoulos, B. de Ruyter: Affective Benefits in Communication: The development and field-testing of a new questionnaire measure. PRESENCE, Aalborg, Denmark, October 2003

11.   J.P. Caughlin, and S. Petronio: chapter: "Privacy in Families". In: Vangelisti, A.L., "Handbook of family communication", p. 379. Lawrence Erlbaum Associates. 2004

12.   K. Fraser, T. Rodden, and C. O'Malley: Home-school Technologies: considering the Family. IDC '06

Community Software Applications

T. B.Dinesh[1] and S. Uskudarli[2]

1 Janastu, Bangalore, INDIA
2 Computer Engineering, Bogazici University
Istanbul, Turkey

Abstract. This is a case study of developing and using community knowledge management software. The context of the case study is a school. During a training workshop staff at a school was introduced to a community knowledge management system. The intent was for them to use it for lesson planning and discussions. Instead, they built a series of applications that they could use to make the school administration more efficient. These applications consisted of Admission, Library, Store and Personnel Management. This case study demonstrates that the ICT need for the next billion is to provide them with systems that they can customize and manage for their needs. An anticipated domino effect would be that they help customize applications for their neighbors' needs, thereby narrowing a digital divide caused by the mystification of application development.

1 Introduction

India has demonstrated how knowledge of English and technical-capacity has yielded a globally competitive IT force that has created a presence in everything from software development to business process outsourcing to research and product development. This is a good example of how capability building builds on itself.

The proliferation of computing and information technology (especially through Internet applications) has enabled users to envision useful applications that would serve their needs. Many such applications would be rather simple to create only if the know how were present. In another words, the avenues for creating what is envisioned by those who envision are lacking.

In this paper, we demonstrate how non programmers are able to create useful applications with a model that enables them to define domain specific information. The model, called Pantoto [1-2], in consideration enables knowledge based community applications that allow user to create domain specific content and communities. With this simple model, users are able to create a multitude of useful applications without resorting to any programming.

Please use the following format when citing this chapter:

Dinesh, T. B., Uskudarh, S., 2007, in IFIP International Federation for Information Processing, Volume 241, Home Informatics and Telematics: ICT for the Next Billion, eds. Venkatesh, A., Gonsalves, T., Monk, A., Buckner, K., (Boston: Springer), pp. 103-112.

We have developed a Web based application based on a knowledge community model called Pantoto. At Janastu [3] we use this model, where we work with a variety of communities and organizations to assist with community knowledge. The aim of this model is to enable communities to create and manage knowledge that is relevant to their context. The online communities that have been developed are essentially simple Web applications. Over the past few years some NGOs, small organizations and communities have used the system for a variety of purposes. Previous cases have been sociologists, disaster response teams, social workers, non governmental organizations, etc. The community SAATHI [4] is such a community application concerning the HIV infection in India.

2   Background and Related Work

Recent development in social network applications such as groups [5-7], blogs [8-9], wikis [10], folksonomies [11-12] have rendered individual publishing trivial. The impact of these technologies is manifested in collaborative inquiries and actions. The Web has enabled a platform that is widely distributed and connected. The social software that is built on it enjoys the benefit of these properties that ease collaborative efforts to be coordinated. The success of such systems is also an indication of how the community orientedness leads to further empowerment through a space that promotes learning and sharing.

There are various community applications that can be installed on websites, home machines, and servers. Caucus [7] is an application that allows groups of people to share and create new information. Information is categorized into segments that are called conferences. Users are part of conferences, can post and read content in each conferences (called Items and responses) in an asynchronous manner. Similarly, Google Groups [5] and Yahoo Groups [6] enable users to communicate regarding topics of interest to them. Some systems have a repository where documents can be uploaded. Wikis allow distributed content management. But in this case the content is the current snapshot without the historical content or separate contributions. Instead wikis favor group over individual ownership of content. There are numerous wiki systems with different features. A recent addition wikis, called Semantic Wiki [13] enables structuring the content with relationships, resulting in semantic processing of the content.

Most of these systems provide some customization capabilities enabling enthusiasts the ability to do their own website or a community site. However, these applications are limited in enabling a community to build a "software application" of sorts or allow members to build/customize such applications to their needs

3   Proposition

Many users are easily able to envision applications that are rather simple, which they are unable to construct due to the non trivial skills required. We propose that the next phase of application building needs those who are not software developers.

Furthermore, these users must be able to maintain the use and evolution of the system. Essentially we are proposing a model for an online knowledge community that is self defined and managed. This proposition is a technology enabling model, where end users are enabled to create and maintain an online space for sharing information and communicating within a domain specific context. Finally, information in this system must be structured – an essentially significant difference from free form online communities, such that the information lends itself to machine processing in order to render information useful in the long term. With access to such applications, these users become empowered as their role extends beyond being consumers to being producers of information technology.

4   Case Study: A K-12 Knowledge Community

This case study presents an account of a workshop held at CHIREC, a K12 school in Hyderabad, India. CHIREC is a progressive school with over 1000 students. Teachers develop structures and processes towards the delivery of effective class room experience for the students. CHIREC is a reasonably affluent private school that employs modern teaching methods and technology. They also have a computer department that supports teachers and students with course material and developing some small applications. Students are well versed with the Internet and most of them have a computer at home.

A few of the students are from outside Hyderabad and some from abroad. We approached this school to see if they would find it interesting to enable a process where the school knowledge - that of the student, teachers, staff inclusive - is pooled into a structured, interactive, and networked space. We studied some of their lesson planning processes and suggested approaches to creating a school knowledge base. A workshop was organized to introduce the teachers to the system where they could collaboratively develop teaching applications. Upon the realization that they would be building the applications, teachers instead voiced their preference for building applications that have been long overdue from the busy computer department. This was quite an unexpected surprise. The teachers decided to go ahead and build applications during the training workshop. This case indicated to us the need for platforms to build applications, and also as how this direction can enable a whole new generation of software builders who are in the right place within the communities for which they build the software.

The teachers had a need for various software applications: admission process management, library catalogues and checkout information, personnel office that caters to students/teachers and parents needs, web-site management, and such. The collective of all these applications, we learnt, is a good way towards enabling the community of teachers to manage their own knowledge. We can foresee that this experience will help them to continuously develop similar applications for their other evolving needs, including handling of lesson plans and such.

4.1 Pantoto Approach

We outline the Pantoto approach. Pantoto Communities software is Web-browser based. All configurations and definitions are done using forms. While some of the forms are related to administration of the software, most common need of a user is to use the forms to define other forms related to their domain of interest. Like a file system with files and access control, a user with an appropriate role can set access control to the folders of the file system. With in these folders, called categories, reside Pagelets -- which are structured, form filled information or rich content. The forms that are created by users are called templates. When a pagelet needs to be added to a category, relevant templates are used to help the user fill in these forms -- which becomes the content. If a form is about a base line survey, the contents of that category will be a database of these surveys. Pantoto handles the meta information management, of users, groups, collation of data and dissemination by searching or reporting. It provides editorship management, which helps the community to delegate and perform admin related tasks concerned to their domain or sub community.

Most of the school applications needed the following process of tasks:

1. Define Roles and access control sets.
2. Define a category tree of various information buckets.
3. Specify a set of templates/forms that need to be active in these buckets.
4. Copy and paste some action links in the text, to be used by application users.
5. Select or configure a presentation for different target groups.

4.2 Example

This section describes some of the things that the *Admissions Process Management* (APM) defined. Admissions personnel work on recruiting applications for the school. In this process, there are several groups with different roles that are in charge of processing the applications. With a simple application that allows them to document the applications according to date, class, name, etc, they are not only able to process the applications but also maintain historical records of the applications, which can be analyzed for reviewing and improving the application management process.

Roles
  Application Issuer, Admission Officer, Admissions Incharge, Administrator

Categories
  School > Admissions > Applications Sold
  School > Admissions > Applications Submitted
  School > Admissions > Applications Approved

Templates defined

Template Name	Fields
Application Issue	Name (person sold to), Application Number, Date Sold

Application Form	Student Name, Parents, Class applied for, Other details
Application Status	Status (Approved/Rejected/Pending), Remarks

Sample forms

Sample forms present in the system can be harvested in order to create new forms. This group found such an approach appealing and used sample forms and customized them. Forms are customized by setting some form properties such as field names and their types.

The content to be presented in the admin context is essentially a description for the category. In this case it is the description of the admissions application.

A look and feel is selected by the APM group. Finally, authorization rights are defined by selecting which roles have access to the categories.

4.3 User Perspective

Given the previous community definition, the system can be used as follows: Application Issuer issues an application (fills form). Admissions Officer receives application (fills rest of form). Admissions Incharge approves some (fills more details). All the information is collated according to templates in the categories. And default reports generated, and search enabled. Using the search, one can find a pagelet and further edit it (as defined by the above process).

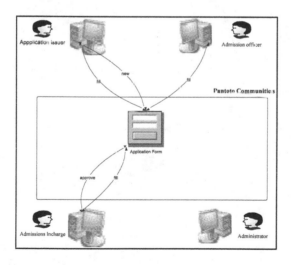

Figure 1: Administrative group's user perspective on creating and filling application forms.

Once application forms are created they lend themselves to any processing offered in the system. One of the automatically available services is context based search, where information can be searched according to criteria.

The context dependent search expression below is a request to find all applications for class 10 that are in pending status. Results of the search result in a report consisting of the application number, the date, that name of the person it is sold to, the parent and the class of application (all fields that have a check mark). The status is not shown as it was not requested. The report may be viewed as a Web page or be exported as a spreadsheet.

No		☑
Date		☑
Name		☑
Parent		☑
Class	10	☑
Status	Pending	
		Search

The following are some screen shots from the application. Due to the private nature of the information most of the application can not be shown, but the following should be sufficiently indicative to the nature of applications built.

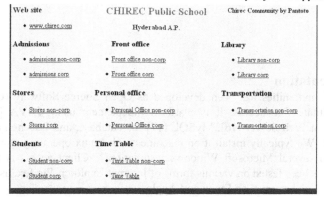

Figure 2: Main Page that gathers access to various applications at the school.

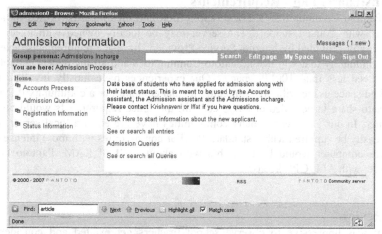

Figure 3: Main page of Admissions Information application

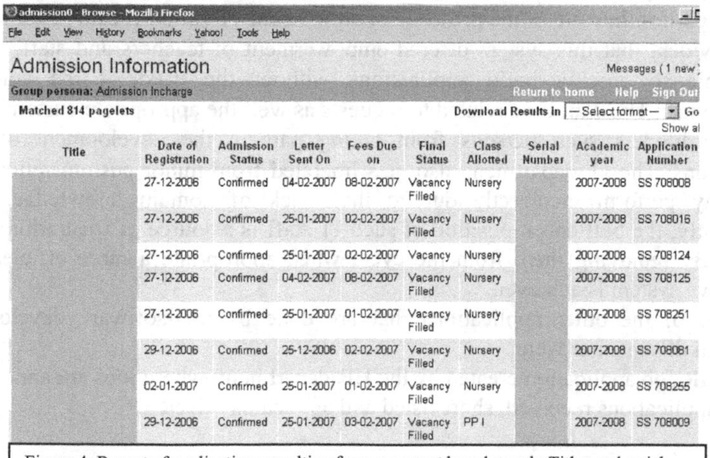

Figure 4: Report of applications resulting from a context based search. Titles and serial numbers are obscured to protect privacy.

5. Implementation

Pantoto Communities has been developed as Open Source Software (OSS) in order to facilitate free access. It is platform independent using JAVA [14-15], Apache Tomcat Web Server [16], MySQL [17] for database, and Lucene [18] as a search engine. We typically install it on machines with Linux operating system, but there are also several Microsoft Windows installations. Client access is through browsers. It has been tested on various forms of Internet Explorer, Firefox, as well as various other Web browsers on Linux and Apple platforms.

6. Installation and Requirements

Pantoto Communities is a Web application and thus must be hosted on a Web server with Tomcat support. The server may be locally owned with in an office network or provided by Internet Service Provider The space requirements depend on the community that will use it.Pantoto Communities and all the dependent software will need less than 100Mb space. Our experiences have mostly involved rather limited space usage with predominantly textual content. For a community that would want to share large video or audio content, the space requirements would be much greater. In our experience, many communities have preferred a local server, which can easily be supplied with a standard PC. For communities with more intense use, a server computer would be advisable with about 1GB of RAM. Pantoto is open source, with APL/GPL licenses.

7. Review

It was impressive to observe school teachers get excited and consider their software needs. Each group built an application in just a few hours. After a server was setup they were able to build, maintain, use and share the software with other relevant parties. In spite of the presence of an in house IT support team at the school, it was evident that this system offered empowerment of teachers and staff. People were able to quickly build applications without the need of the computer professionals. The wait time related to requests as well the appropriate customization seriously hinders such persons from taking part in the development of such applications. The IT department also gets liberated from minor customizations that they may perform incorrectly due to their lack of domain knowledge. More importantly, the bottleneck position of such IT staff is a source of frustration for all parties. By removing them from the cycle when appropriate a more efficient and productive system is achieved.

Some of the other applications that are done by non-software development people, in this manner were:

- HR Job application created by the HR department, where jobs are announced, applications received, short-listed and applicants selected.

- An NGO that works with disabled people built a patient management system for their every day needs.
- An NGO developed a baseline survey and processing application.
- A crafting community built various web-sites that are cross linked to each other.
- An organization has used it for almost all of their internal information management needs, where several small applications interface define how the information is collected the related work flow.

8. Conclusions

Our experiences demonstrate that by using such a system like Pantoto Communities, people who are not computer savvy are able to create very useful Web applications. For many cases Web applications are not very sophisticated. They involve contributing content, searching, and reporting. For community or team applications they also involve communication. By providing means for developing applications based on these patterns, we enable the building of a significant number of custom applications. In an age where fast information access is expected while a great portion of the global population is left on the dark side of the digital divide it is essential to deliver enabling technologies. We are encouraged through our experiences, where we encounter case after case that non programmers are easily able to create applications such as demonstrated in the case described in this paper (application handling team within a school).

We continue to learn from each case and strive to improve Pantoto Communities, which we develop using technologies that enable our project. We maintain a low cost development process and are engaged with the communities who are the target users of this system. Another interesting observation is that that in-spite of the rush to join large companies and to earn large salaries, there are those who are interested in developing community oriented low-cost social applications.

We foresee that our next steps would be to enable simple sms based mobile applications, integration with other services such as GIS, synchronization to offline servers and such. Most significantly, to improve the usability of Pantoto Communities software based on the experiences of the teachers and staff at CHIREC.

Acknowledgements

Pantoto Communities is the result of a collaborative effort. Its implementation and its utilization have been impacted by numerous sources. We gratefully thank all those who have generously contributed to this effort -- volunteers who wrote code, those who contributed free servers space and offered maintenance, and those who provided encouragement.

References

1. Pantoto Communities. url=http://pantoto.com, (extracted March 2007)
2. S. Uskudarli and T. Dinesh. Pantoto: A participatory model for community information. In *Proceedings DyD'02: Development by Design 02*, (2002).
3. Janastu – Let it Be People. url=http://janastu.org, (extracted March 2007)
4. SAATHII, Solidarity and action against the HIV infection in India - online resource center. http://saathii.org (extracted March 2007).
5. Google. Google Groups. url=http://groups.google.com.(extracted March 2007).
6. Yahoo! Yahoo! Groups. url= http://groups.yahoo.com.(extracted March 2007).
7. Dutches BOGES (Board of Cooperative Educational Services), Caucus: Online Conferencing, url= http://www.dcboces.org/conference (extracted March 2007).
8. Pyra Labs. Blogger. http://www.blogger.com (extracted March 2007).N. P. Group. Connotea - organize. share. discover. http://www.connotea.org, (extracted 2007).
9. B. A. Nardi, D. J. Schiano, M. Gumbrecht, and L. Swartz. Why we blog. *Commun. ACM*, **47**(12) (2004) pp 41–46.
10. W. Cunningham and B. Leuf. *The Wiki Way. Quick Collaboration on the Web.* (Reading, Mass. Addison-Wesley , 2001)
11. C. Marlow, M. Naaman, D. Boyd, and M. Davis. Ht06, Tagging Taper, Taxonomy, Flickr, Academic Article, ToRead. In *HYPERTEXT '06*: Proceedings *of the seventeenth conference on Hypertext and hypermedia* (New York, NY, USA, ACM Press , 2006.), pp 31-40.
12. del.icio.us. del.icio.us, social bookmarking. url=http://del.icio.us (extracted March.2007).
13. Max Völkel, Markus Krötzsch, Denny Vrandecic, Heiko Haller, and Rudi Studer. Semantic Wikipedia, *In Proceedings of the 15th international conference on World Wide Web, WWW 2006.* (May 2006)
14. D. Flanagan. *Java in a Nutshell, Fourth Edition.* 4th. (O'Reilly & Associates, Inc, 2002)
15. Sun Microsystems. The Source for Java Developers. Sun Developer Network. url=http://java.sun.com (extracted March 2007).
16. The Apache Software Foundation. Apache Tomcat. url=http://tomcat.apache.org (extracted March 2007)
17. MySQL. Mysql 5.0 reference manual. url= http://dev.mysql.com/doc/refman/5.0/en/index.html, (Extracted March 2007).
18. Erik Hatcher. Lucene Intro. Java.net – The Source for Java Technology Collaboration. url= http://today.java.net/pub/a/today/2003/07/30/LuceneIntro.html, (2004).

Being Social @ Work: Designing for Playfully Mediated Social Awareness in Work Environments

Dhaval Vyas[1], Marek R. van de Watering[2], Anton Eliëns[2] and Gerrit C. van der Veer[3]

1 Human Media Interaction Group, Twente University,
the Netherlands
2 Deptartment of Computer Science, Vrije Universiteit Amsterdam,
the Netherlands
3 School of Computer Science, Open Universiteit,
Valkenburgerweg, the Netherlands

Abstract. Awareness within work environments should not be seen limited to important work-related information, activities and relationships. Mediating somewhat casual and engaging encounters related to non-work issues could also lead to meaningful and pleasurable experiences. This paper explores a design approach to support playfully mediated social awareness within an academic environment. Using ethnographic exploration and understanding the current and aspired practices, we provide details of two broad (and some times overlapping) categories of interaction for supporting and enhancing playfully mediated social awareness amongst staff members: 1) Self-Reflections and 2) Casual Encounters. We implement these two categories of interaction in an intelligent, asynchronous, large screen display called *Panorama*, for the staff room of our computer science department. Panorama attempts to mediate non-critical, non-work related information about the staff-members in an engaging manner to enhance social awareness within the department. We particularly emphasize on the soft design issues like reflections, belonging, care, pleasure and playfulness utilized in our design approach. The result of a two-phase assessment study suggests that our conceptualization of social awareness and the Panorama application has the potential to be easily incorporated into our academic environment.

1. Introduction

Conceptualizing 'awareness' within public and private settings has been an important issue in Human-Computer Interaction (HCI) and Computer Supported Collaborative Work (CSCW) research. The term awareness, however, is ambiguous.

Please use the following format when citing this chapter:

Vyas, D., van de Watering, M. R., Eliëns, A., van der Veer, G. C., 2007, in IFIP International Federation for Information Processing, Volume 241, Home Informatics and Telematics: ICT for the Next Billion, eds. Venkatesh, A., Gonsalves, T., Monk, A., Buckner, K., (Boston: Springer), pp. 113-131.

Early technologies to support awareness – like media spaces [2], have often been specialized for mediating selective work related activities and relationships, through computationally integrated audio-video links between geographically dispersed co-workers [7,14]. In the initial media spaces, the use of videos to mediate awareness was criticized for its limited view-capturing possibilities supporting mainly face-to-face communications, and for privacy related issues [12]. At the same time, it is debatable to what extent these systems could convey the precise awareness of other people, their activities or their contexts.

The scope of technology design is broadening with the growing interest and need to support personally meaningful, authentic, sociable and rich everyday experiences. The notion of mediated awareness has evolved from the objectively observable aspects encompassing mainly the peripheral settings to conveying subjective aspects such as love and intimacy [1, 21, 34], playfulness [1, 12, 28] and other related issues.

In big organizations, social awareness is sometimes neglected in the tension between heavy workloads, time clashes, a lack of social encounters between employees, and a lack of suitable platforms that allow one to construct and convey one's identity [3]. In this paper we provide details of our work on developing a design approach for playfully mediated social awareness within work environments. As Gaver defines [11], playfulness is about creating new perspectives, ideas, and goals, and exploring new ethical and aesthetic standpoints, and not only about entertainment or spending time. Playful systems allow users to playfully and artfully express their own creativity to establish curiosity, exploration and reflection as key values.

A main question that we answer in this paper is how we can design technologies for conveying non-work related, non-critical information about staff-members to enhance social awareness in an academic department. We start with an ethnographic exploration utilizing contextual interviews, naturalistic observations and cultural probes to understand staff members' current and aspired practices of being socially aware of others and of the environment as a whole. Our approach in the fieldwork was focused on understanding social interactions limited not only to work or routine activities but also sentimental, pleasure and play related acts. Based on the results of our fieldwork, we decided to focus on conveying two types of information that are unselective in the sense that they are somewhat open-ended and at the same time engaging, playful and explorative. They are: ability to have Self-Reflections (e.g. making other people aware about one's personal and professional interests), and Casual Encounters among the staff members (e.g. having a verbal or visual encounters in common areas). We implement these two categories of interaction in a large screen display called Panorama, situated in the staff-room of our department. The Panorama interface is inspired by notions of art and attempts to convey information about staff members in a compelling, and engaging way. Panorama supports an asynchronous, 'shared-initiative' interaction in which members can publish their personally meaningful messages (self-reflection) onto the system and, at the same time, the system can detect meaningful interactions amongst the members (casual encounters) and artfully represent them on the display.

In the rest of the paper, we first outline the background work that enabled us to conceptualize social awareness and especially focus on awareness related to non-work activities. We then provide a brief description of the methods used in the fieldwork and some results. Utilizing the results we describe the design of Panorama and provide details of our assessment study. Finally, we discuss several design strategies utilized in our approach for enhancing non-critical social awareness in a work environment. We discuss several design issues like reflection, belonging, curiosity, embodiment and playfulness used in our design approach.

2. Social Awareness

Our aim in this section is to provide some background research on social awareness to conceptualize non-work related, non-critical awareness within the University environment. Schmidt [27] notes that the word 'awareness' is a highly elastic English word and can mean different things in different situations. In this paper, we will focus on a type of technology that supports awareness between different people (office colleagues, family members, friends, lovers, etc.) and not on the technology that is aware of its own and its surrounding states and reacts accordingly – the context-aware systems [e.g. 6, 15]. The former can be categorized as technology for social awareness, since the focus is on supporting relationship between people either for productive (e.g. in the work environments) or for non-productive causes (e.g. in the domestic environments). We will provide an overview of early work on social awareness and point to new developments of the concept in non-work related situations.

2.1 Early Work on Social Awareness

The earlier technologies that were used to convey awareness through closely coupled audio-video links between offices were termed 'media spaces' [2, 7, 14]. Their initial use was to connect work between geographically dispersed offices and work environments. The main expected benefit of using media spaces was to support productivity in work environments by creating possibilities to engage in task-oriented conversations from a distance and, at the same time, to have a general orientation to the presence and activities of colleagues at the other end. Awareness from this perspective is defined as the following:

> "Awareness involves knowing who is 'around', what activities are occurring, who is talking with whom; it provides a view of one another in the daily work environments. Awareness may lead to informal interactions, spontaneous connections, and the development of shared cultures – all important aspects of maintaining working relationships which are denied to groups distributed across multiple sites."
> – Dourish and Bly [7, p.541]

Through media spaces, it was assumed that geographically dispersed office members would work as if they were at the same place. Unfortunately, these assumptions never materialized [27]. Most awareness systems developed to support the work environments focused on the very aspect of productivity in users' everyday work life. In some recent examples of awareness systems [e.g. 24, 26, 33] awareness is supported through indications of the presence of colleagues, availability of their biography, their project descriptions, information about their daily schedules and office calendars.

2.2 Social Awareness beyond Work-Related Activities

With new business needs and emergence of novel computing technologies, the focus of technologically mediated awareness has shifted from only users' work environments to their everyday interactions. The scope of awareness has extended from the mere physical space of the users, to conveying users' emotions, love, social status and other broader social and cultural aspects. Gaver suggests that, as the context in which these (awareness) technologies are used changes, the form and ways to interact with these technologies should also change [12].

In domestic environments these technologies are used to convey, for example, emotional connections between distant lovers [5, 21, 31, 34], awareness within families [18, 19, 32] and ways to keep in touch with family from a distance [25, 22]. In public domains, these technologies are used to establish playfulness and evocations between strangers [1, 12], developing social and cultural respect within a large community [13], and many others. Even in office environments these technologies are deployed for exchanging information about the moods and attitudes between co-workers [29, 30]. All these systems embody certain assumptions about the basic objectives for conveying awareness, the information that should be conveyed and the media through which this might be conveyed.

2.3 Conceptualizing Social Awareness

Bødker and Christiansen [3] suggest that social awareness is a very subtle aspect of our overall awareness, which can be accessed only 'indirectly' through a granular understanding of space, mediators, human conduct and culture. Social awareness can only be felt; it cannot be seen or measured in a precise manner. To be aware of somebody we need to feel his or her presence in a somewhat temporary and subtle way. Because, if presence is too apparent we tend to take it for granted. These authors conceptualize social awareness as a conscious feeling of belonging, relatedness, and care, prompted by the environment.

Taking a sociological stand point, Glaser and Strauss [16] argue that the phenomenon of awareness is central to the study of interaction. They termed a notion of awareness context – "the total combination of what each interactant in a situation knows about the identity of the other and his own identity in the eyes of the others" [p.670]. They suggest that to understand the awareness phenomenon it is very important to see interactions in a broader context.

Glaser and Strauss's conceptualization leads to a reflective approach, which suggests that awareness technology should allow interactants to reflect on a three-way relationship of: "how I see myself", "how I see others" and "how others see me." A similar position is also taken by Bødker and Christiansen.

> "…for social awareness to be prompted 'I' must have the opportunity to be reflected in my environment, and 'I' must be able to see how others are reflected, just as they must be able to see the reflections of 'me'."

– Bødker and Christiansen [3, p.10]

We conceptualize social awareness as reflections that are supported by 'cues' and 'traces' of different activities in the department. "A trace of human activity is recognized as 'social' when it allows someone to acquaint themselves with others without receiving explicitly expressed information about them" [3, p.6]. These cues and traces users leave in the environment make it compelling and emotionally valuable for the next person. When the next person chooses the same environment, he intentionally or unintentionally adds his own cues and traces to the same environment that eventually would turn the physical settings into a social world. Sometimes, these vague and low-fidelity cues and traces might be valued more for community building than bold and high fidelity cues [12].

3. Designing for Playfully–Mediated Social Awareness

By playfulness we do not mean winning or loosing and turn-taking with a final result. Gaming systems like PS-2, Xbox, Gameboy or PC games are already covering a huge market of entertainment industry. But in our case, we do not see entertainment or playfulness being limited to exclusive devices. Following Gaver [11], we see users as active and creative beings for constructing their own entertainment. In this paper we offer a design concept for enhancing social awareness, which also has a playful side to it.

As a first step towards designing for playfully mediated social awareness in a co-located academic department, we sought to understand staff members' current and aspired practices of social awareness within the department. We carried out an ethnographic investigation utilizing naturalistic observations, contextual interviews and cultural probes. From the data gathered in our investigation, we found two main categories of interaction for being socially aware: Casual Encounters and Self-Reflections. These two patterns of interaction were then implemented in a large screen display called Panorama. A two-phase assessment study of a prototype of our Panorama system showed that the concept of casual encounters and self-reflections could potentially serve well in our department.

3.1 Ethnographic Field study

We used a method called interaction analysis [20] to inform our ethnographic exploration. It is an interdisciplinary method to investigate interactions of human beings among themselves and with objects in their environment. Even though this technique was originally used for video analysis, it provides a number of useful foci for understanding the social awareness phenomenon in an academic environment. We focused our exploration on the following categories:
- Forms of awareness
- Activities of awareness
- Agents of awareness
- Places of awareness
- Contents of awareness

Forms of awareness describe different methods of communication that are used for mediating awareness information. These can be either synchronous (e.g. face-to-face, phone calls) or asynchronous (e.g. e-mail, instant messaging tools, post-it notes). The methods for communicating awareness information can be explicit providing direct indications or implicit leaving room for multiple interpretations.

Activities of awareness describe the type of activities within the environment that could mediate awareness information. These can be task-oriented (i.e. a routine work activity) or social in nature (i.e. lunch, coffee break). Often these activities overlap so it is important to take into account the possible relationships between different activities.

Agents of awareness are the people and the objects or artifacts within the environment that mediate awareness, directly or indirectly. People can be seen as individuals and also as constituting groups (e.g. research groups). In this case it is important to understand the roles that the ethical and political issues (e.g. position hierarchy) play in contributing to social awareness. We also need to take into account the role of students in forming social awareness within our educational environment.

Places of awareness, in a broad sense, describe the geographical as well as the 'social spaces' where interactions take place, including the hot spots of interaction. This can be seen as a multi-layered concept: personal vs. private spaces of staff members within an office, a floor, a building and the whole environment. Inherent to the observations made in this category of awareness is the question: "how does the spatial layout influence the structure of interaction?"

Contents of awareness refer to the actual information being mediated through different interactions. Contents of awareness can be staff members' activities, presence, social and political status, achievements, and so on. This can be explicit (i.e. a note saying that a person will be back at a certain time) and implicit (i.e. artifacts used as symbols or the information at a 'glance'). Both are open to different interpretations by different people, the implicit content being more so.

Using these categories as a base for our exploration, we used three methods: naturalistic observations, contextual interviews and cultural probes.

In the naturalistic observations, we used video and still cameras to capture staff-members' activities in the staff-room, the printing-room, the canteen and other common areas where social communication happens. One of the authors spent several hours during a week and noted staff members' everyday activities and their social encounters. Using a video camera, we also followed some of our colleagues to get insights into their everyday interactions e.g. walking to the canteen, to the printer room and to the staff room.

Next, we carried our contextual interviews and arranged a cultural probes [13] study with 10 participants. Eight of the participants were the current staff members with a mixture of PhD students, senior academics, administrative and PR members. We also asked two bachelors students to participate in this study to get a broader perspective. These participants were selected based on their availability and willingness to participate in a 6 weeks long study.

In the contextual inquiry, we asked questions regarding their social dynamics. For example: What type of information would the staff members in our department like to know about other members? What types of information would they be willing to share with others? What are their privacy concerns? What common areas in the department do they use often to gather information about others? What are the common tools of communications they use outside their offices? Especially in the staff room, what are the most common activities performed by the members and how often? And lastly, how important is being socially aware of other members in the department? The information was recorded in an audio device and written notes were also taken.

In the cultural probes study, we provided participants with a collection consisting of a disposable camera, a set of color pencils, post cards, maps, drawing pencils, a marker, scissors, glue, set of post-it notes and three popular magazines in a probe package; and asked the participants to create a personalized workbook and a logbook of their activities. In the workbook there were some open-ended and some specific question about their everyday interactions within the department. Instructions were also provided about when they should use the camera or other materials.

3.2 Fieldwork Findings

In our investigation we found two broad categories interaction for being socially aware of others: Self-Reflections and Casual Encounters. In this paper we will not provide the detailed results of our study, we will briefly discuss our findings focusing only on these two categories. It is important to note that these two categories should not be seen as definitive and mutually exclusive but as broad concepts for informing design.

3.2.1 Self-Reflections

In the fieldwork we observed several attempts of staff-members to let others know about their identity either in groups or individually by providing information about their achievement, status and announcements. We term this type of interaction as self-reflections. Several artifacts and devices were used as a carrier for mediating information about self-reflection. These artifacts and devices included notice boards, staff-room door (Fig 1), printing room door, post-it notes attached to one's office door and other artifacts available in common areas.

The purpose of self-reflection varied from work-related to personal and even sentimental reasons. On the door of our staff room (Fig. 1) there were indications about staff members' personal achievement (e.g. winning in a city marathon), announcement of an event (e.g. music concert), provocative educational clips from magazines (e.g. Business Week), sharing some personal experiences (e.g. holiday postcards) and announcing birth of newborn babies.

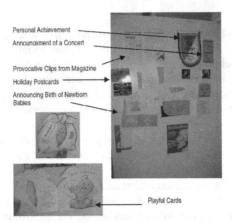

Fig. 1 Self-Refection objects found on the staff room door

The activity of self-reflection was mainly found in the form of asynchronous interaction, in which senders could publish their information in a physical or digital form and receivers would come across these via their habitual activities at work.

Sometimes email and web-based tools were also used for self-reflections. During the contextual interviews one participant mentioned about a web-based system that they used for making other people working on the same project aware of each other's activities. "*I don't use it always but I publish my agenda on this web site so that other people can see what I am up to. Same way I can see other people's agendas and plans.*"

In the cultural probes and contextual interviews, we found that being socially aware of other members and students in the department was not the most important need, but all the participants agreed that if there is an opportunity they would really like it. Fig. 2 shows some examples of participants' expressions towards the overall department.

(a)   (b)

Fig. 2 Personal Expressions conveyed by staff members

Fig. 2 also provides indications about how the staff members wanted to convey their identity to the whole department. In some cases members wanted to convey their professional status (Fig. 2a), in others, they wanted to convey their personal thoughts (Fig. 2b). Fig. 2b is an art piece called– Souplesse originally created by a French artist Chaïm Soutine[1] (1893-1943). The image has a great personal value for a senior researcher who came across it while he was a PhD student.

One of the flexibilities supported by self-reflections was its reconfigurability. Staff members could, at anytime, publish their information in a place that is publicly reachable and in the same way could take the information back if they wanted. We also observed the changes in the physical space because of the self-reflections. In one departmental secretary's office we found a huge collection of post-it notes stating different 'states of her presence' (see Fig.3). At any time when she needed to leave her office she would look for a ready-made post-it with relevance and stick it on her office door. This was a work specific activity, as she was responsible for about 20-30 staff members in the department.

Fig. 3 An aware office door? A collection of Post-it notes found in an employee's office

Fig. 4 A PR officer's announcement on the notice board in the staff room: It says, roughly, "Please, send us 'nice' news to put into our website"

On a different note, sometimes announcements were made on the main notice board of our staff-room. Fig 4 shows an announcement by the PR officer of the department. Email or other digital forms of communication were not used for this particular activity. It was assumed that the staff room is a central point of social and informal activities.

3.2.2 Casual Encounters
We found in our field study that most staff members had very limited time for explicit social interaction while working and that most encounters were initiated and defined by the "*dynamics of the moment*" (as one interviewee pointed out), thus by the context. Casual Encounter was a kind of interaction, where staff members, during their routine activities, interact with the other members and objects within the surroundings that provided hints and cues of social awareness. See Fig. 5

1. http://en.wikipedia.org/wiki/Chaim_Soutine

Fig. 5 Everyday Casual Encounters. Direct and Indirect interaction with people and objects in the department.

Several examples of direct communication were seen, e.g. informal meetings in the staff-room, casual coffee-room chatting, chatting while queuing in the canteen and the printing room. Through these verbal and visual encounters staff members get information about others. These communications included information about professional activities as well as personal and social activities.

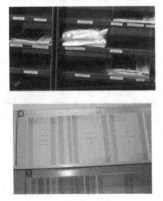

Fig. 6 Indirect mediation of awareness. Staff   Fig. 7 A scrap from a foreign employee.
    Postboxes and Printing shelves.

There were also instances where indirect communication between staff members occurred. E.g. while checking the mail-box (see fig. 6) and faxes from the staff room and collecting prints from the printer room, staff members could see mail and prints belonging to other members. This can give an indirect indication about other members' presence or absence.

Maps used in the cultural probe study also gave a lot of indications about frequently visited places in the department and in the University. Most instances of casual encounters were closely related to the routine activities of staff members. These included coffee and lunch breaks and also some instantaneous activities like going into the staff room for using the fax machine or collecting post, for example. Fig. 7 shows a scrap from a foreign employee who used the microwave situated in the staff room.

The staff room was a common place for most social activities within the department, such as celebrations of different social events like employees' birthday and celebrating after getting funding of a new project. Normally, in this case the employee would use email to announce this amongst his group or friends. In some cases we observed play related activities. Some senior searchers liked playing cards with old friends to freshen their minds. The staff room played an important role in establishing relationships between staff members. In summary, our staff room played a role of social organizing.

3.3 Panorama: Designing for Social Awareness

For designing playfully mediated social awareness we treated the two interaction categories: Self-Reflections and Casual Encounters, as our design concepts. This means that the technology that we design should incorporate these two categories of interaction. To apply playfulness in the design we wanted to provide an opportunity for the staff members to artfully and creatively contribute to our departmental settings. It was evident from our study that the staff-room in our department was the centre for the most of social and informal activities. We intended to put a large screen display in our staff room that would allow staff members to receive socially meaningful information from the environment and to publish relevant information onto the display. The two design concepts were then implemented in a large screen display called Panorama. Fig. 8 shows a prototype version of the Panorama application.

As informed by our design explorations (section 3.2), Panorama utilizes information about Self-Reflections and Casual Encounters in the following way.

Self-Reflections are explicit user initiated interactions. For staff members this means that they can contribute towards the ongoing activities of the overall environment with their personal and non-critical information or data. Here, Panorama serves as a tool that allows staff members to support their social needs, such as sharing non-work related but highly sentimental news (e.g. announcing the birth of a new born child), personal achievements (e.g. best paper award), personal interests (e.g. favorite books, favorite conferences), etc. In this case, Panorama does not passively receive feeds from members. It in fact filters and alters contents and represents this in a manner to show co-occurrence with the real environment.

Casual Encounters are implicit system initiated interactions. In this case, Panorama proactively collects information about the ongoing activities within the department and offers resources of potential interest from the environment. Panorama serves as a mechanism by which staff members can be socially aware by knowing each other's presence, social events and relevant non-critical activities within the department. In this case, even though users passively receive information from the technology, they can actively comprehend the implications of their action (either alone or in groups) on the Panorama.

Fig. 8 The Panorama prototype representing an 'idle' environment in the department

Broadly speaking, Panorama receives explicit and implicit awareness information about the environment and the people and transforms this onto its display. The Panorama interface is like a virtual gallery, where on the wall and on the floor information about social awareness is presented. Both the frames on the wall and the floor are moving to indicate the passing of time. Fig. 8 represents the 'idle' environment when activity level is minimal. As activity level increases it transforms the representation first into the 'live' environment (representing the normal activity level) and then into to 'chaotic' environments (representing hectic activity level). We used motion and noise sensors to detect the activity levels in the common spaces like the staff room, the printing room and the main corridor. In both cases the activity level within the department is represented by the change of speed, color, abstractions (e.g. using shaders) and overlays of 3D objects and particles. Elsewhere [36] we have reported Panorama's representation logic in more details.

For designing Panorama we used a technology called ViP, which we previously developed for an augmented reality theatre production [9]. ViP (Virtual Poetry) is a complex 'representation' system based on DirectX9. It allows projection of live video feeds, digital video clips, texts and sequence of images on an immersive 3D space. The ViP system allows a variety of visual effects, including texture mapping of image feeds on 3D objects, overlays of multiple image textures, as well as particle systems with streaming image feeds projected on sprites.

The goal of the Panorama system is to enhance social awareness by providing interpersonal and rich information related to staff members and their everyday interactions in the department. The placement of the Panorama application in the staff room of our department should be seen as a facility to support staff members' creativity and playfulness and not as a tool that attempts solve problems. The Panorama interface in the staff-room will allow different users to speculate about what is happening in the department. This non-selective information will allow affective, engaging and reflective interactions among the members.

3.4 Assessment of Panorama

Methods for assessing technological aspects of a system may be impractical or unsatisfactory when evaluating systems that are meant to support subjective and interpersonal aspects [35], such as understanding their social awareness. Previous researches [17, 23] have shown that mixed-reality and artistic interfaces can better be evaluated using a combination of argumentation ('art criticism') and informal conversation with users. To validate our understandings of social awareness (as discussed in section 2.3) and to assess the effectiveness of Panorama in the staff room we organized our assessment in two phases.

Part 1: Individual meaning construction through 3 different scenarios

Part 2: Social meaning construction through group discussions

Fig. 9 Phase 1 of Panorama assessment (in a Laboratory)

In the first phase, we invited eight employees of our department to a laboratory. Without providing explicit information about Panorama, we demonstrated three different scenarios of Panorama, representing different environments in the department: Idle, Live and Chaotic. During the session we first asked them to individually write down: what Panorama represents, the difference between the three scenarios and the system's suitability in the department. After this we introduced some discussion points to observe their social meaning construction about the system. See Fig. 9. The discussions were recorded in an audio device and the transcripts of their written answers were also collected for further analysis of our system.

Fig. 10 Phase 2 of Panorama assessment (in the **Staff room**)

In the second phase, we installed the Panorama system in the staff room (see Fig. 10). The main purpose for this assessment was to observe the behaviors and reactions of staff members towards Panorama and check its effects in a natural environment. We asked questions similar to those in the lab assessment, but the whole experiment was situation dependant in the sense that the passers-by could comment on almost anything. We took notes of their comments and noted their behaviors.

Results: The lab assessment led to some interesting perspectives on Panorama. It was clear to all participants what Panorama was about. Some described it as, "*it reflects the dynamics at our department*", "*it demonstrates what's the department in a virtual way*", "*a lazy way to get information about the department*", and so on. Most participants could easily recognize the objects presented on the Panorama: posters, announcements, events, images of staff members, but it was difficult for them to make a clear narratives of the sequence of the presentation. The presentation of Panorama was appreciated by most participants. Some said, "*it could also be used as a PR resource to attract new students to the University*." The three different scenarios of Panorama were also easily distinguishable into idle, live and chaotic environments. A tradeoff between information and impression was observed. Some participants (mainly students) appreciated the dynamic visuals, overlapping images and fast flow of information in scenario-3 (chaotic environment); compared to others (mainly senior staff members) who appreciated the slow but comprehensible flow of information in scenario-1 (idle environment). Scenario-2 (live environment) was considered to be the best by all the participants as it was a combination of a nice representation of the dynamic side of the department and still being informative.

In the staff room assessment, we noted that a main aspect of the Panorama system was curiosity. We did not explicitly invite anybody for this assessment. All participants came to the staff room to do their routine activities or take a short break from work. We observed that many of the viewers were curious to see their pictures in the department staff members' list. Interestingly, privacy did not seem to be an important issue. There were two reasons for this: first, Panorama provided non-critical information about staff members and mainly the information that was in fact published by the staff members themselves; and second, staff members (like other academics) were interested in conveying their status and identity. One of the viewers waited for some time to see himself on the big screen. Others commented, "*I would like to see myself on the screen.*"

Did Panorama improve social awareness? We do not pretend to measure this effect. But we found that Panorama certainly increased curiosity and provided pleasant experiences amongst the participants, and to a certain extent improved their knowledge about the social environment. We believe that the social benefit offered by Panorama was a result of mainly the personal nature of the content and party the dynamic representation and its placement in the staff room. When installed in the staff-room, we observed that Panorama provided a reason for members to communicate about different ongoing activities in the department. E.g. a conversation: "*Whose trophy is this?*"… "*I think its Jan's.*" An interesting thing about this example was that the same announcement of this person's achievement of 'winning in a city marathon' was already published on our staff room door (Fig. 1) but very few people knew it. When presented on Panorama it became a point of talk amongst the viewers. In this particular case, we observed that the viewers started talking about other aspects related to this instance.

4. Discussion: Design Strategies for Playfully-Mediated Social Awareness

Our design approach demonstrates the use of several interesting design strategies that are useful to enhance social awareness in the work environments.

Awareness as reflections. A main strategy that we applied in designing Panorama was the focus on reflections. Panorama allows its users to reflect on themselves and on other members of the department. In order to support this, it allows users to explicitly and implicitly leave cues and traces of their activities and preferences. Through the mechanism of self-reflection, for example, members in the department could know each other's personal and professional interests and the things one is up to. Panorama provides opportunities for viewing non-rational information that may trigger a commitment to reading and commenting on information that is related to the personal traces. It provides a common virtual space that allows members to know about each other.

Awareness as belonging. The panorama system embodies staff-members, their artifacts and their activities in the sense that their presence is reflected on the system. According to Fels [10] this type of embodiment can lead to an aesthetic feeling of belonging when users can relinquish the control over to the system. Panorama embodies the presence of the staff-member in a compelling and artistic way that leads to an emotional response of belonging to a community. In a big organization like our department, this could lead to social benefits even when it is difficult to establish face to face interactions with other members. This way panorama serves as a platform to support awareness as feeling of belonging.

Awareness as a choice. The use of an awareness system in the public domain may sometimes lead to privacy issues. Not all members may like a system that records their activities without notice. Organizational politics, organizational hierarchy and cultural diversity may even lead to the rejection of such an awareness system. Panorama utilizes social awareness in an academic environment as an option or a choice and not as an obligation: a person is present only if 'he wants himself to be publicly known and present' [3]. As a mechanism to support self-reflections, the members can add their views and their personal information to the system making their presence and their views available to the community.

Awareness in embodiment. The representation dynamics on panorama co-occurs with the real-time activities in the department. E.g. when the activity level increases to a certain level the presentation of panorama gets changed to indicate the hectic work environment. This offer staff members a two-level communication mechanism. At the first level, staff members receive information about announcements, news, and so on from the different objects floating on the screen. And at the second level, the presentation of these objects provides indications of the kind of mood or emotion the department is going through, e.g. normal, idle, or chaotic.

Awareness in (playful) exploration. Unlike media spaces [2], where continuous, high quality video and audio links were provided to support awareness, the Panorama interface utilizes unselective, random information in the form of casual encounters and self-reflections. The Panorama interface provides information in a compelling manner, which makes the members explore possible facts hidden in the given information. Panorama provides a 'new way' of interacting with other staff members within the department. Members could intentionally leave cues and traces of their existence to make the environment playful. Nevertheless, this being unselective information allows open and rich awareness amongst the staff members. The randomness and non-critical aspect of Panorama allows staff members a sort of freedom-of-interpretations. Members can construct their own views and make their stories about the department based on the information provided on the Panorama screen.

Non-critical & pleasurable awareness. Our focus has been on the non-critical awareness. Our staff room is used as a place to have a break from heavy work-load, stress and obligatory tasks related to work. During the field study, we observed members chatting and playing cards. Panorama adds a suitable technology in the staff room. Panorama does not focus on the precision of information but on how the information is experienced by the viewers through the traces it generates for supporting social awareness. Additionally, the information that is presented on the Panorama screen does not require full attention from the users. It is possible to ignore such information, and the receiver may choose not to interpret the details of someone else's traces in great detail.

Awareness beyond intelligence. The notions of seamlessness, disappearance and intelligence as propagated by ubiquitous computing [37] and ambient intelligence [8] are primarily based on the technological intelligence. Their technology-oriented conceptualization of context is very limited and sometime unachievable, especially when these approaches attempt to predict users' intentions and activities. Users' everyday encounters may involve interaction with many heterogeneous media and tools and users may adapt or interweave these to support their activities [4]. Additionally, viewing users as 'passive' receivers of information is an incomplete view. Panorama provides an opportunity for the staff members to be an active, playful and artful creator of their own environment. Panorama utilizes the intelligence aspect not to predict staff-members' behaviors or activities but for depicting them in an artistic way to enhance social awareness within a work environment.

5. Conclusion

Social awareness is in essence a relatively novel concept in the design of smart environments. This type of design profits from recent developments in domains like Ambient Intelligence [8], Ludic Design [11] and Virtual Art [17]. Combining inspirations from these fields allows an addition to the work environment that provides for causal encounters and self-reflections beyond the focus of business or work. This, in turn, will support, but not enforce, a deeper and more "personal" awareness of people and social events. Our artistically inspired design project resulted in understanding the value of design sensibilities like reflections, belonging, care, exploration, and playfulness. Our conceptualization and application for social awareness has demonstrated valuable outcomes.

Acknowledgments

This work was partially funded by a generous grant from Microsoft Netherlands. Most of the work reported here was carried out when the first author was associated with Vrije Universiteit Amsterdam. We would like to thank all our participants and colleagues. Thanks also go to Zeljko Obrenovic for his comments and Cees Visser for providing technical support.

Reference

1. K. Battarbee, N. Baerten, M. Hinfelaar, P. Irvine, S. Loeber, A. Munro, and T. Pederson, Pools and Satellites – Intimacy in the City. *Proceedings of DIS'02*. ACM Press: NY, (2002), 237-245.
2. S. Bly, S. Harrison, and S. Irwin, Media Spaces: Bringing People Together in a Video, Audio, and Computing Environment. *CACM*, vol. 36, no. 1, 1993, 28–46.
3. S. Bødker, and E. Christiansen, Computer support for social awareness in flexible work. *Computer Supported Collaborative Work*, Springer Netherlands, 15: 2006, 1-28.
4. M. Chalmers, and A. Galani, Seamful Interweaving: Heterogeneity in the Theory and Design of Interactive Systems. *Proceedings of DIS'04*, ACM Press: NY, (2004). 243-252.
5. H. Chung, C-H. Lee, and T. Selker, Lovers' Cup: Drinking interfaces as new communication channels. *Proc of CHI'06*. ACM Press: NY, (2006), 375-380.
6. K. Cheverst, N. Davies, K. Mitchell, A. Friday, and C. Efstratiou, Developing a context-aware electronic tourist guide: some issues and experiences. *Proceedings of CHI'00*. ACM Press: NY, (2000), 17-24.

7.   P. Dourish, and S. Bly, Portholes: Supporting Awareness in a Distributed Work Group. *Proceedings of CHI'92*. ACM Press: NY, (1992), 541–547.
8.   K. Ducatel, M. Bogdanowicz, F. Scapolo, J. Leijten, and J.C. Burgelman, Scenarios for Ambient Intelligence in 2010. *ISTAG Final Report*, (2001), IPTS, Seville, Feb.
9.   A. Eliëns, Odyssee – explorations in mixed reality theatre. *Proceedings of GAME'ON-NA'2006*, Naval Postgraduate School, Monterey, USA, Sept 19-21, 2006.
10. S. Fels, Designing Intimate Experiences. *Proceedings of IUI'04*. ACM Press: NY, (2004), 2-3.
11. W. Gaver, Designing for Homo Ludens. *I3 Magazine*, No. 12, June, 2002, 2-6.
12. W. Gaver, Provocative Awareness. *Computer Supported Collaborative Work*. 11: Springer Netherlands, 2002, 475-493.
13. W. Gaver, T. Dunne, & E. Pacenti, Design: Cultural Probes. *Interactions*, 6, 1, ACM Press:NY, 1999, 21-29.
14. W. Gaver, A. Sellen, C. Heath, and P. Luff, One is not enough: Multiple views in a media space. *Proceedings of INTERCHI'93*. ACM Press: NY, (1993), 335-341.
15. H-W. Gellersen, M. Beigl, and H. Krull, The MediaCup: Awareness Technology embedded in an Everyday Object. *1st International Symposium on HUC'99*, LNCS; Vol 1707, Springer, (1999), 308-310.
16. B.G. Glaser, and A.L. Strauss, Awareness Contexts and Social Interaction. *American Sociological Review*, Vol.29, No.5, 1964, 669-679.
17. K. Höök, P. Sengers, and G. Andersson, Sense and Sensibility: Evaluation and Interactive Art. *Proceedings of CHI'03*. ACM Press: NY, (2003), 241-248.
18. D. Hindus, S. Mainwaring, N. Leduc, A. Hagström, and O. Bayley, Casablanca: Designing social communication devices for the home. *Proceedings of CHI'01*. ACM Press: NY, (2001), 325-332.
19. H. Hutchinson, W. Mackay, B. Westerlund, B. Bederson, A. Druin, C. Plaisant, M. Beaudouin-Lafon, S. Conversy, H. Evans, H. Hansen, N. Roussel, B. Eiderbäck, S. Lindquist, and Y. Sundblad, Technology Probes: Inspiring Design for and with Families. *Proceedings of CHI'03*. ACM Press: NY, (2003), 17-24.
20. B. Jordan, and A. Henderson, Interaction Analysis: Foundations and Practice. *Journal of the Learning Sciences*, 4: 1, 1994, 39-102.
21. J. Kaye, and L. Goulding, Intimate Objects. *Proceedings of DIS'04*. ACM Press: NY, (2004), 341-344.
22. P. Markopolous, N. Romero, J. van Baren, W. IJsselsteijn, B. de Ruyter, and B. Farshchian, Keeping in Touch with the Family: Home and Away with the ASTRA Awareness System. *Proceedings of CHI'04*. ACM Press: NY, (2004), 1351-1354.
23. M. Mateas, Expressive AI: A hybrid art and science practice. *Leonardo*, 34 (2), 2001, 147-153.
24. J. McCarthy, T. Costa, and E. Liongosari, UniCast, OutCast & GroupCast: Three Steps Toward Ubiquitous, Peripheral Displays. In G. Abowd, et al. (Eds): *Proceedings Of Ubicomp 2001*, LNCS 2201, Springer-Verlag Berlin Heidelberg. (2001), 332-345.
25. E.D. Mynatt, J. Rowan, S. Craighill, and A. Jacobs, Digital family portraits: Providing peace of mind for extended family members. *Proceedings of CHI'01*. ACM Press: NY, (2001), 333-340.
26. J. Redström, T. Skog, and L. Hallnäs, (2000) Informative Art: Using Amplified Artworks as Information Displays. *Proceedings of DARE'00*. ACM Press, NY, (2000), 103-114.
27. K. Schmidt, The problem with 'awareness': Introductory remarks on 'Awareness in CSCW'. *Computer Supported Collaborative Work*. 11: Springer Netherlands, 2002, 285-298.
28. A. Sellen, R. Harper, R. Eardley, S. Izadi, T. Regan, A. Taylor, and K. Wood, Situated Messaging in the Home. *Proceedings of CSCW'06*. ACM Press: NY, (2006), 338-392.
29. P. Sengers, K. Boehner, S. David, and J. Kaye, Reflective Design. *Proceedings of Aarhus-2005 conference on Critical Computing*. ACM Press, NY, (2005), 49-58.

30. N. Streitz, C. Röcker, T. Prante, D. van Alphen, R. Stenzel, and C. Magerkurth, Designing Smart Artefacts for Smart Environments. *IEEE Computer*, March, 2005, 41-49.

31. R. Strong, and W. Gaver, Feather, scent, and shaker: Supporting simple intimacy. *Proceedings of CSCW'96*. ACM Press: NY, (1996), 29-30.

32. A. Taylor, L. Swan, R. Eardley, A. Sellen, S. Hodges, and K. Wood, Augmenting Refrigerator Magnets: Why Less is Sometimes More. *Proceedings of NordiCHI'06*. ACM Press:NY, (2006), 115-124.

33. K. Tollmar, O. Sandor, and A. Schomer, Supporting social awareness @ work: design and experience. *Proceedings of CSCW'96*. ACM Press: NY, (1996), 298-307.

34. F. Vetere, M. Gibbs, J. Kjeldskov, S. Howard, F. Mueller, S. Pedell, K. Mecoles, and M. Bunyan, Mediating Intimacy: Designing technologies to support strong-tie relationships. *Proceedings of CHI'05*. ACM Press: NY, (2005), 471-480.

35. D. Vyas, and G.C. van der Veer, Rich Evaluations of Entertainment Experience: Bridging the Interpretational Gap. *Proceedings of 13th European Conference on Cognitive Ergonomics (ECCE-13)*. Zurich, Switzerland, (2006), 137-144.

36. D. Vyas, M.R. van de Watering, A. Eliëns and G.C. van der Veer, Engineering Social Awareness in Work Environments. *Proceedings of HCI International 2007*, Beijing, China, (in Press).

37. M. Wieser, The computer for the 21st century. *Scientific American*, 9, (1991), 933-940.

Shaping social beliefs: A community sensitive health information system for rural India

Vikram Parmar, David V Keyson and Cees deBont
Social and Contextual Interaction Design
Faculty of Industrial Design
Delft University of Technology

Abstract. This paper presents critical issues concerning the community sensitive personal health information system in rural India, from an industrial design perspective. Literature in current ICT based applications, point to the fact that, current efforts related to personal health information dissemination have gained limited acceptance at community level among rural population. This is probably due to limited understanding of community sensitive information needs, societal structure and user beliefs of the rural community. To understand the underlying social values and users beliefs related to personal health information (PHI), a preliminary study including field interviews and review of currently deployed ICT projects was conducted. This paper presents the preliminary results, indicating several social and design challenges towards the development of a PHI system. Further the paper proposes a design framework, which includes design as a primary tool to shape existing user beliefs to positively influence the technology acceptance process of PHI system.
Keywords: Personal health, Community behavior, Information distribution

1 Introduction

In rural India, the delivery of relevant personal health information and medical treatment is still recognized as a large challenge for government and private sectors [1, 2]. At the government level, efforts to disseminate PHI and medical treatments currently occur at three levels (Figure-1). In particular, the role of Primary Healthcare Center (PHC) is to run outreach programmes, organize health awareness and treatment camps in villages which falls under their vicinity. However the government health care reach-out programmes have not been able to keep up with the growing health care demands in villages. The partial success of government healthcare system could be attributed to large geographical distances between urban and rural areas, limited medical staff, and poor infrastructure to accommodate new medical schemes from pharmaceutical companies.

Please use the following format when citing this chapter:

Parmar, V., Keyson, D. V., deBont, C., 2007, in IFIP International Federation for Information Processing, Volume 241, Home Informatics and Telematics: ICT for the Next Billion, eds. Venkatesh, A., Gonsalves, T., Monk, A., Buckner, K., (Boston: Springer), pp. 133-143.

Towards supporting government health initiatives, several external efforts from non government organization and multinational companies have been initiated. These initiatives involve organizing health camps with private hospitals, distributing free medicines, and use of information and communication technology to provide distant healthcare or tele-medicine facilities.

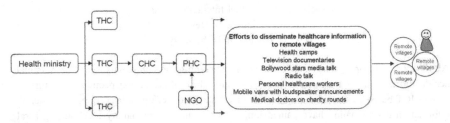

Fig. 1. Existing Public Health Information Efforts

1.1 Need of PHI system

Currently, the ICT health related applications offered at tele-centers or on PDA platforms tends to focus on disease treatment related information, rather than providing insight on prevention. The advances of health care in the diagnosis and treatment may have helped add years to users life, but have not yet rendered the community at large, healthier. This situation clearly indicates the need to educate the rural communities towards having a better understanding of disease and their basic preventive measures. For instance, in India every year 500,000 children under age five die due to diarrhea [3]. Precautionary measures such as feeding oral rehydration salts in the primary stage of illness could save few lives. To educate rural users information system are needed which could nurture knowledge among villagers, such that their personal health can be improved via their own initiative and efforts. Here, an information system could be defined as a tool to offer relevant information to rural users and involves network of all communication comprised of people, machines and methods to collect, process, transmit and disseminate data [4, 5].

Despite several ICT efforts such as tele-centers or use of PDA platforms to reach remote villages with limited healthcare facilities eg teledoc, which offers distance diagnosis, the acceptance of ICT based healthcare applications in rural India has been limited. This situation could be partially attributed to limited understanding of rural societal structure and attitude of rural users towards personal health issues. In reviewing the societal structure of rural areas, strong hierarchy at work and home environment, male dominance in decision making at home, orthodox religious practices and overall low awareness about global development was identified. Furthermore, field interviews revealed that, due to stigmatization, women in rural areas finds it difficult to access appropriate healthcare. Stigmatization is based on an existing social values and beliefs, which are the outcome of existing close mindset, and superstition owing to religious practices [6]. A study by Spector [7, 8] stated that, ignorance of these culturally divergent beliefs and traditional health care practices may lead to failure of health information systems. In addition, issues such as lack of privacy to share and receive information related to personal health care are inhibiting the acceptance of PHI systems. A study by Dourish & Anderson [9] noted that privacy concerns are not something that can be retrofitted to technologies, but are fundamental to their structure and usage models.

In above context, to accentuate ICT as a mass media information tool, the information needs related to existing community thinking, social values and beliefs should be considered as fundamental issues in developing PHI systems. This should result in an acceleration of acceptance of the knowledge sharing mechanisms to improve the well being of the community. Furthermore, Byrne & Sahay [10] pointed out that there is a need to reconfigure the existing individual based approach where information is only received or delivered to one or two users via PHI systems to a community- sensitive approach where maximum number of users could be reached. In order to investigate the above issues from an industrial design perspective, the paper aims to present preliminary findings about existing inhibiting factors in rural communities with specific reference to personal hygiene issues concerning rural women and factors influencing the acceptance of PHI systems. These inhibiting factors have been explained as an outcome of field interviews and review of ICT based case studies in rural India. The paper concludes with proposed research approach towards shaping the social beliefs for developing community sensitive personal health information system.

2 Current Study

The current research is a part of on-going doctoral research at the Industrial Design Department in Delft, The Netherlands. In reviewing the ICT literature, rich data on development of information systems for developing countries capturing multiple view-points from various fields of discipline was reviewed. For instance in social anthropology Metcalfe & Joham [11] described their research on oral culture, and have argued that modern technology, such as UHF citizen band radio, can be highly effective in supporting knowledge exchange between groups with a strong oral tradition. From the view-point of information infrastructure Rolland & Monterio [12] addressed the standardization versus localization debate, and argued that universal solutions are unlikely to be successful in multiple location spanning different social, political, institutional and strategic context. From a knowledge management framework, Okunoye & Karsten [13] provided a detailed discussion of the specific use of technologies such as e-mail, database, and telecommunications in six African countries to access knowledge sources. However, there is a lack of body of knowledge in literature on the correlation between design and social cultural issues involving the social process of groups, communities and societies. Furthermore, how design can be used as a research tool towards developing community sensitive information systems needs to be researched. To address the above gap in literature the research reported here presents an industrial design approach to research on underlying socio-cultural issues in rural context towards developing personal health information systems.

The study intends to build design approach by integrating components from "Community organization framework by Kenny,S [14]. This includes the Activist's framework involving: community participation, social change, advocacy and self determination. In particular, the current study will focus on social change, which occurs at three levels- structural (entrust decision making structures to facilitate community self determination), ideational (participants begin to understand their interdependence and the values of mutuality and compassions), level of skills (where citizens become skilled in participating and articulating concerns identifying needs and resolving conflicts). In collaboration with non government organization, the project will be piloted in western India.

3   Method

To understand the role of ICT in personal health, users social values, and their perceptions about new technology development, two research methods were applied: structured and unstructured field interviews and case study research method advocated by Yin, R [15]. The interviewing team included an industrial designer in conjunction with local NGO employees. Note: To narrow the scope of current research and test the proposed design process, personal hygiene problems related to village women and girls has been undertaken as a problem case.

3.1 Structured and unstructured field interviews

The structured and unstructured field interviews of (n-20) villagers and (n-20) ICT service providers assisted in developing a qualitative assessment of (a) demographic data, (b) daily routine and schedules, (c) existing social system and traditional beliefs (c) current practices and efforts to access health information (d) user ICT exposure and their perceptions about new technology (e) identify the information needs and different user segments, and (f) ICT success and failures in villages.

3.2 Review of cases

To establish a broader understanding of the existing ICT success and failures, in addition to ICT based health care projects, one e-governance was also reviewed. Being one of the initial e- projects in India, these projects were evaluated to gain empirical evidence from their design and deploying experiences. A brief explanation about selected projects is given below:

Tele-doc [16]: It is an e-health programme offering door to door medical service. The health care information is delivered by village based field worker, who records and transmits diagnostic data to an IT enabled central clinic via java enabled mobile telephone.

Electronic Medical Record (EMR) [17]: Mainly involves collecting data for better understanding of disease pattern in a community, which could lead to optimal resource allocation during outbreak. The information is recorded via a hand held device.

N-logue [18, 19]: Offers distant health care in the area such as cardiac care, remote patient monitoring and veterinary care. An information transaction relies on 35/70 kbps internet connection.

Gyandoot [20] : Is an intranet based Government to Citizen (G2C) service delivery portal offering twenty two applications namely agro-market Information, Income Certificate, Domicile Certificate, Caste Certificate etc. The gyandoot centers are mainly connected through dial-up and WiLL technology.

Note: Detail analysis of the projects is not presented in this paper. If required given references could be used to read more information about the selected case studies.

The selected cases were evaluated from the following perspectives:

- *User participation*: the level of user participation and how user requirements were dealt with.
- *User interface/Interaction model:* user interface issues related to input and output of information at user and system level were analyzed.
- *Technology acceptance*: issues concerning technology acceptance and approaches utilized.
- *Communication between different stakeholders*: ways in which communication between rural user, local stakeholders, and technology providers was established, towards achieving user centric solutions.
- *Awareness generation*: To analyse the strategies applied to generate project awareness among rural users.

4 Results

The preliminary findings from the structured and unstructured interviews and review of the projects revealed few social, community, and design challenges. Issues mentioned under each challenge will be included in the design and development of community sensitive personal health information systems.

4.1 Social challenges

Stigmatization: Due to low social status of women in rural India, freedom to express their ideas and problems openly is still a distant dream for rural women and girls [21, 22]. As a result, women with personal hygiene issues mostly do not seek treatment due to existing self and society based stigmatization. Due to embarrassment, women hesitate to discuss their personal health, [23, 24]. In unavoidable circumstances, they seek treatment from local quacks who are scientifically unqualified for offering health treatments.

Superstition: Owing to superstitions, women are not allowed to visit holy places during their menstruation periods. Additionally, due to lack of exposure, many women think that menstruation is a punishment for some evil doing [25].

Trust: It was observed that due to an inefficient formal medical healthcare system there is a high prevalence and trust on traditional medical care practitioner among village women.

Privacy: Low privacy level exists due to existing social norms. In rural India, privacy is curtailed owing to the fact that interaction in public or even private places is often subject to external observation and intervention [26]. This makes women, hesitant in discussing their personal hygiene issues with each other or even to health worker.

Male dominated society: The current study observed that, majority of ICT projects were offering male oriented information. The requirement of several user groups in the rural communities such as village women, adolescent girls, elderly, and youth were ignored perhaps owing to male dominated society [6, 27].

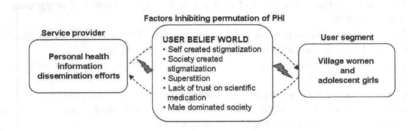

Fig. 2. depicts user belief world inhibiting the permutation of PHI information between information service providers and village women.

4.2 Community sensitive needs

Collective capacity building: Existing ICT applications have seldom offered women specific information to improve their social status in the Indian society. There is a need to offer functions, which could develop certain skills or competence to improve their performance ability. With increase efficacy, women could gain dignity.

Collective empowerment: From review it appears that, there are limited ICT applications which addressess women health related issues or have stimulated group participation among village women. Introducing strategies which involve group participation from women could amplify their exposure about new developments. Collective participation may offer opportunity to display their own skill sets in front of other village women, which could strengthen their intra-personal trust.

Collective action: Community cohesions and inclusion are necessary to support community action. Currently there is a need to educate communities as a whole towards having a better understanding of primary health related issues and their basic preventive actions [28].

Collective Knowledge sharing: In reviewed cases, it seems that offered ICT application doesn't supports sharing of problems or success stories among rural users at community level. There is a need for a platform where group discussion involving village women could be organized to induce community knowledge sharing.

4.3 Design Challenges

Privacy: How to design a system which ensures privacy while receiving information related to personal health issues, while at the same time allow sharing of information at community level.

Trust: There is a low awareness about offered ICT applications among rural users. Low awareness has led to low usage of PHI systems. The challenge is to seek component of design that can play a role in generating awareness about PHI applications and aid in building trust among users.

Attract communities: Given the weak position and the closed mindset of village women in rural communities about sharing personal health issues, the challenge is, to collectively motivate village women to access relevant personal health information and induce community action towards removing existing stigmatization.

Multiple user incorporation: In current ICT projects, there is a limited possibility of disseminating information to multiple users due to close physical environment and limited screen size for offering information. The challenge is, how to present personal health information to multiple users.

Well defined application: Existing ICT projects are mainly focused on providing internet access for web browsing, rather then offering any well defined application. In order to have well defined applications, the challenge is, how users in concern could be involved to generate content and define application and what role design could play to have user participation in early design stages.

5 Conclusions and proposed research framework

While formulating information dissemination strategies, seldom have efforts been made towards incorporating existing user social values and beliefs in ICT based PHI systems. As a result, the reacheability and acceptance of current PHI system in rural area have been limited. This has further led to information gap between health service provider and rural users. A study by Guizzardi [29] and Awusabo-Asare [30] demonstrated the persuasive power of ICT and multimedia for providing desired information and training components, without disturbing the social and behavioral patterns of users in developing countries.

While addressing existing social beliefs of rural users and low acceptance issues related to PHI systems, different design strategies will be explored to understand user requirements and develop PHI system. Design strategies would be based on activity organization framework, where process of social change occurs at three stages as mentioned earlier, namely structural, ideational, and skill level [14]. The design propositions will be evaluated via interactive system design variables [31] namely :

Interactivity: will involve issues related to representation of information to users i.e. audio-visual based, graphic based, or touch based, depending on users skill set. *Content:* to increase users sense of ownership about PHI system, queries coming from rural users will be included in a content generation process. Later gender specific content could be collected by mapping queries pattern in rural areas. *Form:* will include flexibility to offer privacy as desired by the rural users and high observability factors to create awareness about the project. *Strategy:* based on existing social system and users belief, several design strategies will be tested as hypothesis. *Connectivity:* will consider issues related to knowledge sharing among rural users via intra-personal communication and explore community to community connection via on-line or off-line information.

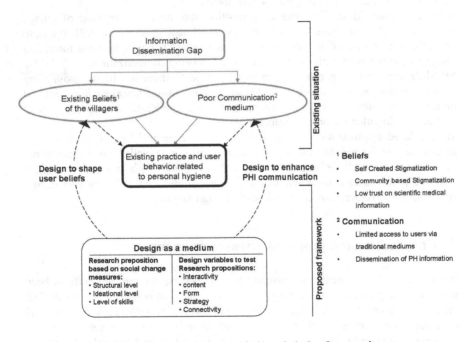

Fig. 3. depicts proposed research through design framework

Interactive system design variable can thus be used as an evaluation factors in the development of a community sensitive PHI system as shown in figure-3. In future, multiple combinations of given design variables will be explored to understand the role of design in development of PHI system. In summary, the result of the current study should lead to the development of integral design methodology and a research platform. This may serve as a tool to extract user requirements, incorporating a broad spectrum of factors which may influence technology acceptance. Industries involved in developing and evaluating ICT projects in emerging rural areas, stand to benefit from the expected outcome.

6 Acknowledgement

The current research is partially funded by the Smart Surrounding project from the Industrial Design Department, Delft University of Technology. We are thankful to NGO Chetna and Gram seva trust for providing us timely support on the pilot site.

7 References

1. Deodhar, N.S., *What went wrong with public health in India.* Journal of Health and Population in Developing Countries, 2000. **3**,: p. 91-98.
2. Mahajan, P. and N. Sharma, *Parents attitude towards imparting sex education to their adolescent girls.* The Anthropologist, 2005. **7(3)**: p. 197-199.
3. USAID. *India's Largest Ever Race Against Diarrheal Deaths* 2005 [cited 2005 24th September]; Available from: http://newdelhi.usembassy.gov/pr072706.html.
4. Hirschheim, R.e.a., *Information systems development and data modeling: Conceptual and philosophical foundations.* 1995: Cambridge & Aston University Press.
5. Wikipedia. *Information system.* 2006 [cited 2006 November 14th]; Available from: http://en.wikipedia.org/wiki/Information_system.
6. Raj, H., *Rural Sociology.* 2005, New Delhi:: Surjeet publications.
7. Spector, *Cultural aspects of women's health and health-promoting behaviors.* Journal of Obstetrics and Gynecologic and Neonatal Nursing, 1995. **24**(3): p. 241-245.
8. Spector, R.E., *Cultural diversity in health and illness.* 1991, New Jersey: Appleton and Lange.
9. Dourish, P. and K. Anderson, *Collective information practice: Exploring privacy and security as social and cultural phenomena.* Human-computer interaction, 2006. **21**: p. 319-342.
10. Byrne, E. and S. Sahay, *Health information systems for primary health care.*
11. Metcalfe, M. and C. Joham. *The "ear" and "eye" digital divide.* in *the International Federation of Information Processing IFIP 9.4 and 8.2 Joint Conference on Organizational Information Systems in the Context of Globalization.* 2003. Dordrecht, The Netherlands: Kluwer.
12. Rolland, H.H. and E. Monteiro, *Balancing the local and the global in infrastructural information systems.* The Information Society, 2002. **18**(2): p. 87-100.

13.   Okunoye, A. and H. Karsten, *Global access to knowledge: Findings from academic research organizations in sub-Saharan Africa.* Information Technology and People, 2003. **16**(3): p. 353-373.

14.   Kenny, S., *Tensions and dilemmas in community development: new discourses,new Trojans.* Community Development Journal, 2002. **37**: p. 284-299.

15.   Yin, R.K., *Case study research: Design and methods.* 1994: America: Sage publications.

16.   Jiva. *TeleDoc: Sustainable Healthcare for Rural India.* 2005 [cited 2005 April 20th]; Available from: www.jiva.com/health/teledoc.asp.

17.   Anantraman, V.e.a., *Handheld computers for rural healthcare, experiences in a large scale implementation.*

18.   Paul, J. *What Works: n- Louge's Rural Connectivity Model.* 2004 [cited; Available from: http://www.TeNet.res.in.

19.   Ponnapa, P.G., *IT for common man, in IT for common man (With n-logue).* 2004.

20.   CEE, *Rural cyber cafes on intranet: A cost evaluation study of project Gyandoot, Dhar, Madhya Pradesh, India.* 2002, IIM: Ahmedabad,Gujarat.

21.   Khanna, A., R.S. Goyal, and R. Bhavsar, *Menstrual practices and reproductive problems: A study of adolescent girls in Rajasthan.* Journal of health management, 2005. **7**.

22.   Singh, A., *Place of menstruation in the reproductive lives of women in rural north India.* Indian journal of community medicines, 2006. **30**(1).

23.   Bang, R., & Bang, A, *A community study of gynecological diseases in Indian villages in Zeidenstein and Moore (eds.) learning about Sexuality: A Practical Beginning.* 1989.

24.   Nandini, O., *A decade of research on Reproductive Tract Infections and other Gynecological Morbidity in India: What we know and what we don't know* Women's Reproductive Health in India, ed. R.a. Jejeebhoy. 2000, New Delhi: Rawat Publication.

25.   Deo, D.S. and C.H. Ghattargi, *Perception and practices regarding menstruation: A comparative study in urban and rural adolescent girls.* Indian journal of community medicines, 2005. **30**(Jan- March).

26.   Hofstede, G. *Geert HofstedeTM cultural dimension.* 2006 [cited; Available from: http://www.geert-hofstede.com/hofstede_india.shtml.

27.   Bharat, S., *India: HIV & AIDS-related discrimination, stigmatization and denial.* 2001.

28.   Blattman, C., R. Jensen, and R. Roman, *A study on assessing the need and potential of community networking for developing countries: A case study from India.* 2002.

29.   Guizzardi, G. and e.a. Stella R., *Rationality and preventive measures: The ambivalence of the social discourse on AIDS. Sexual Interactions and HIV Risk eds. L. V.Campenhoudt, M. Cohen, G. Guizzardt and D. Hausser.* 1997. 159 - 180.

30.   Awusabo-Asare, K., *HIV/AIDS education and counseling: experiences from Ghana.* Health Transition Review, 1995. **Vol-5**: p. 229 - 236.

31.   Benyon, D., P. Turner, and S. Turner, *Designing interactive systems-People, Activities, Context, Technologies*. 2005.

"Can we trust the Indians with our data?" An examination of the emergence of information privacy laws in India

Ramesh Subramanian

Information Systems Management, School of Business, Quinnipiac University, U.S.A.

Abstract. This paper looks at the nature and current state of evolution of privacy laws in India. India is an emerging economy, but the Indian ITeS environment has already emerged into a mature and highly competitive destination to outsource a variety of business processes from technically advanced nations. There is, however, a tension that exists between the IT industry's needs and the Indian societal needs in general. One of the causes of such tension pertains to the issue of privacy. An important facet of the IT industry is information privacy – an aspect demanded and expected by its global customers. But the notion of privacy is hardly global. Different countries have different notions of privacy, often based on cultural norms, resulting in widely differing privacy laws. This paper studies the evolution and development of privacy laws from the context of four main players, namely, the law and legal environment, governmental policies, the IT industry and the citizenry of India. The study shows that while India has made several strides in matching the privacy needs of its global clientele, there are several areas which require further work. To some extent, the democratic structure in India, as well as its security needs have made it difficult and cumbersome to enact privacy laws, and more work is required in this area.

1 Introduction

In the last two decades, India has been the beneficiary of the global outsourcing boom. Starting with IT services in the late 1980s the Indian companies providing services to outsourcing companies in the US and UK have steadily grown to encompass other service areas such as business process outsourcing, customer support, research and development in fields ranging from computers science, information technology, manufacturing design and bio-technology, direct marketing, education, health and financial services including tax services and even the entertainment industry such as animation services.

Please use the following format when citing this chapter:

Subramanian, R., 2007, in IFIP International Federation for Information Processing, Volume 241, Home Informatics and Telematics: ICT for the Next Billion, eds. Venkatesh, A., Gonsalves, T., Monk, A., Buckner, K., (Boston: Springer), pp. 145-155.

India seems to be a natural destination for global outsourcing. It has a large population of English-speaking technicians, managers, marketers, health professionals and analysts. India's geographic location and the resultant time-differential between itself and technically advanced countries such as the US, Canada and countries of the EU give it an added advantage – when it is night in, say, the US, it is day in India. This gives US companies the possibility of 24-hour shifts which are accomplished by just shifting the work to their Indian counterparts at 5:00pm every day. Global networking as well as other technology developments such as distributed collaborative systems enable seamless transfer of business processes between India and the US, UK and Australia. In addition, even in industries which do not require the daily transfer of job processes between India and US/UK, the availability of Indian workers who are willing to work at nights in order to fulfill the day-time service requirements of US companies, plus the notable wage differential between India and the US provide additional reasons for ensuring the continued boom of outsourcing IT enabled jobs and processes to India in the foreseeable future.

Today, the outsourcing and IT-enabled services industry (ITeS) in India is booming. The Indian IT enabled services sector grew at a rapid rate in the last fifteen years. The earnings from IT-ITES exports was US$ 13.3 billion (61.9 percent of total industry revenues) in 2003-04 and was expected to touch US$ 17.9 billion (63.7 percent) in 2004-05 [1]. Several analysts predict that India will continue to grow in the ITeS arena. According to Noshir Kaka, a partner in McKinsey & Company, "...the total addressable market for global off shoring is approximately $300 billion, of which $110 billion will be offshore by 2010. India has the potential to capture more than 50 per cent of this opportunity and generate export revenues of approximately $60 billion by growing at 25 per cent year-on-year till 2010 [2]."

But this growth is not without its pitfalls. Outsourcing (also known as off-shoring) of business processes has led to job losses in the US and other European countries. This has led to widespread backlash among citizens in these countries, who have been quick to point out some of the problems that have inevitably ensued due to off-shoring. These include communication and collaboration problems exacerbated by distance, differences in work ethics, differences in culture, quality of service issues, and more recently (and ominously), security issues. As the global spread of the Internet increases rapidly, so does the propensity for crime based on exploiting the Internet. These crimes are generally referred to as "cybercrimes," and pertain to criminal activities in which computers and computer networks, notably the Internet, are the tools, targets and locations of criminal activity. As Indian companies grow and become major players in the outsourcing market, Indian professionals working at various locations in India are increasingly involved in directly handling personal data pertaining to citizens of foreign countries, especially from North America and Europe. This raises the issue of data security and safeguarding of privacy of the data.

Certain well-advertised security lapses in Indian ITeS companies have recently come to light which expose the vulnerability of such data to mishandling, theft and other exposure. In April of 2005, three former employees of Mphasis, a BPO company in India, were arrested for defrauding four Citibank account holders in New York to the tune of US$ 300,000. Later, on June 23, 2005, the London-based tabloid, The Sun, reported that one of its reporters was able to buy information about 1,000 UK bank accounts and personal data associated with the accounts from an individual working at an Indian web design company in Gurgaon, a New Delhi suburb [3]. These incidents were widely publicized in the US and UK media, and led to a Forrester Research Report cited in a Rediff.com news article [4] that warned that such incidents will greatly curb the outsourcing boom to India . These incidents, as well as the publicity and the Forrester Reports sent shockwaves to the Indian BPO and outsourcing sectors, which clearly saw the potential for loss of business arising from lax security and protection of data. These developments spurred calls for greater focus on security and privacy in the Indian ITeS sector towards the end of 2005.

The strongest calls to enhance data security and data privacy in Indian ITeS companies have come from the Indian outsourcing industry and NASSCOM (National Association of Software and Service Companies), India. NASSCOM is the main industry association that has historically taken a leadership role in promoting the Indian software industry abroad, in developing standards for the Indian IT industry, in acting as a lobbying group to the government, and in acting as a clearing house for IT industry-related information to domestic and foreign customers.

In this paper we will track some of the governmental, legal and industry-based measures that seek to ensure data security and privacy in India, and, where relevant compare the measures with similar measures that exist in North America and EU countries. The objective of this essay is two-fold. The first is to determine the state of existing instruments to secure privacy in the Indian context. The second is to see if there are significant gaps between the requirements and the reality of the situation in India. Based on these we will finally provide an analysis of privacy in India, and our conclusions and directions for future studies in the area.

In the remaining sections we will discuss the issue of data privacy in India from the points of view of the law, government policies, industry policies and standards, and the people, especially the software industry workers in India.

2. The Indian Constitution's position on an individual's privacy

Privacy is not explicitly guaranteed by the Constitution of India. Article 21 of the Constitution, which was signed in 1949 by Jawaharlal Nehru, the first Prime Minister of India, and went into effect in 1950, states that "no person in the country may be deprived of his life or personal liberty except according to procedure established by law." [5]. This does not explicitly state anything about an individual's right to privacy. The first connection between Article 21's granting of "personal liberty" and an individual's privacy rights in India was established in the 1964

Supreme Court ruling in the Kharak Singh v. State of Uttar Pradesh case [6]. Kharak Singh had complained in his lawsuit that his right to privacy was being violated by the police of the State, who made domiciliary visits to his place of residence and harassed him. In that case, even though the Court repelled Kharak Singh's argument, the minority judgment emphasized the need to recognize the right to privacy "as it was an essential ingredient of personal liberty" [6, para 4]. Since that time, the right to privacy has gradually become accepted as a right granted through Article 21 of the Constitution, and has been applied to various situations including those arising from developments in technology.

In 1994, in the Supreme Court case of R. Rajagopal v. the State of Tamil Nadu, Judge B.P. Jeevan Reddy held that "though the right to privacy is not enumerated as a fundamental right it can certainly be inferred from Article 21 of the Constitution." [6, para 10] Over the years, especially in the mid-twentieth century, even in countries where privacy was considered essential to human existence and personal liberty, the concept of privacy was gradually extended to include matters pertaining to "health, personal communications, family, personal relations and a right to be free from harassment and molestation." [6, para 8].

Despite the gradual recognition of a citizen's right to privacy in India, there is still no general data protection law in India. There are, however, laws that regulate the environment of electronic commerce in India, which is discussed in a later section.

In the following section we will discuss the governmental initiatives and policies pertaining to IT development including data privacy issues.

3. Governmental initiatives in IT and Software development

Even though software outsourcing and on-site software development services were provided by Indian IT firms since the late 1970s, it was the advent of economic liberalization policies in 1984, under Prime Minister Rajiv Gandhi, that gave an impetus to IT development in India. The new policies greatly liberalized the import of computers, peripherals and software to India. Several IT companies generally benefited from this. However, the policies fell short, and did not completely remove many of the import restrictions or the restrictions on travel by Indian software engineers to locations abroad. The foreign exchange shortfall sharply restricted currency exchange between the Indian rupee and the US dollar, which further curbed Indian technocrats from traveling abroad for business purposes. In 1989, India went into an economic recession, and in 1991, Rajiv Gandhi was tragically assassinated, and P.V. Narasimha Rao became the Prime Minister. The country's balance of payment situation became serious in 1991, and India turned to the IMF for assistance. This was followed by a structural adjustment program. The main aim of this program was to increase India's competitiveness through free flow of foreign technology. A New Industrial Policy (NIP) was announced in 1991. Manmohan Singh, the Finance Minister, carried out the economic reforms. Foreign Direct

Investments (FDIs) were permitted in all sectors. Restrictions on software imports were eased further [7].

This led to a tremendous growth in software companies in India. Indeed, India, with its multitude of trained engineers and software professionals, was "at the right place, at the right time," to exploit the emerging need for low cost software and IT enabled services among technically advanced countries. Realizing the vast potential to move India into the echelons of technically advanced countries through using the vehicle of information technology, the Indian government began to take some critical steps towards fostering and engendering growth in this sector. In 1998, Prime Minister Atal Behari Vajpayee set up a "National Task Force on IT and Software Development." The stated goal was to come up with ideas and strategies to make India an IT superpower and one of the largest generators and exporters of software in the world in ten years (i.e. 2008). The task force, consisting of government bureaucrats, ministers, industry officials, IT entrepreneurs, military officers, policy makers, academics and selected Indian IT professionals around the world, solicited suggestions from all interested parties by setting up a web site to post suggestions. The resulting ideas and suggestions were collected and developed into an "Information Technology Action Plan," which consisted of 107 "objectives," categorized under several areas such as "Info-Infrastructure Drive," export targets for IT software and services, strategies for creating IT penetrations and awareness, Citizen IT interfaces, IT in Government, and development of Data Security Systems and Cyber Laws [8]. Objective number 102 specifically called for the establishment of "A National Policy on Information Security, Privacy and Data Protection Act for handling of computerized data shall be framed by the Government within six months." [9].

Despite this high-level proposal, the implementation of some the objectives have been spotty. This is particularly true in the area of developing laws to protect privacy. In its 2003 "Privacy and Human Rights Report," the group Privacy International reported that no legislative action concerning privacy had been taken in India. However, with the aid of the IT Action Plan, as well as pressure from NASSCOM, the software and services industry association, the government of India passed the Information Technology Act in 2000. Thus it becomes evident that in the case of IT-related laws and regulations, the industry has been very active in moving the government forward.

4. Legal protections in the Internet Age

As noted in an earlier section, the Constitution of India, Article 21 provides for privacy protection to its citizens, even though it does not directly do so. Privacy has become included as a one of the protections afforded by the Article through common law precedence set over the years by various rulings.

The Telegraph Act of 1885 provides protection from wiretapping. However, this law has been flouted on several occasions, until the Supreme Court ruled in a 1996 decision in Peoples Union for Civil Liberties (PUCL) vs. The Union of India & Another, that "wiretaps are a 'serious invasion of an individual's privacy.'" [10]. However, the right to privacy is available and enforceable only against the State. Thus, "if the offender is a private individual then there is no effective remedy except in tort where one can claim damages for intruding in his privacy and no more. Tort itself falls in the gray area." [11].

In order to keep pace with technology developments, and in keeping with its aim to become a leading provider of software and software services in the word, India enacted its first IT-related laws in the year 2000. The Information Technology Act (2000). The Act provides a comprehensive regulatory environment for electronic commerce, and also addresses computer crime, hacking, damage to computer source code, breach of confidentiality and viewing of pornography. The Act also contained some sections that required cyber-cafés to maintain detailed records of customers' web browsing habits and provide them to the authorities upon request. However, after a public outcry, these sections were dropped.

Despite the enactment of the IT Act, the tremendous pace of the technology has ensured that privacy can easily be violated. As noted by Agrawal, citing an article by Satyantan Chakrawarty in *India Today*, November 17, 2003, "sometimes the officials transgress their authority and enter the private domain of the people thus infringing their privacy. The Research and Analysis Wing (RAW) had access to bugging, surveillance and counter surveillance equipment. A variety of devices can be used by an investigating agency, like, e-logger, GSM monitor, laser ear, e-mail interceptor, and spy cavities." [11].

In March 2002 the Indian Parliament passed the Prevention of Terrorism Act (POTA). This was done mostly under the scenario of increasing threat due to terrorist activities over the disputed territory of Kashmir, and under the shadow of the September 11, 2001 terrorist strikes in the US. This Act gave law enforcement sweeping powers to arrest suspected terrorists, intercept communications, and curtail free expression. Critics, including the opposition party at that time, and human rights groups criticized the Act, saying that based on past experience, the law could be used to infringe on people's privacy and freedom. This, despite the fact that Chapter V of POTA, which deals with the interception of electronic communications, also creates an audit mechanism that includes some provision for judicial review and parliamentary oversight. The over-abiding question is how effective the checks and balances will work in practice.

The above discussion is by no means a complete listing of privacy-related laws enacted in India. But they do provide a good idea of the background and history of privacy and the law in India over the years.

This brings us to the subject of the role of the media, the public and the industry, over the years, in shaping privacy policies and developing cyber laws and privacy laws in India.

5. Privacy laws: the role of the media, industry and the public in a democracy

The IT-industry's premier organization, NASSCOM, has been at the forefront of efforts to bringing India's IT-laws in line with, or at least close to technically advanced nations in Europe and North America. In this, the NASSCOM has been aided by the Indian media organizations who have kept up the public's focus on the risks that data theft and inadequate data protection pose to the Indian public as well as the customers of Indian ITeS companies. The Indian software industry primarily employs members from India's vast middle-class, who also have access to the wide array of news media and news outlets. Thus the efforts of the industry organization, coupled with the democratic processes that allow an open media to disseminate good as well as bad news, and offer critical assessments of the government and the industry, is slowly beginning to raise an awareness of the importance of data privacy among the industry as well as the public employed in the IT sector. Free access to unbiased media, and frequent media exposés have played an important role in educating the public on the value of privacy, while warning the industry leaders of the potential dangers to the IT industry itself, if data was not adequately protected, and privacy was not adequately maintained. This is especially critical to the Indian ITeS industry, as much of its customer base is located in technically advanced countries with sophisticated and well developed laws concerning the protection of data and privacy.

Given this background, NASSCOM has taken a lead in driving public policy concerning data protection and privacy, as well as providing certain directions and standards for IT organizations in India. NASSCOM promotes the concept of "trusted sourcing," which is the term it gives for its efforts in promoting data protection and privacy amongst the Indian IT industry players. The NASSCOM web site has large and comprehensive sections on Information Security and Privacy, Indian Privacy Law and Data Protection. NASSCOM defines "privacy" as "as a combination of maintaining the confidentiality of information and restriction of the use of the information, as authorized by the information owner." [12]. It then provides a list of US and UK laws that pertain to privacy, for the information of Indian IT outsourcing companies.

Over the years, NASSCOM has become particularly concerned about Indian data protection and privacy. This is an area which also seems to be under the cross-hairs of the Indian policy makers, though for a completely different reason. In the post September-2001 world, Indian policy makers have increasingly focused on acquiring surveillance powers and use technologies such as provided by the Internet, as well as other digital forensic tools, to track down terrorists and other extreme elements. This notion of national security is at odds with the notion of privacy that is sought by NASSCOM and other industry groups. In a newspaper article that appeared in May 2005, NASSCOM's president Kiran Karnik expresses his concerns thus: "I feel deeply concerned about the obsession we have with 'security'... which seems to provide a cover-all for anything and everything. It seems to permit the government and its multiple security agencies to do anything from tapping telephones to intercepting mail to seeking identity and sites accessed by cyber cafe users."[13]

Sunil Mehta, Vice-president of NASSCOM, states that "as Internet penetration in India increases, e-governance initiatives grow in reach and more and more 'personal identifiable information (PII)' becomes digitized, many of us are increasingly concerned about privacy and security breaches. I really believe there should be a genuine public debate in this country among all stakeholders around the kind of privacy laws that we, as citizens, really need." [13].

In addition to NASSCOM, the Indian public has also gradually become aware of possible privacy violations that could be caused by technology. The Indian public's access to the Internet has increased, due to the lower costs of computers and Internet access, and due to marketplace pressures as well as governmental policies. At the same time, its awareness and knowledge of use and misuse of personal information has also increased. This has resulted in pressure being exerted on the government to enact and defend laws pertaining to its privacy.

The above statements and emerging public consensus on the issue tend to illustrate the complexities involved with formalizing and legalizing the notion of privacy and privacy protection. While NASSCOM has pioneered and pushed Indian policy makers into enacting IT-related laws, it is also concerned that under the guise of national security, many of the laws, including those pertaining to privacy, made never be implemented in India. NASSCOM has thus become the champion of IT-related laws, including those that protect privacy. The government, on the other hand, is interested in promoting India's IT growth, and in legislating new laws as they pertain to IT misuse. However, there seems to be a hesitation in enacting privacy laws that might restrict its powers in enforcing national security.

In addition to shaping public policy, NASSCOM also provides various guidelines to IT companies on various ways to secure organizational, network and private data in it web site. The aim of this is clearly designed to maintain Indian IT companies' competitive advantage in the global marketplace, and to assure customers that the India ITeS industry is actively taking steps to protect the privacy of its customers' data. By undertaking all of the above activities, NASSCOM seeks to actively promote India's prowess in the global ITeS arena.

6. Analysis and conclusions

In the Indian attempts at establishing high-level data security and privacy standards, we clearly see Christopher Stone's [14] "hand of the marketplace" at work. To elaborate, Christopher Stone, in his book *Where the Law Ends,* states that there are three hands associated with managing a firm to achieve socially desirable behavior. As elucidated by Jeff Smith [15] in a Panel titled "Information Privacy: Management, Marketplace and Legal Challenges," conducted during the ICIS 2004 conference in Washington, D.C., Stone's "three hands" are: the hand of management, the hand of law, and the hand of marketplace. Smith suggests that managers and executives may not have adequate incentives to shape or follow privacy initiatives. However, that is not the case when the same organization is faced with marketplace issues, such as lack of competitiveness due to lack of privacy standards. In such a situation, such executives would take all the necessary actions needed to shape or influence public policy and get appropriate laws enacted. In doing so, they may sometimes complement or act in opposition to public attitudes that will also play an equally important role in shaping public policy discussion in a democratic environment. The Indian IT industry clearly sees the risks to its well-being and growth that might occur due to compromises in data security and privacy, and is pushing for privacy standards and appropriate laws from the government. However, at the same time, the industry as well as the public balk at the idea of increased security needs that is cited by the government in the implementation of existing Information Technology and privacy laws. Thus, the current Indian scene as regards privacy is hardly clear, especially in the absence of clear-cut privacy laws. What is clear is the overall desire of the Indian IT industry and the Indian government in using the current outsourcing boom to its maximum potential. In doing so, each entity has its own unique reasoning and judgment, which act against each other in some situations, and complement each other in other situations.

Some useful questions for further research in this area could include:
1. The attitudes of Indian IT executives with regards to privacy
2. Cultural studies of Indian software professionals to gain an understanding on their attitudes to privacy.
3. Comparison of Indian privacy laws with US/UK privacy laws.

In conclusion, the answer to the question: "Can we trust the Indians with our data?" is a qualified 'yes.' India is definitely making progress in enacting data-privacy and data-protection laws. However, in continuing to do so, the policy makers have to counterbalance national security threats as well as the need to provide a secure environment that is in tune with the needs of its customers from technically advanced nations. In addition, there is a general consensus on the fact that the Indian legal system is currently very slow, and cases take a very long time to prosecute. In order for India to continue on its path to becoming an IT superpower, a conscious effort has to be made to enact appropriate IT laws that specifically apply to privacy and security of data, and to speed up the legal processes pertaining to IT-related cases. This would require a massive effort focused on raising an awareness of, as well as training the policy-makers, judicial system and citizens on the privacy and security issues that technology developments inevitably herald. Further, the political and legal system should be flexible enough to identify and act swiftly on the new and emerging technologies that are sure to come in the future.

References

1. NASSCOM Industry Trends (2003-2004). Para 2. Retrieved April 17, 2006 from http://www.nasscom.org/artdisplay.asp?cat_id=795

2. NASSCOM-McKinsey Report, December 12, 2005. Para 7. Retrieved April 17, 2006 from http://www.nasscom.org/artdisplay.asp?Art_id=4782

3. Jaikumar Vijayan, 2005. "Alleged data theft in India grabs security spotlight," *CIO Asia,* June, 2005. Retrieved April 10, 2006 from http://www.cio-asia.com/ShowPage.aspx?pagetype=2&articleid=1803&pubid=5&issueid=52

4. Rediff.com, April 8, 2005. "Call Center theft may bust India's BPO boom," *Rediff.com.,* Retrieved April 17, 2006 from http://www.rediff.com/money/2005/apr/08bpo.htm

5. Human Rights Watch report, 1999. "Selected Articles of the Indian Constitution." Retrieved on April 17, 2006 from http://www.hrw.org/reports/1999/india/India994-15.htm

6. Agarwala, B.D. 1996. "Right to privacy: A case-by-case development." *Practical Lawyer,* Eastern Book Company. Retrieved on April 17, 2006 from http://www.ebc-india.com/lawyer/articles/96v3a2.htm

7. Subramanian, Ramesh, 2006. "Indian and Information Technology: An Historical and Critical Perspective," in the *Journal of Global Information Technology Management* (JGITM), Vol. 9, No. 4, 2006.

8. Privacy International, 2003. "Privacy and Human Rights Report, 2003," Excerpted from *Information Technology Action Plan, Special Web site on National Taskforce on Information Technology and Software Development, 1998.* Retrieved on April 17, 2006 from http://it-taskforce.nic.in/index.html

9. Privacy International, 2003. "Privacy and Human Rights Report, 2003," Excerpted from *IT for all -2008, Special Web site on National Taskforce on Information Technology and Software Development, 1998.*Retrievd on April 17, 2006 from http://it-taskforce.nic.in/it2008.htm

10. Privacy International, 2003. "Privacy and Human Rights Report – Republic of India, 2003. Para 7. Retrieved April 17, 2006 from http://www.privacyinternational.org/survey/phr2003/countries/india.htm

11. Agrawal, Rachika, 2004. "Privacy and emerging technology: Are Indian laws catching up?" *Lawyers Collective,* February 2004. Retrieved April 17, 2006 from http://www.nwmindia.org/Law/Commentary/privacy.htm

12. NASSCOM, 2006. "Information Security and Privacy – Overview." Retrieved on April 17, 2006 from http://www.nasscom.org/artdisplay.asp?cat_id=678

13. Indian Express, 2005. "Need for an effective privacy policy," *Indian Express,* May 30, 2005. Retrieved on April 17, 2006 from http://www.nasscom.org/artdisplay.asp?Art_id=4358

14. Stone, Christopher, 1975. *Where the Law Ends:The Social Control of Corporate Behavior.* New York: Harper and Row.

15. Yolande Chan,, Mary Culnan, Kathleen Greenaway, Gary Laden and H. Jeff Smith, 2005. "Information Privacy: Management, marketplace, and legal challenges," *Communications of the Association for Information Systems,* Volume 16, 2005.

Off Their Trolley -- Understanding Online Grocery Shopping Behaviour

Lillian Clark[1] and Peter Wright[2]
1   Department of Computer Science, University of York, UK
2   Art & Design Research Centre, Sheffield Hallam University, UK

Abstract. The artefact or object-based models commonly used in interaction design for describing users are inadequate for understanding the complexity and variability of online consumer behaviour, while traditional models of consumer behaviour do not reflect the user's ability to shape their shopping experience online. To address this gap a framework has been developed for modelling online consumer behaviour and in this paper this framework is used to develop a survey of online grocery shopping in the UK. Analysis of the survey reveals several issues of concern, particularly dissatisfaction with product search capabilities and a conflict between the online consumer's desires for both empowerment and experimentation.

1   Introduction

It is axiomatic that interaction design begins with a thorough understanding of the user, and this understanding is often developed and communicated through conceptual models of the user that are grounded in specific activities or artefacts [4-6, 13]. The task of user modelling becomes particularly difficult in the context of online shopping systems. Consumer behaviour itself, regardless of venue, is highly complex in nature [14, 15], varies greatly for different demographic groups and can vary even for the same consumer depending on context [12]. This level of complexity and variability cannot be adequately reflected in models that are grounded to a particular task or artefact, and reliance on single-aspect models leads to neglect of the whole sphere of online consumer behaviour [1, 20]. Adding to these difficulties is the fact that online consumers differ from "terrestrial" ones in that they are also able to initiate and shape their shopping experiences through the use of interactive shopping systems [7, 9, 17]. Consequently, traditional models of consumer behaviour are also insufficient for modelling online consumer behaviour as these traditional models rely on the premise of a primarily passive and reactive consumer [10, 11, 18].

Please use the following format when citing this chapter:

Clark, L., Wright, P., 2007, in IFIP International Federation for Information Processing, Volume 241, Home Informatics and Telematics: ICT for the Next Billion, eds. Venkatesh, A., Gonsalves, T., Monk, A., Buckner, K., (Boston: Springer), pp. 157-170.

Therefore in order to develop the understanding of online consumer behaviour needed for effective interaction design, we need a way of modelling users that facilitates identification and exploration of the various aspects relevant to online consumer behaviour.

To address this need, we have developed a framework for modelling online consumer behaviour and demonstrated its use in developing design personas, identifying behavioural patterns, and illuminating potential interaction problems. In this paper we will examine how this framework can be used to further explore the diversity of online consumer behaviour by developing and administering a framework-based survey designed to examine the behaviour of online grocery shoppers in the UK.

2. The e-Consumer Framework

In Clark & Wright [2] we presented the e-Consumer Framework (e-CF) as a structure for conceptual modelling of online consumer behaviour. The e-CF, which was derived from existing literature and research into both online and general consumer behaviour, is based on seven parameters of online consumer behavioural (Fig. 1).

Fig. 1. The e-Consumer Framework (e-CF)

This multi-dimensional framework provides a comprehensive yet practical platform for conceptual modelling of online consumer behaviour, facilitating identification, description and prioritisation of relevant behavioural aspects while recognising the complexity and variety of online consumer behaviour. To date, we have demonstrated how the e-CF provides a structure for collecting and processing qualitative data and subsequent design persona development. In addition, e-CF based summaries of qualitative data can be used to develop insight into usage patterns and identify potential interaction issues both within and across domains.

3. Rationale For An e-CF Based Survey

In our previous study we examined online grocery shopping behaviour by observation and interview of eight participants who identified themselves as regular users of online supermarkets. In addition to demonstrating how personas could be built from individual e-CF based descriptions of each participant, we also aggregated the results for all online grocery participants into an e-CF based summary which enabled identification of various behaviour patterns common to most or all of the participants and uncovered some potential issues of concern to interaction designers including conflicts between the participants' desire for empowerment and their desire for experimentation, a lack of loyalty to terrestrial outlets of the online supermarket, a degree of difficulty in finding certain items, an avoidance of polychronic activity and a seeming indifference to site design.

The e-CF based ethnographic study illuminated the complexity of the online grocery shopper's behaviour, particularly the variety of aspects that influence such behaviour. By developing an e-CF based survey of online grocery shopping, we can use quantitative data to explore the diversity of online grocery shopping behaviours and identify common features and issues relevant to interaction design.

4. The Survey

To construct the survey, we developed over 60 closed questions each designed to cover one or more e-CF themes. Questions were designed to measure either perceived behaviour or attitudes, with themes duplicated with alternative wording where possible to minimise response bias [3]. The first question asked of all respondents was as follows:

Which of the following statements most closely describes your current level of grocery shopping?
I do most of the grocery shopping for my household
I share grocery shopping duties with other members of my household
I occasionally go grocery shopping
I never do the grocery shopping

In addition to exploring the themes of Self-Efficacy and Environments, this question acted as a primary filter, as those respondents who indicated that they never did the grocery shopping could then be immediately eliminated from the rest of the survey.

Respondents were then asked several questions concerning gender, age, occupation and household size so that demographic profiles could be built. The next set of questions was intended to explore various e-CF themes in general online shopping behaviour and non-Internet (terrestrial) food shopping.

e-CF Themes	Behavioural Questions asked of all respondents
Logistics Environments	Are there particular religious, ethical or health considerations that affect your grocery shopping? (Y/N)
Connections	Where do you do most of your non-Internet food shopping?
Connections	On average, how often do you buy your groceries from a supermarket, grocer or any place other than the Internet?
Self-Efficacies	Aside from groceries, have you ever bought any of the following types of products online?: Books, Music/Films, Travel, Electronics, House/Garden, Clothing, Toys/Gifts, Computer Hardware/Software, I have never bought anything online

The next set of questions was intended to explore the extent of various behaviours manifested in food shopping and terrestrial food shopping in particular. For these questions, a 5-point Likert scale was used for responses.

e-CF Themes	Questions on general Food Shopping Behaviours (Never, Rarely, Sometimes, Frequently, Almost Always)
Beliefs	Do you store your credit/debit card details at your favourite online shopping sites?
Self-Efficacies	Do you every find online shopping confusing?
Self-Efficacies	How often do you cook means from scratch?
Affects Logistics	Do you tend to buy the same brands or types of groceries over and over?
Economics	How often do you compare prices before deciding where to buy your groceries?
Logistics	How often do you study the label on a new item before purchasing?

The next set of questions was intended to measure attitudes towards food and food shopping in general, using a 5-point Likert scale.

e-CF Themes	Questions on Attitudes (Strongly Disagree, Disagree, Neutral, Agree, Strongly Agree)
Self-Efficacies	I am comfortable using my computer to access the Internet
Self-Efficacies	I like to try new things out on the computer myself, rather than ask someone to help me
Environments	Being able to grocery shop at any time of day is important to me
Environments	Buying organic or Fair Trade products is important to me
Affects	Food shopping is boring
Affects	I enjoy cooking for my family and friends
Environments	Grocery shopping is easier to do if I'm on my own
Affects	I don't like someone else picking out my groceries for me
Affects	I enjoy food shopping
Affects	I like to try different places to buy my groceries

Through a filtering question, respondents were then split into two groups -- those who currently did any part of their grocery shopping online (OGS) and those who did not currently do so. The OGS were then asked questions about their online grocery shopping behaviours and attitudes as follows:

e-CF Themes	Questions on Behaviour when shopping for groceries online
Beliefs Connections	Where do you do most of your online grocery shopping?
Connections	Overall, where do you buy most of your groceries? (Online, From a Supermarket, From a Grocer or other local shop, Other)
Environments	On average, how often do you buy your groceries online?

e-CF Themes	Questions on Behaviour when shopping for groceries online (Never, Rarely, Sometimes, Frequently, Almost Always)
Beliefs Connections	If you need to go to a supermarket, do you go to the same vendor that provides your online grocery shopping?
Beliefs Environments	How often do you check out Special offers or items on sale?
Environments	How often do you do your online grocery shopping from your home computer?
Economics Logistics	How often do you time your online grocery shopping to take advantage of cheaper delivery charges?
Logistics Environments	How often do you use the Search box to find an item?
Logistics Environments	How often do you scan or browse categories to find an item?
Logistics	How often do you use the "Notes" or "Instructions" feature?
Logistics	How often do you use the "My Favourites" or "Last Order" feature?
Logistics	How often do you have problems finding items?
Affects Logistics	How often do you try new products or brands?
Beliefs Affects Logistics	How often do you buy something on impulse?
Environment	How often do you do your online grocery shopping alone?

e-CF Themes	Questions on Respondent Attitudes (Strongly Disagree, Disagree, Neutral, Agree, Strongly Agree)
Economics	Buying Groceries online saves me money
Environments	I don't like being interrupted when grocery shopping online
Affects	I feel more in control of my grocery shopping when I do it online
Environments	I don't mind talking to people while doing my online grocery shopping
Connections Logistics	Buy groceries online hasn't affected the types of things I buy
Environments	My favourite online grocery site is easy to use
Affects Connections	I'm more likely to buy something new if I see it in a supermarket or shop than online
Economics Connections	The best thing about buying groceries online is that I spend less money than I would in a supermarket
Affects	I miss being able to pick out my own produce when shopping online
Affects Connections	If I had the time, I would prefer to buy my groceries in person rather than online

e-CF Themes	Questions on Respondent Attitudes (Strongly Disagree, Disagree, Neutral, Agree, Strongly Agree)
Environments	I prefer not to be distracted when online grocery shopping, as I need to concentrate on what I'm doing

e-CF Themes	Thinking about the last time you bought groceries online, please rate the vendor on... (Excellent, Good, Acceptable, Below Average, Poor)
Environments	Ease of use
Logistics	Quality of Products
Logistics	Product Selection
Logistics	Quality of Service
Environments	Web Site appearance
Economics	Price

e-CF Themes	Thinking about the last time you bought groceries online...
Beliefs	Do you store your credit/debit card details on that site?
Beliefs	Do you store your login details for that site?
Environments	Do you have the web address of the site stored in Bookmarks or Favourites?

While the intent of this phase of the survey was not to build a specific e-CF based profile of those who did <u>not</u> currently do any part of their household grocery shopping online (NOGS), several questions were developed for this group in case more comparable information was required.

e-CF Themes	Questions on frequency of Respondent Behaviour when shopping for groceries online (Never, Rarely, Sometimes, Frequently, Almost Always)
Beliefs	How often do you use credit or debit cards to pay for your food shopping?
Beliefs	How often do you check out Special offers or items on sale?
Logistics	How often do you use the supermarket nearest your home?
Environments	Do you try to do your grocery shopping at a particular time of day?
Environments	Do you try to do your grocery shopping on a particular day of the week?

e-CF Theme	
Connections	Have you ever tried to buy your groceries online?

5.   Administering The Survey

The survey was built and administered online using the QuestionPro platform (www.questionpro.com) and ran from February to April 2006. Respondents were solicited from within the UK, and the opportunity to win a £50 gift certificate was offered in order to encourage participation and valid responses, as respondents needed to identify themselves to be eligible for the prize draw. The results from the survey are detailed in Appendix A.

6. Implications For Interaction Design

In conducting this survey, our goal was to explore the diversity of online grocery shopping behaviours and identify common features and issues relevant to interaction design. To achieve this goal we transformed the survey results shown in Appendix A into an overall profile of the 46 respondents who identified themselves as OGS follows.

e-CF OGS Profile
Self-Efficacies (Technical, Product, Online Shopping)
Good levels of technical and product knowledge. Experienced online shoppers.
Beliefs
Evenly divided on financial trust, but somewhat more likely to trust online supermarket than other online vendors.
Loyalty to vendor's terrestrial outlets weak (but pull-thru not measured). Less than half look at online promotions, impulse buying drops dramatically online.
Economics
Little propensity to comparison shop, many perceive online grocery shopping as cost effective and spend less than in supermarket. Last site viewed as having good-excellent prices, and many prefer to time their shopping for cheaper delivery slots.
Affect
See online grocery shopping as gaining control over time, but losing control over selection, and most would prefer to shop in person if they had the time despite rating both online vendor's product selection and quality as good or better. Food shopping (regardless of venue) and cooking viewed as pleasurable activities. While there is a marked tendency to repeatedly buy the same products/brands regardless of venue, the inclination to experiment with product purchases decreases when online, with only a weak correlation between online and terrestrial behaviours. Experimentation with vendors was rated slightly higher
Connections
Slightly less than half the grocery shopping done online, as most continue to terrestrial shop on a regular basis (bi-weekly or more). The terrestrial environment strongly seen as the platform for product experimentation. Online shopping not perceived as having much impact on the types of products bought, slightly less than half use the same grocer for online and terrestrial and a third like to vary their vendor.
Logistics
Tendency to make a shopping list decreases somewhat online, My Favourites/Last Order is the strong preference for driving selection process. Browsing slightly preferred to Searching, no correlation between selection methodology and likelihood of encountering problems, but most report encountering at least some problems finding items. Despite concerns about controlling selection, very few use the Notes or Instructions features. More likely to store login/registration details with vendor than card details.
Environments
Mostly shop from home, once a month or less. Variable attitudes towards distractions, but half prefer not to be interrupted. Grocery shopping viewed as being easier to do alone, and more likely to online shop alone. Half saw Fair Trade/Organic as important, a third had religious, ethical or health considerations that affected their food shopping. Most perceived their online grocer's site as easy to use and rated site appearance highly.

From this profile we can identify and explore a number of issues relevant to interaction design.

Self-Efficacies: There was little diversity in the levels of Self-Efficacy (skills, knowledge and confidence) amongst the OGS, a result that would encourage the development of online supermarket interactions based on a relatively high level of experience and expertise in online shopping, grocery purchasing and Internet usage. However these results may present a biased picture as those less familiar with the Internet are less likely to respond to an online survey in the first place. In fact, our previous ethnographic study of online grocery shopping behaviour uncovered a greater level of diversity in the levels of technical self-efficacy than in this survey, suggesting that design based on high levels of technical expertise can present barriers to both existing and new users who are less skilled in these areas.

Loyalty: Respondents often used different vendors for online and terrestrial shopping, an issue that would at first glance not seem relevant to interaction design. However, given the continued frequency of terrestrial shopping amongst the respondents and the fact that the major online shopping sites in the UK are run by the supermarket chains, this lack of loyalty would naturally concern vendors who would in turn develop marketing activities taken to encourage vendor loyalty. Such activities will naturally need to be reflected in interaction design considerations, such as promotion of loyalty card schemes.

Searching and Browsing: Category browsing was more popular with respondents than use of the search facility. While there was no correlation between product location strategy and frequency of online shopping, there was a reasonably strong correlation between use of the search facility and the Notes/Instructions feature. This could suggest that use of the Search facility is more common for those shoppers particularly concerned about controlling product selection. It should also be noted that there was little correlation between browsing or searching activity, or between either activity and the likelihood of encountering problems in locating items. However, over half the respondents reported that they sometimes encountered problems finding items, and 15.6% said these problems were frequent. These results imply that regardless of product selection method used, finding items may be an issue for many online grocery shoppers and interaction designers need to consider how to improve search and scan facilities.

Empowerment: Respondents clearly had concerns about the level of control they had over their grocery shopping. On one hand, 73.9% agreed that being able to shop at any time of day was important, over 40% saw online grocery shopping as more cost-effective than terrestrial and levels of reported impulse purchasing dropped substantially online. However, the vast majority of respondents agreed they missed the experience of picking their own produce, half did not like having their grocery items picked out by other people, and over half said they would prefer to do their grocery shopping in person if time allowed. Unsurprisingly, less than a quarter of the respondents agreed with the statement that online grocery shopping gave them increased control. It is clear that the current methods of product selection in online supermarkets are working against the online consumer's need to feel in control of their shopping experience.

Experimentation: While levels of reported new product purchasing activity decreased only slightly online, the number of those claiming they never or rarely did so rose substantially and over three-quarters of the respondents agreed they were more likely to try new products in a supermarket than online. These results suggest that customers feel their ability to experiment is constrained when shopping online.

Polychronic Activity: While the survey did not specifically ask what other activities respondents engaged in while online grocery shopping, 52.2% of the respondents said they did not like being interrupted when online grocery shopping, and 31% said they preferred not to be distracted as they needed to concentrate when online grocery shopping. 30.3% said they minded talking to others while shopping. These results support our earlier observations that online grocery shoppers do indeed view their activities as requiring a degree of concentration, with some degree of tolerance for interruption.

Site Usability and Appearance: A large majority of the respondents gave positive ratings to the appearance and particularly the ease of use of their favourite online grocery site.   The site features "My Favourites" and "Last Order" were particularly popular with respondents. Product search tools and Special Offers features were less popular while use of the "Notes" and "Instructions" feature was very limited, despite respondent concerns about controlling their product selection. This would seem to indicate that online grocery shoppers do not have any particular concerns about site design or usability, but are not making full use of site features, even those that could address their product selection issues.

7. Conclusions and Suggestions for further research

Online grocery shopping in the UK has been particularly successful to date [8, 19], however it is clear there is still considerable room for improving the user's experience, especially their perception of control over their grocery shopping. Consideration needs to be given to helping online shoppers locate products through more intelligent search functionality and/or more intuitive taxonomies (a search for "rice pudding" should not produce the same results as "pudding rice") and barriers to use of site features that enhance control (such as the ability to provide specific product instructions to the vendor) needs to be examined. Addressing the online grocery shopper's need to experiment is a more difficult challenge, especially as presenting the user with extra information or displays is quite likely to conflict with their desire to control their shopping experience. One possible way to address both the user's desire to experiment and to control their grocery shopping experience is through Virtual Reality interfaces that can enhance product perception through telepresence [16].

Administering any type of consumer survey online needs to be carefully considered. Schiffman and Kanuk [14] point out that the anonymity of the Internet-based survey provides an environment where respondents can on one hand be more forthcoming in their responses but on the other hand also invent fictional profiles. To these concerns we should also add the self-selecting nature of an online survey in that it will naturally attract respondents who are comfortable with the Internet and have a reasonable level of engagement with the topic in question. Consideration should therefore be given to administering future iterations of this survey terrestrially as well as on the Internet, ideally with the cooperation of one or more UK supermarkets.

Several intriguing trends and correlations appeared in the survey results that were outside the scope of this particular study but certainly warrant further investigation. For instance, an e-CF model of those respondents who did not currently buy groceries online (the so-called NOGS) could be developed. Such a model, especially if compared to online grocery shopper models, could provide additional insights into those factors that inhibit or encourage online shopping behaviours.

REFERENCES

1. L. Clark and P. Wright, A Review of Common Approaches to Understanding Online Consumer Behaviour, in *Proceedings of the IADIS International Conference e-Society 2005*, Qawra, Malta, pp. 211-218.
2. L. Clark and P. Wright, e-CF: A Framework for Understanding Online Consumer Behaviour, 2007. (Awaiting publication).
3. D. Clark-Carter, *Quantitative Psychological Research* (Psychology Press, Hove, 2004).
4. A. Cooper, *The Inmates Are Running The Asylum* (SAMS Publishing, Indianapolis, 1999).
5. A. Cooper and R. Reimann, *About Face 2.0: The Essentials of Interaction Design.* (Wiley Publishing, Indianapolis, 2003).
6. A. Dix, J. Finlay, G.D. Abowd, and R. Beale, *Human-Computer Interaction* (Pearson Education Limited, Harlow, 2004).
7. A.F. Firat and A. Venkatesh, Liberatory Postmodernism and the Reenchantment of Consumption, *Journal of Consumer Research* **22** pp. 239-267 (1995).
8. IMRG, (August 1, 2005), Tesco has announced bumper half year results; http://www.imrg.org/802569750045BDAD/(search)/78440CC46A72170B80256F250041 1D6C?Opendocument&highlight=2.
9. J. McCarthy and P. Wright, *Technology as Experience* (The MIT Press, Cambridge, 2004).
10. J.U. McNeal, *An Introduction to Consumer Behavior* (Wiley, New York, 1973).
11. R. Markin Jr., *Consumer Behaviour. A Cognitive Orientation* (New York, Wiley, New York, 1974).
12. D. Miller, P. Jackson, N. Thrift, B. Holbrook, and M. Rowlands, *Shopping, place and identity* (Routledge, Padstow, 1998).
13. J. Preece, Y. Rogers, and H. Sharp, *Interaction Design* (John Wiley & Sons, New York, 2002).
14. L.G. Schiffman and L.L Kanuk, *Consumer Behavior* (Pearson Prentice Hall, Upper Saddle River, 2004).
15. M. Solomon, G. Bamossy, and S. Askegaard, *Consumer Behaviour: A European Perspective* (Pearson Education Limited, Harlow, 2002).
16. K.S. Suh and S. Chang, User interfaces and consumer perceptions of online stores: The role of telepresence, *Behaviour & Information Technology* **25**(2) pp. 99-113 (2006).
17. I. Szmigin, *Understanding the Consumer* (Sage Publications Ltd, London, 2003).
18. C.G. Walters, *Consumer Behavior: Theory and Practice* (Richard D. Irwin Inc, Homewood, 1976).
19. N. Wingfield and E. Anthes, Selling Food Online To Get Further Boost as Amazon Joins In, *The Wall Street Journal Europe*, June 24th 2003, page A6.
20. M. Wolfinbarger and M.C. Gilly, eTailQ: dimensionalizing, measuring and predicting etail quality, *Journal of Retailing* **79**, pp. 183-198 (2003).

Appendix A – Survey Results

	Frequency		Valid %	
	OGS	NOGS	OGS	NOGS
Gender				
Male	23	19	50	33.3
Female	23	38	50	66.7
Age:				
Under 24	2	3	4.3	5.3
25-34	24	19	52.2	33.3
35-44	13	19	28.3	33.3
45-60	6	15	13	26.3
60+	1	1	2.2	1.8
Occupation:				
Working Full-time	37	43	80.4	75.4
Student	4	11	8.7	19.3
Retired	1	1	2.2	1.8
Homemaker	0	1	0	1.8
Other	4	1	8.7	1.8
Household Size				
1	8	12	17.4	21.1
2	22	24	47.8	42.1
3	6	14	13	24.6
4	8	4	17.4	7.0
5+	2	3	4.3	4.3

	%of OGS
Which of the following statements most closely describes your current level of grocery shopping?	
I do most of the grocery shopping for my household	69.6
I share grocery shopping duties with other members of my household	23.9
I occasionally go grocery shopping	6.5
Are there particular religious, ethical or health considerations that affect your grocery shopping?	
Yes	37
No	63
Where do you do most of your non-Internet food shopping?	
Tesco	32.6
Sainsburys	15.2
Asda	6.5
Iceland	4.3
Morrisons	8.7
Waitrose	8.7
Netto/Aldi/Lidl	2.2
Other	21.7

	% of OGS
On average, how often do you buy your groceries from a supermarket, grocer or any place other than the Internet?	
Less than once a month	6.5
Once a month	10.9
Once every 2 weeks	13.0
Once a week	52.2
2 or more times a week	17.4

	% of OGS
Aside from groceries, have you ever bought any of the following types of products online?	
Books	93.5
Music/Films	87.0
Travel	78.3
Electronics	67.4
House/Garden	47.8
Clothing	60.9
Toys/Gifts	69.5
Computer Hardware/Software	67.4
I have never bought anything online	0.0

	% of OGS
Where do you do most of your online grocery shopping?	
Tesco.com	69.6
Sainsburys To You	13.0
Asda.com	2.2
Ocado/Waitrose	8.7
Other	6.5
Overall, where do you buy most of your groceries?	
Online	40.0
From a Supermarket	53.3
From a Grocer or other local shop	2.2
Other	4.4
On average, how often do you buy your groceries online?	
Less than once a month	35.6
Once a month	24.4
Once every 2 weeks	24.4
Once a week	15.6
2 or more times a week	0.0

OGS on general shopping	N%	R%	S%	F%	A%
How often do you cook means from scratch?	2.2	2.2	17.4	52.2	26.1
Do you every find online shopping confusing?	8.7	50.0	39.1	0.0	2.2
Do you store your credit/debit card details at your favourite online shopping sites?	32.6	8.7	23.9	2.2	32.6

(N=Never, R=Rarely, S=Sometimes, F=Frequently, A=Always)

OGS on terrestrial shopping	N%	R%	S%	F%	A%
How often do you study the label on a new item before purchasing?	0.0	17.4	23.9	34.8	23.9
How often do you compare prices before deciding where to buy your groceries?	10.9	41.3	23.9	15.2	8.7
Do you tend to buy the same brands or types of groceries over and over?	0.0	0.0	15.6	53.3	31.1
How often do you do your grocery shopping alone?	2.2	8.9	20.0	33.3	35.6
How often do you buy something on impulse?	0.0	15.6	46.7	37.8	0.0
How often do you try new products or brands?	0.0	11.1	66.7	20.0	2.2
How often do you make a list before shopping?	8.9	17.8	17.8	28.9	26.7

(N=Never, R=Rarely, S=Sometimes, F=Frequently, A=Always)

OGS on general shopping	SA%	A%	N%	D%	SD%
I like to try different places to buy my groceries	2.2	28.3	34.8	30.4	4.3
I enjoy food shopping	26.1	32.6	34.8	6.5	0.0

OGS on general shopping	SA%	A%	N%	D%	SD%
I don't like someone else picking out my groceries for me	6.5	43.5	32.6	15.2	2.2
Grocery shopping is easier to do if I'm on my own	39.1	30.4	19.6	8.7	2.2
I enjoy cooking for my family and friends	32.6	45.7	13.0	4.3	4.3
Food shopping is boring	6.5	19.6	32.6	30.4	10.9
Buying organic or Fair Trade products is important to me	22.2	28.9	31.1	11.1	6.7
Being able to grocery shop at any time of day is important to me	43.5	30.4	19.6	4.3	2.2
I like to try new things out on the computer myself, rather than ask someone to help me	24.4	48.9	22.2	4.4	0.0
I am comfortable using my computer to access the Internet	89.1	8.7	0.0	0.0	2.2

(SA=Strongly Agree, A=Agree, N=Neutral, D=Disagree, SD=Strongly Disagree)

OGS on online grocery shopping habits	N%	R%	S%	F%	A%
How often do you do your online grocery shopping alone?	6.8	2.3	9.1	27.3	54.5
How often do you buy something on impulse?	4.5	38.6	43.2	13.6	0.0
How often do you try new products or brands?	2.2	24.2	53.3	20.0	0.0
How often do you make a list before starting?	24.4	20.0	20.0	17.8	17.8
How often do you have problems finding items?	0.0	28.9	53.3	15.6	2.2
How often do you use the "My Favourites" or "Last Order" feature?	11.4	9.1	15.9	34.1	29.5
How often do you use the "Notes" or "Instructions" feature?	34.1	38.6	13.6	9.1	4.5
How often do you scan or browse categories to find an item?	2.2	15.6	37.8	37.8	6.7
How often do you use the Search box to find an item?	8.9	11.1	44.4	22.2	13.3
How often do you time your online grocery shopping to take advantage of cheaper delivery charges?	15.6	20.0	15.6	24.4	24.4
How often do you do your online grocery shopping from your home computer?	0.0	11.1	20.0	20.0	48.9
How often do you check out Special offers or items on sale?	8.9	17.8	28.9	24.4	20.0
If you need to go to a supermarket, do you go to the same vendor that provides your online grocery shopping?	4.5	15.9	38.6	18.2	22.7

(SA=Strongly Agree, A=Agree, N=Neutral, D=Disagree, SD=Strongly Disagree)

OGS on online grocery shopping	SA%	A%	N%	D%	SD%
I prefer not to be distracted when online grocery shopping, as I need to concentrate on what I'm doing	4.8	26.2	42.9	26.2	0.0
If I had the time, I would prefer to buy my groceries in person rather than online	19.0	38.1	21.4	21.4	0.0
I miss being able to pick out my own produce when shopping online	26.2	45.2	21.4	7.1	0.0
The best thing about buying groceries online is that I spend less money than I would in a supermarket	7.1	35.7	38.1	14.3	4.8
I'm more likely to buy something new if I see it in a supermarket or shop than online	28.6	45.2	14.3	11.9	0.0
My favourite online grocery site is easy to use	9.3	69.8	18.6	2.3	0.0
Buying groceries online hasn't affected the types of things I buy	9.3	55.8	14.0	20.9	0.0
I don't mind talking to people while doing my online grocery shopping	2.3	32.6	34.9	25.6	4.7
I feel more in control of my grocery shopping when I do it online	7.1	16.7	38.1	28.6	9.5
I don't like being interrupted when grocery shopping online	4.5	47.7	38.6	9.1	0.0
Buying Groceries online saves me money	13.6	27.3	29.5	22.7	6.8

(SA=Strongly Agree, A=Agree, N=Neutral, D=Disagree, SD=Strongly Disagree)

OGS rating of last site used	Excellent %	Good %	Acceptable %	Below Avg.%	Poor %
Ease of Use	4.8	57.1	35.7	2.4	0.0
Quality of Products	9.5	52.4	28.6	9.5	0.0
Product Selection	9.5	61.9	28.6	0.0	0.0
Quality of Service	21.4	52.4	23.8	2.4	0.0
Web Site appearance	19.0	52.4	28.6	0.0	0.0
Price	16.7	61.9	21.4	0.0	0.0

OGS behaviour on last site used	Yes %	No %	Don't Know%
Do you store your credit/debit card details on that site?	50.0	45.5	4.5
Do you store your login details for that site?	65.9	31.8	2.3
Do you have the web address of the site stored in Bookmarks or Favourites?	47.7	47.7	4.5

Containing Family Clutter

Laurel Swan[1], Alex S. Taylor[2], Shahram Izadi[2] and Richard Harper[2]

1 School of IS, Computing and Mathematics, Brunel University, UK
2 Microsoft Research, Cambridge, UK

Abstract. In this paper, we present material from an ongoing ethnographic investigation of family life. Drawing on selected fieldwork materials, we look at the ways families deal with household clutter, and in particular how clutter can be contained in bowls and drawers. Based on this research, a case is made for rethinking digital media management in domestic settings. We argue that existing solutions, largely based around the PC, inhibit the casual storage and loose organization of content, properties afforded in both bowls and drawers. We explore a design perspective that aims to address this by building on physical properties of the bowl, using salient properties from fieldwork material to sketch out an early concept of an augmented bowl designed to hold physical and digital content.

1 Introduction

Where there is order, where things are classified and given a rightful place, there will always be matter out of place, always disorder, always mess [see 7]. In our ordered worlds, clutter is ever-present, and nowhere more so than in the family home: letters arrive on the doormat, children come home and throw their things on the floor, dirt accumulates and the laundry builds up. Chaos looms.

Our central argument in this paper hinges on the way families deal with clutter. For most families, the ideal of the perfectly ordered house sits uneasily with the reality of family life, and a constant balance must be negotiated between the family members assorted paraphernalia and a 'tidy enough' house. Families, of course, do not always systematically maintain this balance and often resort to intermediary solutions to deal with the resultant clutter. Using materials from an ethnographic study of family homes, we will argue that this is a practical, commonplace approach to everyday life at home and will show how containers, such as bowls and drawers, help enable this economy of living.

Please use the following format when citing this chapter:

Swan, L., Taylor, A. S., Izadi, S., Harper, R., 2007, in IFIP International Federation for Information Processing, Volume 241, Home Informatics and Telematics: ICT for the Next Billion, eds. Venkatesh, A., Gonsalves, T., Monk, A., Buckner, K., (Boston: Springer), pp. 171-184.

Using this as a basis, we aim to explore an alternative perspective to managing and arranging digital media. We consider how new digital technologies are adding to the proliferation of *stuff* in homes and yet, by and large, fail to assist in the containment of clutter. Instead, the digital realm offers increasingly sophisticated solutions for managing and organizing media that require prolonged and sustained interaction. These tools allow family members to archive images, edit video, create music compilations and much else besides, but often, indeed very often, these tools demand more time and effort than is available [12]. Of course, people do sometimes want to spend time and effort organizing, archiving and editing digital media; however, due to the constraints and demands of family life, this is not always possible and the design of current digital technologies does not allow for this variability of effort.

In the following, we will begin by touching on the main themes of HCI research related to domestic technology and consider these with respect to the minimal effort given to managing household clutter. We then detail materials selected from our ongoing ethnographic investigation of family homes. We foreground the casual ways that families store and loosely organize materials, and draw specific attention to the at-handedness, visible function and flexibility of physical containers such as bowls and drawers. We discuss how these containers afford minimal effort to contain clutter of particular kinds: items *en route* to somewhere else, items with a limited life span, items where their sentimental character makes disposal problematic, or items that no one knows what to do with and therefore have no 'proper' home.

Drawing on this material, we will then discuss the implications of our analysis for the management of digital media solutions in the home. In referring to digital media, we confine ourselves to content held on devices like mobile phones, digital cameras and music players, as opposed to materials generated by email and the internet. Finally, to address design directly, we outline some design ideas we have been exploring to deal with digital media in lightweight ways. Our ideas are encapsulated in a presented design sketch, in which we investigate how the properties of a physical bowl might be augmented. Although it might appear an unlikely candidate for research, our hope is for the bowl, as an idea, to illustrate how we might think about designing for the casual, low effort practices we use to manage clutter in the home.

1.1 Household Clutter in HCI

In much of the research surrounding the home in HCI and its related design fields, little (if any) attention has been given to the general problem of untidiness and clutter. Despite its all too familiar presence in home life, the domestic environment appears sanitized, clean, and clutter-free. For example, where technological concerns have been paramount, as in the ongoing and widely dispersed Smart Home Programme and select areas of Ubicomp, much attention has been given to the use of and interaction with sensors [13], networked appliances [2] and home automation [19]. Other efforts have been concerned with monitoring, both of security [3] and the health of a home's inhabitants [14]. While laudable for other reasons, these projects are vulnerable to the oft-made criticism from the ethnomethodological perspective, a criticism that holds that the 'work' or effort routinely put in to making places like the home unique is regularly rendered invisible in technological visions [e.g. 20]. Ignored in such projects, for instance, is the considerable work required to keep the home in order [1,22] and, relevant to the evidence presented here, the efforts and resources enlisted to keep clutter at bay.

More detailed investigations of home life have partially addressed such failings [5,11,23]. These works have not however placed direct attention on clutter per se nor the tools or behaviors used to manage it. Rodden et al. [17], for example, have discussed the role of 'stuff' as an important component of designing technology for domestic settings. However, their 'stuff of the home' tends to be of a purposeful, functional nature, whereas the stuff in the households we examine is occasionally interacted with, but more often disregarded, left to coalesce in hidden places. Similarly detailed investigations into home life have looked at the collaborative aspects of practical activities such as TV viewing [16,21] and photo sharing [6,9]. While such studies pay heed to activities that take up considerable time and thought, they again remain concerned with a discrete, purposeful engagement with the home environment. The practices surrounding the containment of household clutter are less purposeful or discrete but are, we would argue, more pervasive, ubiquitous and indeed continuous.

2   Fieldwork

The data we present to explore these arguments are drawn from an ongoing, ethnographic study of family life. They have been chosen from a larger corpus of field investigations, spanning 18 months, with 12 families living in the UK. Excerpts from interviews and observations with three mothers constitute the core of the materials used. This limited but focused explication will illustrate some of the rich and varied ways in which homes and the stuff within them are organized.

2.1   Effortless containment

To begin with, we consider the following from Nicola, the mother of two sons, aged six and ten. In her open plan kitchen/dining room, three stacks of bowls sit near the work surfaces, seemingly ready to prepare or serve food. It is immediately apparent, however, that they have been appropriated for an assortment of bits and pieces. Here she describes the origin of this usage:

> I suppose it's because you have stuff [said with emphasis in a pejorative tone] and you need to put it somewhere and bowls seem quite a good receptacle in that they just swallow everything up. Ummm,... [pauses] completely without any thinking or planning... (see Fig. 1)

Figure 1. Nicola's three bowls.

The *stuff* Nicola refers to is a seemingly haphazard mixture of sunblock, cheque stubs, door locks, mobile phones, and much else besides. In an attempt to keep clutter at bay, Nicola has appropriated a class of common household items, bowls, to act as repositories for this varied paraphernalia. The ability of bowls to 'swallow everything up' makes them well-suited to containing the family's flotsam and jetsam with a minimum of effort. As we shall see, this technique has become part of the organization of her home. She continues, describing her husband's use of bowls:

> ... sometimes he'll plug into them. So he knows for example that- it's never talked about, but he'll know that batteries go in that bowl, keys go in that bowl and, if you have paper work that needs sorting, it'll go in that little pile. So I guess he tunes into it almost subconsciously. They are my systems, but they become the home systems I suppose. And they're really not- it's rather a grand word to call them systems actually.

On the face of it, then, we see that bowls and piles are considered useful in a home because they help family members achieve, in an ad hoc, lightweight way, some semblance of order with minimal effort. As our next excerpt illustrates, however, the easy-to-hand use of bowls on Nicola's part is not a wholly satisfying system. Although she refers to piles in the following excerpt, Nicola's remarks are directed at the general clutter on show in her house:

> I think a file, somehow, would just get forgotten about more than just a visible pile that's actually irritating me. That's part of it. Part of it is that I don't like clutter, even though you wouldn't know it [gestures around house]. I don't like all these piles of things everywhere so if I deliberately make a pile then it's sort of a motivation to get rid of it as well.

Unlike things that are filed away, visible piles and bowls full of stuff attract attention, reminiscent of the things we leave out to trip over to act as reminders [15]. Nicola's bowls summon attention because householders can see at a glance that things are in them, waiting to be 'properly sorted'. For Nicola, the bowl serves not only as a to-hand solution, but also stands as a slightly irritating reminder of the tidying and organizing that needs to be done. As such, they serve as a partial or *temporary* solution to the problem of tidying up, sufficient in the short term.

Another of Nicola's bowls, this one tucked out of sight behind the kitchen door, raises another important property, that of *layering*. Pointing to the bowl, Nicola runs through its contents:

This is old mobile phones that we're going to chuck out but I think actually I'll get them recycled somehow. Film for the camera, batteries- the inevitable batteries because if you have kids all their toys need batteries, the A-to-Z. You know, sort of bits and pieces but if you dig down to the bottom I'm sure there are things in there that I have long since forgotten about. So it isn't very organized in that respect. The things on the surface are important, but in some sense it's like geology.

Nicola's suggestion that there are things long since forgotten about under the surface and her reference to geology conjures up the sense of excavation common to clutter containers. Stuff is thrown in to the bowls in a way that is almost without thought and the layering that results is achieved because of the bowl's depth and its sidedness. Items are kept together in ways we are immediately familiar with; newer items remain on the surface whereas the older and/or smaller content seep towards the bowl's sediment. The physical layering thus becomes a queue for recollection, management, and for navigation through the accumulated layers.

2.2   Types of clutter

Our next examples examine the myriad forms clutter can take and how placing clutter out of sight or having it hidden can serve quite particular purposes. Emma has a 'junk drawer' with a broken front, located amongst the kitchen cabinets (Fig. 2). In contrast to Nicola's piles and bowls, Emma's drawer is not particularly noticeable; when closed, it looks like any drawer, save for its broken front. Inside the drawer is a jumble of string, spare plugs, cards, sunglasses and bicycle lights. There is no explicit system of separation or organization; it simply appears to be clutter. Emma's description, however, reveals that there is some form of order to the drawer, albeit a loose one:

This is where I just put things where I- you know where you think you really want to throw it away but you don't feel that you can... so it's a combination of those things and little things that I don't have a home for but I should have a home for, like the tape measure, and the rulers, and the paper clips, and things.

Emma's description of the things "you really want to throw away but you don't feel you can", conveys some of the essence of clutter. Her use of the word 'home' regarding the paper clips and rulers is also telling; it gives a sense of things having a right and proper place. Presumably these little household tools deserve a 'home' due to their usefulness and ubiquity, but paradoxically their 'home' ends up amongst the homeless, in the clutter.

Digging deeper, it emerges that there is further categorization within the clutter. Emma elaborates while sorting the contents into several small piles:

Those are dice, but again they should go, there's a little bag we have upstairs for dice so that should be, they should all be in the dice bag... Lego, that needs to go in the Lego box...more dice, they should all go in the dice bit...

In Emma's drawer are items from various larger collections stored elsewhere in the house. This is a particular type of clutter; it is "matter out of place" [7]. These pieces do have a 'home', they are simply not in it, and Emma's description of them "going places" gives the sense that they are in transit, albeit perhaps temporarily on a stopover in the junk drawer.

Figure 2. Emma's junk drawer.

Of course, it is not always so clear where items of clutter belong or what status they hold. While adding things to a pile she has designated rubbish, Emma holds up a card, explaining that it was from the last Harry Potter movie and "was terribly precious for a short period of time". The fact that a sizable proportion of things in junk drawers can be disposed of upon sorting out is interesting. It suggests that items can go into the drawer with one status and come out with another, that something "terribly precious" can transform into rubbish within the drawer. Items such as media associated with new movies derive some of their value from their newness; when the novelty wears off, their status plummets. The drawer can thus act as a holding place, a safe spot for things with a temporary shelf life to live until that life expires.

In the next excerpt we see that clutter bowls and junk drawers can function as repositories for items with problematic status:

> ...that's an air freshener for a car that [smells the wooden apple shaped object]- err, smells horrible, but it was in the car when we bought it so we've hung onto it for sentimental reasons... when we bought our car that we have now it was new and for some reason it was in there. I don't know why it was just- I think the kids thought it was exciting that it came with an apple as well. You know 'new car *and* wooden apple!' [laughs] so for some reason we still have it.

Although Emma's drawer might not, on first glance, seem an obvious place for archiving memorabilia, her wooden apple raises an interesting point. Namely, not all sentimental objects are guaranteed a place on the mantelpiece, as it were, and junk drawers and bowls give refuge to items of ambiguous value.

2.3   Battling clutter

We want to build on this idea of ambiguity in our final example, taken from an interview with Olivia, mother to two girls, aged six and nine. Olivia's family home is especially tidy, and on first glance does not seem to be a promising arena for studying clutter. There is none visible, and Olivia herself claims that she does not keep "stuff" and throws away as much as she can. Delving further, however, we are able to find little hints of clutter, and more interestingly, Olivia's efforts to keep them at bay. Tucked into the corner of a cupboard of wine glasses is a small bottle of homeopathic drops. The bottle of ointment, a gift from her daughter to help her (the mother) to unwind, presents a small problem of classification for Olivia:

> I thought well- I couldn't think where to put it actually, and you can't see it when you close the door... I mean really it could be put in another drawer. But this is me, I think to myself 'Why is that out? Put it away.' So it may not be in the right place but I put it away because I can't stand stuff lying about.

Although Olivia's gift is placed out of sight in a cupboard, we discover it does in fact have its right and proper place. The overriding criteria appears to be that stuff cannot be left lying about and therefore a bottle meant for a drawer is put away elsewhere. Unbeknownst to her daughter, stress is relieved not by using its content but by hiding the bottle from view.

Olivia has recently had her kitchen and adjoining utility room redesigned with banks of closets, cupboards and drawers, and feels that she now has "places to put stuff". Peering into various drawers, we find collections of like things, neatly separated by containers, dividers, trays, plastic bags, etc. Indeed, the drawers are the epitome of organization, and it does seem as if Olivia has perhaps eradicated the specter of clutter by categorizing it to the nth degree in all its minutiae. In a drawer of tools and household implements, however, we get a glimpse that all is not as it seems. This drawer has, besides a tray full of tools and a case of socket wrenches, a biscuit tin of batteries and a plastic tub of keys. Olivia explains that the tub is specifically for keys, separated out into a plastic bag, and keyrings. When the number of keys is remarked upon, she replies: "I have no idea what they're for, but I've kept them because that's where they go."

Olivia has thus taken something of uncertain status found in nearly every household—in this case, keys to unknown locks—and has given them a home. In doing so, she has not resolved their status; she has no more idea of their rightful destination than either Nicola or Emma would, but by giving them a designated place "where they go" she has organized them and attended to them, compartmentalizing and thereby minimizing what one might call their ambiguity.

Exploring further in the key tub, we find several un-key-like items. Olivia's response is illuminating:

> They're just things, aren't they? I don't know what to do with them so I put them in here... [pointing to a glass sphere]. That's a ball off the garden swing. It's of absolutely no use but it's beautiful so I couldn't throw it away, could I? So I've put it in here.

In the glass ball off the garden swing, there are echoes of Emma's wooden apple car freshener, of an item having the dual status of being junk and sentimental at the same time. Although Olivia tackles the business of classifying the miscellany of the household with fervor, and has closets, cupboards, drawers and dividers to help her, ultimately she too ends up with a small tub somewhere full of 'just things'.

2.4   Containing disorder

Reflecting on the prior examples—Emma's drawers, Olivia's categorisations and Nicola's bowls and piles—we see that the containers and the material within have a number of distinctive properties. Containers that demand low levels of interaction, like bowls and drawers, allow our three households to deal with clutter with minimal effort. These devices afford at-handedness; their placement near to where clutter accumulates offers a simple and lightweight resource for containing or hiding things. Moreover, bowls and drawers allow the placement of things in them without careful thought or deliberation. Part of their success is due to their visible functionality— anyone can see what they are for, no labeling is needed and no expert training is required before tossing something in; as we have seen, even husbands know how to use them. The intelligibility of these devices is further represented by their layers and the 'geology' of the stuff they contain, both serving to show the history of their use.

3   Managing digital media in the home

In the remains of this paper, we wish to contemplate how these practices associated with managing clutter in the home might be applied to the digital realm. To develop our ideas we have chosen to focus on digital media such as digital photos, music and video, even though the fieldwork materials described above could of course be applied to a variety of digital technologies. This is in part due to the increasing adoption of digital media players and recorders in the home, a trend that suggests digital content will be entering and staying in our homes in ever-greater quantities. More importantly, What intrigues us about the currently available software solutions for managing digital photos, video, music, etc. is that they retain a fairly conservative perspective on organization, one that arguably overlooks the kinds of practices we believe hold an important, if not elemental place in the home.

3.1   Digital media on the PC

Before reflecting on our own design explorations, we want to briefly consider the PC, probably the most commonly used solution for storing, managing and organizing digital media. By reflecting upon the use of the PC, we hope to provide a clearer position on some of our ideas that follow.

The PC provides the necessary hardware and software to perform a host of functions on diverse media formats such as digital photos, video, music and so on. However, this PC-centric model of handling digital media contrasts with the minimal effort practices and casual storage afforded by bowls and drawers. As presented in the fieldwork, bowls and drawers function as a lightweight method for holding content, one that is readily adopted in the home. Bowls and drawers store and loosely organize as a natural consequence of placing objects within them, and therein lies their appeal; very little if any effort is required for bowls to work in an intelligible way. Indeed, it is the limited rather than abundant number of features that make it compelling.

In contrast, the PC's ability to perform a range of activities related to storage, organization *and* manipulation demands a level of complexity that makes it unwieldy and thus difficult to incorporate into everyday routines. Because of this complexity, no casual way exists to simply contain or store digital media—there is no equivalent to an object simply placed in a bowl or drawer and minimally organized by its size and when it was placed there. There is an in-built formality to both containing (or 'uploading') content and organizing it on the PC that is manifestly not the case with physical containers. Consequently, the PC is better suited to the more formal storage and organization of content that requires highly focused interaction, the sorts of activities that are put off in the family home for more time-bounded and infrequent occasions.

3.2   Digital media containers

To contemplate this problem and consider the practical issues, we have started to sketch out a conceptual design space. The primary motivation underlying our initial design forays has been to support the casual and informal organization of digital media by providing lightweight methods of interaction that are intelligible to the user. The practical focus thus far has been on augmenting a physical bowl in order to explore some of the empirical ideas above and to use this exercise to draw lessons for further design iterations.

The current design 'sketch' (only partially implemented) is based around a semi-transparent physical bowl capable of holding both digital and physical content (Fig. 3). The basic idea is that when devices such as cell phones and digital cameras are placed inside the bowl, their content is copied and displayed on the bowl's sides. As more content is added, existing items fall deeper to the bottom. Similar to the bowls in our fieldwork, our augmented bowl becomes a temporary holding place where digital content can be casually added and viewed, and loosely arranged, before later, maybe much later, finding a place elsewhere.

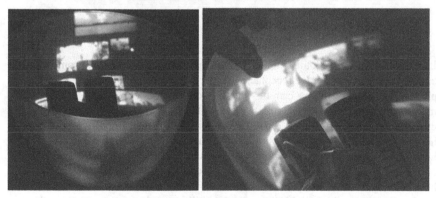

Figure 3. Bowl sketch built using projection system and translucent glass bowl.

Containment
In our early mock-ups of the above sketch, a primary motivation has been to support the minimal effort qualities of clutter containers. We wanted the simple act of placing a device in the bowl to accomplish the containment of digital as well as physical media. One way in which we aimed to do this was by preserving the familiar, physical properties of a bowl and thus retaining the intelligible and lightweight interactions that are afforded. In short (and echoing Nicola's comments

above), we used a bowl shape to exploit the properties bowls exhibit, properties that allow people to "tune" into their use "almost subconsciously".

For similar reasons, we wanted the bowl to have only limited functionality. The limited features that were chosen to facilitate informal and casual use that would, again, be intelligible. For example, we imagined that image thumbnails might be moved by simply moving the associated device in the bowl or alternatively by simply interacting with the thumbnails directly. Moreover, the projected thumbnails would be 'stretched' as they were moved from the rounded bottom of the bowl to its relatively flat sides (see Fig. 4). This 'stretching' was seen to exaggerate the effect that would be obtained by moving a projected image from a tightly curved to flat surface: a visible and intelligible property of the bowl's physical form.

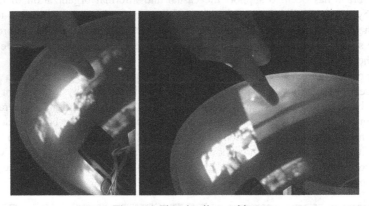

Figure 4. Thumbnail stretching.

Storage

It is, we have suggested, the simplicity of use and to-handedness that promote bowls as particular sorts of storage receptacles. As we have seen in contrasting the PC with physical containers, items can be literally tossed into bowls and drawers with minimal expectation of order. Like we saw with Nicola and her home's bowls, and even Emma's dedicated junk draw—in her kitchen—this minimal organization of household stuff into containers is routinely bound up with where it can coalesce and how it interleaves with a household's comings and goings. We have aimed to build on this by designing the augmented bowl to operate as a standalone container, with a home having the choice to place the bowls in different locations.

Contemplating the individual storage capabilities of these augmented bowls, it is evident the size of the bowl clearly restricts the extent to which media can be organized. The point in exploring the bowl as a digital media container, however, has been precisely to limit the organizing capabilities. Our aim has been to explore a just-good-enough solution for loosely storing grouped items (as opposed to assuming that increasing the storage capacity is automatically preferable). Next, in introducing the idea of surface ecologies, we will comment on how we see a more involved and explicit organization of media might be accomplished.

We have considered in our designs how some media may be obscured as more items are added. Rather than a limitation, we see this to be an intelligible feature: as with a conventional bowl, as items are placed in it, other content is obscured. To view lower lying items, the top layers must be sifted through, moved apart or removed. In terms of detaching media from its associated device, we have tried to maintain the idea of layering that both Nicola and Emma referred to where newer items remain atop a bowl's content and older items end up, over time, constituting a container's sediment. In our design, content can be 'peeled' away from its device and left on the top 'digital' layer until obscured by other content. To detach the media, a device's thumbnails are held down in the bowl with a finger as the device is pulled away. In general, we have sought to explore is how properties such as fullness, layering, and loose temporal ordering might hold true for a digital container such as the augmented bowl.

Surface ecologies

Arguably, other augmented surfaces, such as tabletops and walls, offer a technically more feasible solution to the problem of digital media containment and storage. The difficulty involved in projecting onto and detecting interactions with tabletops and walls has been subject to extensive research. What is evident from our observations is that tables and walls do not lend themselves to the same types of containment and storage functions afforded by bowls and drawers. This point is best illustrated by example. Consider how horizontal surfaces such as tables play into the patterns of home life. As we and others have observed, tables are ideally suited to the display and organization of materials, particularly with collaborative activities; the physical nature of the table lends itself to having content spread over it and people arranged around it for the purposes of sorting, organizing, viewing, playing, eating and so on. Usage is thus driven by bounded activities, something all the more pertinent in the family home where table-use is regulated by a household's daily rhythms and negotiated by family members. Any containment afforded by tables is consequently constrained by who and what has overall rights to the table. The table has a social as well as physical character in the home that means any storage is time limited and bound by an established social order.

Bowls, in contrast, serve a very different function. We have suggested that one of the reasons why clutter bowls and drawers exist in the home is to keep disorder at bay, to contain and store it, sometimes out of sight. Tables and walls place clutter on show, revealing to others our house's disorder and possibly worse, acting as a reminder of our own idleness. As Olivia demonstrates in placing her bottles of ointment out of sight, the-need-to-put-away can be a moral imperative.

A sensitivity to the actions and activities afforded by tabletops, walls, containers, etc. gives an indication of how bowls might operate within the larger environment. In essence, bowls can be seen to be part of a wider ecology of surfaces in the home. This notion of surface ecologies—of different surfaces working together and sometimes competing—stands in contrast to the multi-purpose solution of the PC, where an effort is focused on centralizing virtually all operations. Thus, we see the presented sketch as something that should be used only under certain conditions, with a constrained range of operations working in concert with the surroundings—both physical and social.

4 Conclusion

In this paper, we have shown how an examination of clutter containers in family homes has been used to rethink the management of digital media. The common use of containers like bowls and drawers to manage the litany of stuff that pervades family homes highlights an easily overlooked quality of our everyday domestic experience; it reveals that sometimes, and through perfectly ordinary, unremarkable routines, we find ways of doing just enough to keep the home orderly—of applying minimal effort to keep disorder and clutter at bay [see 23].

Such minimal effort techniques, we have argued, are at odds with the established computing paradigm and, relevant to the presented work, the operations commonly required to store and organize digital media. The dominant PC-centric model demands a level of engagement and attention for transferring media from and to devices, such as cameras, music players, mobile phones, etc., that is far removed from the ease with which objects can be effortlessly placed in containers. The proliferation of media recorders and players for the home has not been matched by a sensitivity towards designing solutions for managing the inevitable growth in volume of media. Instead, efforts have been largely placed on making ever-bigger storage solutions and ever-faster ways to search them. Only the research on visualization techniques has sought to properly address media's proliferation [e.g., 4], and yet this research only succeeds to work within the constraints of the problem, rather than address the fundamental character of the media we capture and store, and our interactions with them.

In our focus on clutter containers, we have attempted to highlight the subtle ways we deal with the material things in our homes. With clutter bowls and junk drawers, we find nuanced ways to keep our homes tidy, to remind ourselves of things we must do, and to sometimes transform the meanings and emotional relations of the objects. Our homes are replete with these simple, embodied practices, so much so that they weave into and bind together the home's social fabric—our homes would not be the same without them.

The sketch of the bowl we have presented is an attempt to explore the need we have to effortlessly handle things. The sketch is also meant to explore how computational resources might be incorporated to build on our intimate familiarity with the physical. On reflection, the sketch has provoked a number of questions that deserve further attention. For example, more thought needs to be given to the functionality envisaged for the bowl. In some respects the mockup appeared to have too many features, encouraging the sorts of prolonged and potentially convoluted interactions we hoped to avoid.

More generally, the presented work has raised a host of questions about digital media containment and possible solutions that address real-world practices in family homes. For instance, the mapping of clutter onto digital media is clearly not a direct one. Further thought needs to be given to the sorts of digital media that might take on clutter-like qualities and consequently what media should and should not be displayed in containers like the augmented bowl we describe. Questions are also raised about the literalness of our interpretations in designing the augmented bowl. Is such a literal translation of physical containers necessary? Also, do such tangible interfaces merely limit our potential, while failing to introduce novel and possibly more appealing methods of engaging with our everyday experiences? Why too should our interactions with digital media be constrained by the properties of the physical world when clearly they do not have to?

As we develop the work above and progress towards a fully functioning prototype of an augmented bowl or other container, we hope to address these questions. The position we take here is that detailed studies of established, real-world practices provide a powerful resource in incremental design. This approach is best complimented, however, with *in situ* prototyping where people's everyday interactions with a solution are used to develop potentially more novel, but still grounded design ideas. What we hope to have done is set the groundwork for a departure from existing notions of storage, changing our expectations of and interactions with digital media.

References

1. Berg, A.-J. A gendered socio-technical construction: the smart house, in *The Social Shaping of Technology*, D. MacKenzie and J. Wajcman (eds), (OU Press, Buckingham, 1999), pp. 301-313.

2. Chung, K. H., Oh, K. S., Lee, C. H., Park, J. H., Kim, S., Kim, S. H., Loring, B. and Hass, C. A user-centered approach to designing home network interfaces. *Proc. CHI '03*, ACM Press, (2003), pp. 648-649.

3. Covington, M. J., Long, W., Srinivasan, S., Dey, A. K., Ahamad, M. and Abowd, G. D. Securing context-aware applications using environment roles. *ACM Symposium on Access Control Models and Technologies, Workshop on Role Based Access Control*, ACM Press, (2001), pp. 10-20.

4. Crabtree, A., Hemmings, T. and Rodden, T. Coordinate displays in the home. *CSCW '02, Workshop on Public, Community and Situated Displays* (2002).

5. Crabtree, A. and Rodden, T. Domestic routines and design for the home. *Computer Supported Cooperative Work* 13(2), (2004), pp. 191-220.

6. Crabtree, A., Rodden, T. and Mariani, J. Collaborating around collections: informing the continued development of photoware. *Proc. CSCW '04*. ACM Press, (2004), pp. 396-405.

7. Douglas, M. *Purity and Danger* (originally published 1966), (Routledge, London, 2002).

8. Drucker, S.M., Glatzer, A., De Mar, S., Wong, C. SmartSkip: consumer level browsing and skipping of digital video content. *Proc. CHI '02*, ACM Press, (2002), pp. 219-226.

9. Frohlich, D. M. *Audiophotography: Bringing Photos to Life with Sounds* (Kluwer Academic, Dordrecht, 2004).

10. Gaver, B. & Martin, H. Alternatives: exploring information appliances through conceptual design proposals. *Proc. CHI '00*, ACM Press, (2000), pp. 209-216.

11. Harper, R. (ed) *Inside the Smart Home* (Springer, London, 2003).

12. Mateas, M., Salvador, T., Scholtz, J., Sorensen, D. Engineering Ethnography in the Home. *Proc. CHI '96*, ACM Press, (1996), pp. 283-284.

13. Mungiatapia, E., Intille, S. S. and Larson, K. Activity recognition in the home setting using simple and ubiquitious sensors. *Proc. Pervasive '04*, Springer-Verlag, (2004), pp. 158-175.

14. Mynatt, E. D., Essa, I. and Rogers, W. Increasing the opportunities for aging in place. *Proc. Universal Usability*, ACM Press, (2000), pp. 65-71.

15. Norman, D. A. *The Psychology of Everyday Things* (Basic Books, New York, NY, 1988).

16. O'Brien, J., Rodden, T., Rouncefield, M. and Hughes, J. At home with technology: an ethnographic study of a set-top-box trial. *ACM TOCHI* 6(3), (1999), pp. 282-308.

17. Rodden, T., Crabtree, A., Hemmings, T., Koleva, B., Humble, J., Åkesson, K.-P. and Hansson, P. Between the dazzle of a new building and its eventual corpse: assembling the ubiquitous home. *Proc. DIS '04*, ACM Press, (2004), pp. 71-80.

18. Shen, C., Lesh, N., Vernier, F. Design: Personal digital historian; story sharing around the table. *Interactions* 10(2), 2003, pp. 15-22.

19. Spinellis, D. D. The information furnace: consolidated home control. *Personal and Ubiquitous Computing* 7(1), 2003, pp. 53-69.

20. Suchman, L. Working relations of technology production and use. *Computer Supported Cooperative Work* 2, (1994), pp. 21-39.

21. Taylor, A. S., Harper, R. Switching on to switch off, in *Inside the Smart Home,* R. Harper (ed), (Springer-Verlag, London, 2003), pp. 115-126.

22. Taylor, A. S. and Swan, L. Artful systems in the home. *Proc. CHI '05*, ACM Press, (2005), pp. 641-650.

23. Tolmie, P., Pycock, J., Diggins, T., Maclean, A. and Karsenty, A. Unremarkable computing. *Proc. CHI '02*, ACM Press, (2002), pp. 399-406.

Digital Photo Sharing and Emotions In A Ubiquitous Smart Home

Gaurav Sondhi and Andy Sloane

School of Computing and Information Technology,
University of Wolverhampton, Wolverhampton, UK

Abstract. Ubiquitous computing has come a long way since Weiser introduced the concept in 1988 where he put forward some ideas as to how the future of computing would allow us to interact more freely. Today this paradigm of computing is affecting us in more than one way from homes, to offices, to travel, to even the way we are presenting ourselves, with smart clothes embedded with technology. When it comes to the home environment we look at objects as personal attributes and form a close relationship with them. Today the PC has become a personal communication tool, which is being used for variety of purposes like Internet browsing, shopping, photo sharing. The combination of Internet and digital photography has allowed people to share photos with friends and families who are geographically separated. And when we look at smart homes of the future we expect networking and the Internet to form the central hub for information for the homeowners, hence providing an environment for anytime anywhere computing. We aim to provide a ubiquitous photo sharing environment for the smart home of the future which will allow the users to receive, store, and distribute images between various devices and allow them to attach emotions and personal feelings to pictures in a convenient and enjoyable way, as home is a place where we express most of our emotions. This paper provides the design scenario of how the photo-sharing environment will be built and evaluates how social relationships can be enhanced by the use of digital data related to emotions and photographs. We will look at the factors, which govern the use of digital image technology to provide the level of social interaction and entertainment expected within the smart home to support positive ways of living. We believe that a photo-sharing environment for a smart home could help people in providing important reminders and alerts during critical family events.

Please use the following format when citing this chapter:

Sondhi, G., Sloane, A., 2007, in IFIP International Federation for Information Processing, Volume 241, Home Informatics and Telematics: ICT for the Next Billion, eds. Venkatesh, A., Gonsalves, T., Monk, A., Buckner, K., (Boston: Springer), pp. 185-200.

1   Introduction

Ubiquitous Computing is concerned with allowing the users timely and efficient access to information that is around us in our daily lives. One of the ways in which this can be achieved is by embedding the information systems into the fabric of our home environment. The technology has to fuse in with the decor of the home so that it can provide constant access to information while being hidden from the user for most of the time. A truly ubiquitous technology is one, which allows the user to ignore its presence, and the user only becomes aware of the system when they interact with it. Information and Communication Technology (ICT) based artifacts and computers would fade into the background while people would be surrounded by intelligent and intuitive interfaces embedded in all kinds of objects [1].

The advent of the Internet has brought this idea of anytime/anywhere access to information a step close within the smart home environment. A "smart home" can be defined as a residence equipped with computing and information technology, which anticipates and responds to the needs of the occupants, working to promote their comfort, convenience, security and entertainment through the management of technology within the home and connections to the world beyond [2]. Smart Home systems could simply offer additional convenience in everyday activities adding to the benefits provided by the mechanical and electrical technologies. Ubiquitous computing is a technology shift where technology becomes virtually invisible in our lives. Instead of having a desktop or notebook machine, ubiquitous computing will allow technology to become hidden in our lives, built into the things we use, embedded in our environment.

Photographs are a very effective way of connecting people socially. Especially with the invention of digital photography, photo sharing has allowed people to communicate and share emotion through pictures when in a face-to-face environment. Photos provide social interaction with the people we share them with and can form the basis for social relationships as they serve as memory triggers, which allow emotions and memories associated with the pictures to be conjured up. If these personal emotions and memories can be captured by the user and stored with the associated picture hence allowing a digital representation of our emotions, it could make a worthwhile addition to the photo-sharing environment in a smart home. As existing technologies are not designed to support lightweight spontaneous interactions between users especially if they are using the Internet as the communication medium, we think that this approach will make the photo sharing more engaging and less demanding for the user.

The invention of digital cameras has had a profound affect on the way in which we take photographs and share them with friend and families, hence constructing social relationships on the way. Digital photography has allowed us to capture the entire moment of our lives into one photographic image. Photos allow people to share experience and events even if they were not physically there. Today photos are used for a variety of purposes ranging from sharing, decorating homes, albums, as gifts on mugs and photo frames. All these forms of usage shows how people relate themselves to their pictures and how it represents their social lifestyle.

Advancing technology continues to support families and their endeavours to use photography as a means to support social interaction. The introduction of digital photography, and its rapid acceptance has created a paradigm shift in the way people record and review images of everyday life. Digital cameras have allowed people to capture, reproduce, and share visual narratives more easily [3]. It has allowed people to instantly review the picture taken with easier duplication and sharing, as well as easier disposal of pictures they don't want. This is both economical and eco-friendly as the cost of throwing away digital images is virtually zero.

The home computer has become a digital archive, taking on storage, retrieval and display duties; however, its location in the home and its aesthetic appearance limit the type of sharing and social interactions that happen. For presentation most people still print out physical photos for display and interaction in the home. People do not often change the photos because of the effort involved. Somehow, the digital photos haven't made the full transition to support existing behaviours of people when sharing the photos. Furthermore, current digital photo frames have not yet addressed these needs in the home. The increase in the number of digital photos people are acquiring makes digital display in the home desirable [3].

To help us design photo-sharing environment for a smart home, we needed to get some idea as to what people like to do with photos and how they relate themselves to it. We therefore carried out a survey to measure the attitude of people towards photo sharing. We looked at how people use photographs and how we can make photo sharing easy and fun. The survey dealt with questions regarding the usage of cameras, the living environment, preference for digital or paper storage, medium for photo sharing, significance of a picture, emotional attachment, intimacy, indexing, usage of internet, reception, storage, and distribution. However one of the main objectives of the survey was to see the influence of digital cameras on photo sharing. The findings of the survey can be found in [9].

1.1   Aim/Purpose

Photo sharing provides great opportunities for creating and maintaining social relationships within the home. This is due to the fact that we as human beings are social creatures who find human presence and communications essential for the enjoyment of life and since home is a place where we express and share most of our emotions; photo sharing is one way in which these emotions are expressed when we are with friends and family. As proposed by Miller [4] well-being can be supported by encouraging and enabling effective action, prediction and control, satisfying social interaction, and mindfulness, physical involvement and enjoyment. When we look at the home environment most if not all of the factors proposed my Miller could be addressed by providing a photo-sharing environment to address these issues. A central device to handle the reception, storage and distribution would encourage effective action from users as they will be able to access information without being in sight of the source and hence will have control over the information.

The aspect of satisfying social interaction and physical involvement could be resolved by allowing users to attach emotions to pictures associated with them. This would help not only the users in being more involved with pictures but also help pictures to act as storyboards and help in creating social relationships. Miller [4] also suggests that an important way of designing for well-being is to design the space that enables people to "do Well-being" for themselves. When we look at the home environment we see the physical space where people spend most of their time and if we could provide an environment where people could relate themselves to some of the attributes of that space, we think it will be a good addition to the smart home.

Looking at the aspects of entertainment within the home, there are several consumer electronic devices that provide multiple interaction mediums to communicate with each other. They include devices such as PC's, Notebooks, PDA's, TV's, Projectors, DVD, and Cameras etc. These multiple interaction mediums form the basis of our space in the home, which we interact with on regular basis and if we bring photo sharing into this space then we need to use these devices. To facilitate a better interaction, we propose a convergence of these technologies and interaction mediums, by providing an In-Home Communication Infrastructure, which can interact with all these devices and provide the comfort and convenience that the user expects.

Although there are digital photo frames which allow users to display images in digital format through the home, what they still lack is in providing ease of use as the user will not always want to use it with friend and families for photo sharing and would prefer a display medium of some other kind like the TV or projector system. If we provide a ubiquitous environment for the user, we cannot simply use one aspect of technology in digital frames, we need to incorporate all the aspects, which the user can associate them with. The home environment should support the same level of rich social interactions and experiences that are associated with traditionally printed photos.

1.2   Methodology

The project follows a human-centered design approach in the sense that we carried out a survey to measure the attitude of people towards incorporating digital photo sharing within the home environment. The nature of the home, and the character of everyday home life is undergoing constant change in definition and as such is required to become responsive to the changing needs of people throughout their lifetime. Since our emotions relating to an event or object change over a period of time, a photo-sharing environment, which could capture this change, will allow the user to be constantly involved with photo sharing and will make the technology more fun and enjoyable. Using digital photos for display in the home allows for rich interaction possibilities such as ease of selecting and displaying, annotation and sharing [3]. Although the Cherish framework [3] looks at the social aspect of digital photo frames within the home, it comes short on emotional aspect of pictures and how we can capture emotions of the user in relation to the picture and preserve it digitally.

To help us design photo-sharing software, we needed to get some idea as to what people like to do with photos and how they relate themselves to them. We carried out a survey to measure the attitude of people towards photo sharing. We looked at how people use photographs and how we can make photo sharing easy and fun. The survey dealt with questions regarding the usage of cameras, the living environment, preference for digital or paper storage, medium for photo sharing, significance of a picture, emotional attachment, intimacy, indexing, usage of internet, reception, storage, distribution of pictures and how we could integrate the system in an ubiquitous environment. Our research revealed two main opportunities for a photo-sharing environment in a smart home which would play an important role in the lives of the people living in those homes: -

1. Having a photo-sharing environment to support various devices and media types.
2. To attach and preserve emotions digitally in association with the pictures.

We wanted to know how we could use emotions associated with a particular picture to annotate it for storage and how this annotation could be used for search and retrieval of photos from a database. Our research explores the needs, goals, and desires of families and includes concepts based on the needs discovered, and a concept validation that evaluates if our proposed solution meets the needs of the home owners, as well as if our understanding identifies real needs. The survey results will allow us to generate a smart home concept application that addresses the needs we identified in our fieldwork. Our aim was to validate if the needs we observed matched the needs as families/home owners perceived them. We also aim to probe the receptivity of our proposed solution by users.

2 Photography and social relationships

Photographs are a good representation of the social status we enjoy in society. They show our social networking with people. Photos allow presentation of oneself as kind of person one would like to be taken as, and allow other people to go along with that pretence gracefully (Goffman [7]). The photo sharing environment should allow people to feel connected to other people by the way emotions may be expressed in response to their pictures. The social interaction within the home can be increased by providing a photo-sharing environment where the user can attach emotions as well as capture the audio conversation they have when they share pictures with friends and families. This could allow the picture to act as a storyboard for people to see/read/hear who were not present at a particular moment.

Even though there are plenty of photo sharing services available like e-mail, Flickr [16], CONFOTO [15] etc, they are primarily web-based services and are more suitable for people who would take large volumes of pictures of anything and everything. It is also not something people associate with their home, as when you are at home its more about possession of items and things you can physically relate to. This is however dependent on an individual's idea of the home and could vary from person to person. People are less attached to something on the web as compared to physical artefacts that they can see in their home. However as Wise [18] puts it, space (home in this case) can be marked and shaped through physical objects. When it comes to photographs Wise has put forward the idea that photographs glow with memories of experience, of history, of family/friends etc, and what creates this glow is the articulation of subject to object, caught up in a mutual becoming home. People are very aware of how their surroundings are viewed by other people and try to express themselves through various objects and possessions. The home environment brings a more personal feel to objects (e.g. a photo frame) for someone who spends most of their time at home. However this could be different for someone whose time is spent in an environment which is not their home but the individual has tried to make space resemble a more homely and friendlier environment (e.g. by putting up photos, posters, objects of interest etc). Wise has forwarded the concept of home as a territory or space to which an individual can add identity through expressions of objects.

A digital photo sharing environment for the smart home will provide friends and families the opportunity to exchange photos as gifts with personal feelings hence supporting the construction of family identity and other social constructs. It could make family members feel better about themselves and the roles they play, and potentially increase the emotional connection between family members.

It could also form part of a communicative technology that might be of use in smart homes. Our research has revealed the following opportunities for this smart home technology to play a role in transforming the lives of the people:

1. By having a photo-sharing environment to support interaction with various devices and media types.
2. To attach and preserve emotions digitally in reference to the picture and allowing the user to capture spontaneous interaction.
3. An evaluation how the use of different data can be used to signal emotions with photographs.
4. Increasing social interactions between people by allowing people who were not present at a particular event to enjoy the experience.

At one time or another we all experience strong feelings that accompany positive or negative emotions. We usually have no problem identifying the emotion that we are experiencing at a given time. Human Beings feel a range of emotions when they view photos. To name a few emotion types of Joy, Distress, Happiness, Sadness, Love, Hate, Envy, Jealousy, Hope, Fear, Satisfaction, Shame, Disappointment etc could be a reasonable addition to pictures. One of the options for users could be providing them with a range of known emotions types and allowing them to select the appropriate emotion to attach to the picture. Event types like seasons, holidays, birthdays, etc could also be used to save pictures.

Another options for users could be saving pictures by relationships with individuals in the picture hence allowing for another retrieval method. People don't want to go through a search structure to get to their photos which can be time consuming and tedious. They want to get to their pictures as quickly as possible. Our emotions can be put into groups, which contain various emotion types experienced, by people on a day-to-day basis. These groups can be categorised as Well-Being, Fortunes-of-Others, Prospect-Based, Confirmation, Attribution, Attraction, Well-Being/Attribution, and Attraction/Attribution. The category labels and emotion types corresponding to each group have been summarised in [14]. We need to map this grouping of emotions with the mental model of the user so that it's easy for them to recognise the particular emotion they are feeling when looking at a picture and affectively attach it. Our picture could sometimes invoke multiple emotions at the same time e.g. feeling of fear and excitement (Could be at various levels) at the same time when doing some extreme sport.

Our photos allow us to reflect back on the past, cater for present and to some extent plan for the future regarding our family/friends, hence looking forward to creating new memories to be shared. Storytelling and reminiscing using photographs are one way of keeping and sharing memories and building family legacy [12]. The respondents from our earlier survey [9] favoured our concept of a photo-sharing environment in a smart home, which could provide reminders about the change in emotions in association with pictures over a period of time as well as changes in our daily routines.

The invention of wireless digital camera's and wireless photo frames will allow for the environment to become ubiquitous as then the user can manage the images through the central device. This will allow the user to, for example display images, which are stored in his camera directly to the photo frame or on any other display medium.

3   Photo sharing In Smart Homes

Home is a place associated very closely with human beings. It's a place where we spend most of our time and interact closely with our friends and family. Previous research has focused on how smart homes can improve human experiences, however those researches have focussed mainly on controlling devices and less on allowing people more control over their lives. One of the things people value the most in their homes is their collection of photos as it represents their social contacts and life events. As revealed from our earlier survey [9], photos bring out emotions in people and they would like digital technology to represent personal emotions on pictures and get emotional satisfaction from the thing they value most.

Digital data coming into the home today includes music in CD-format, video in DVD, digital photos, and there is already digital radio and TV-channels. Multimedia Entertainment is slowly becoming more and more readily available which is allowing the users to experience a more augmented experience. In order to make it as easy as possible for the occupants of the smart house to interact with the various smart appliances, the medium of communication must be as natural as possible [9]. Sloane et al [5] summarize the range of information used in the home and outlines the movement of information and the actors involved in its use. It also shows the diversity of information usage in the home. Our survey revealed that digital technology has had a great impact on digital photography and has allowed more people to become involved with photo sharing Fig 1. With the advent of the Internet and with it becoming a part of more and more people's lives, sharing photos with friends and families has become easier.

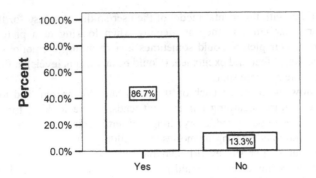

Fig. 1. Digital Technology has made Photo sharing easier.

We need to understand the roles of the smart home as well as what part presentation of digital photos have to play in our surroundings. In the future where the communication between various devices will be ubiquitous, it will become easier for the user to interact with the data on devices, which are not in their line of sight. When it comes to photo sharing our central device will allow the user to receive, store, distribute and view the pictures without having to interact with the actual device on which the pictures were originally stored. We hope that our research will help us in providing a framework for a smart home environment where photo sharing and emotional attachment to the pictures can be represented in a digital format.

The survey [9] helped in finding out the expectations, needs and desires of the users and will help us in creating a sense of desirability for the application. Our photo-sharing environment will allow them to achieve the sense of who they are and how they would like to be represented. By providing the users with a compelling and entertaining environment to share pictures in, we could create a sense of comfort and familiarity with the user that we hope fosters increased usage of the application and further enjoyment of their pictures and memories. This could be achieved by providing a high degree of on screen activity for the users to engage themselves in.

When we bring together the technologies involved in smart home of the future and a photo-sharing environment, there should be clear guidelines as to what this kind of technology should provide the users with. Friedewald et al [7] points out what we need to keep in mind when developing smart homes: -

1. It helps its inhabitants live a healthy, happy and safe life.
2. It performs tasks automatically to relieve the stress of managing the house.
3. It integrates home, work, learning and leisure activities.
4. It does not annoy people with the technological details of how it actually works.

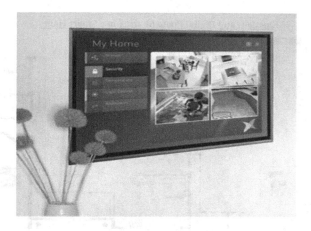

Fig. 2. Home automation solutions provided by ConvergeX

The above points to some extent have been realised by researchers of technologies who are now working with many developers to achieve these in the home environment. An example of this is the ConvergeX [20] home automation platform in the UK (Figure 2), which provides home automation services for new properties being developed as well as the old properties where owners want their technology platforms to adapt to their specific requirements. However Friedewald's suggestions are mainly technical and cover the technological aspects of the technology. They fall short on the emotional domain when it comes to building technology in the smart homes, which could assist with our emotional attachment to objects/space. Our research extends the above technical details to incorporate the following features:

1.   To support the affective well being of the inhabitants, and
2.   To support building/maintaining of interpersonal relationships.

If the photo sharing system could absorb some of these guidelines for providing the user with a ubiquitous environment to share photos with friends/family and allow them to attach emotions to pictures digitally, it should provide for a fun and enjoyable experience. The key for a successful photo-sharing environment lies with designing a product that is both entertaining and emotionally engaging. This could be achieved by making the picture a central feature of the application with which the user can interact with hence allowing the user to experience the sharing environment and the memories that the pictures often facilitate.

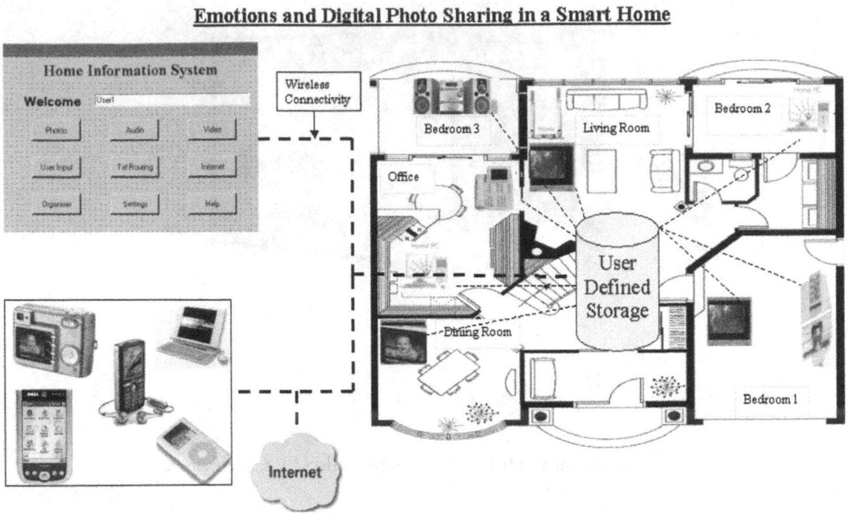

Emotions and Digital Photo Sharing in a Smart Home

Fig. 3. Digital Photo sharing in a networked smart home.

The scenario in Fig 3 will require interaction with various communication/networking mediums. What the HIS will provide is a simpler way to interact with these devices for the home user i.e. if the user wants to transfer data from one device to another which are located in different location in the home without actually having to physically interact with the devices, the HIS will allow for this facility. For example, if the PC is located in the bedroom and is Wi-Fi enabled, the user can use the HIS (in the living room) to communicate with it and transfer data from the PC to the central storage and then view it on the TV as a slide show. The storage requirements of data could vary from one person to another and the scenario needs to be incorporated in the design of the HIS with options for future expansion regarding storage requirements.

The most immediately apparent difference between looking at static images on a web page and sitting down with your friend and a stack of photos is the absence of voice. Speaking while sharing photos is not only natural, but is also socially expected [11]. Our survey [9] revealed that adding text and audio to the pictures will help in elaborating the memories associated with photos. It will help attaching emotions to the pictures. The users could add text by using a standard keypad, writing by hand to give it a more personal feel, or by making use of the voice-to-text technology. This could be used to annotate picture by the user and could be used for search and retrieval of pictures from the database using the comments as a search criteria.

The scenario in Fig 4 shows how a user might receive photos for storage from another device in the house. This could involve a user trying to download pictures from a digital camera, which might be in the one of the rooms in the house to the central server using Wi-Fi as the communicating medium. The user will have option of creating a new folder or saving in an existing folder on the server database. Once this is completed, the user can decide if they want to download the whole collection from the camera at one go or view and download each picture individually. This will give them the option of only storing the pictures they want and rejecting other pictures. It will also allow the users to name the pictures while they are being downloaded individually rather than the pictures being saved with some random number with a ".JPEG" extension. This was evident from our survey results in [9] where respondents were very positive about the scenario of providing them the option of downloading individual pictures and naming them at the same time from the source storage. Although there are other options apart from the name, which could be added to the picture while its being downloaded, e.g. place, event, relationship etc, we thought we would provide these options to the user when they view these pictures or want to make changes to them, or attach emotions. However if the users suggest that they would like to attach some more information to the pictures while they are being downloaded, the interface could be changed to accommodate that requirement.

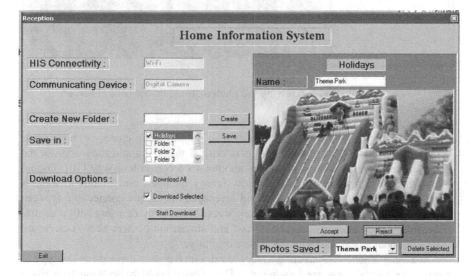

Fig. 4. Receiving photos from a device for storage on the central server

Viewing of pictures and adding emotions through different options available to users will allow them to feel more connected with the pictures and the task they aim to achieve i.e. of photo sharing in a home environment. The user will be able to select the directory in which the pictures are stored to view them and have access to various options like maximising the photo, deleting, editing, adding emotions, e-mailing and saving the changes. The picture will also represent the emotions, audio, or the text that the user has attached to it, although the best way to represent these is still undergoing changes and will form the basis for our next survey when the users test it. Fig 5 shows the "View Photo" screenshot where the user can select the source where the pictures are saved, select the folder they want to view, and read the text associated with that picture.

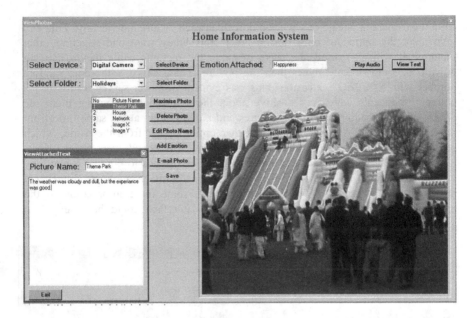

Fig. 5. Viewing the photos stored on the central server.

Recognising that a picture is a memory also implies that pictures can be a nexus of communal bonds. Because of this, it is critical that the application address the basic human need to connect with one another in a compelling way [10]. Digital photo sharing in a smart home will allow family members and friends to forge a bond with each other that reinforces and leverages the unique connection between memories and important moments in their lives. It will provide users with a central point from which memories can be relived and shared with others as well as record their emotional attachment with the picture digitally.

Attaching emotions or creating a storyboard with a picture depends on the type of picture the user/viewers are looking at. The picture could be to do with a place visited, an event, family photo, moments in life, work, pleasure etc. Although there are some pictures, which will have the same emotional response from people, some pictures can generate different types of emotions in different people. To cater for this variation we are trying to give the user the option of attaching emotions based not only on different emotional categories, but also based on relationship types and the other attributes mentioned earlier that could be associated with the picture to elicit emotions. The user will also have the option of attaching an audio story with the picture, which will help build social relationships or strengthen an existing relationship. Audio will also help people describe an event in a way, which might not be available through the standard emotional categories. Fig 6 tries to demonstrate some of the options available to users for attaching emotions to photos.

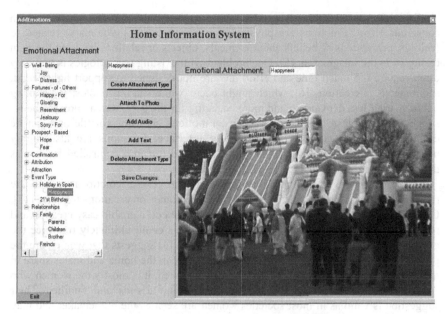

Fig. 6. Attaching emotions to pictures.

We now have digital cameras, which are equipped with some form of wireless connection. This will allow us to send the picture directly form the camera to the central server or view them on the handheld device. It will also allow photos to be displayed on display mediums directly from the camera as long as they are connected by a network connection. The figure below illustrates how such distribution of photos within the networked home might occur where the user might select a source device, which holds the pictures, and then view those pictures on a viewable platform as a slide show or send them to be saved on another device.

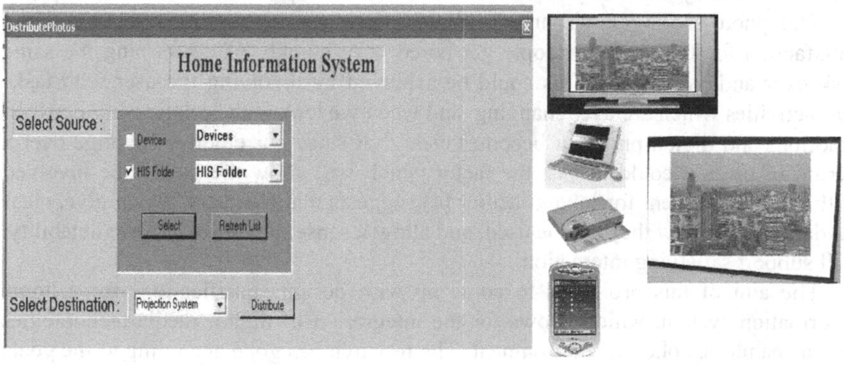

Fig. 7. Distributing images to other platforms for viewing.

Emotions are mental states that arise spontaneously, rather than through conscious effort. Emotions are physical expressions, often involuntary, related to feelings, perceptions or beliefs about elements, objects or relations between them, in reality or in the imagination [5]. One problem with existing technologies is that they often require too much time and effort and are not designed to support lightweight, spontaneous interactions [6], which might occur while sharing photos. By making photo sharing less demanding and more engaging for the user, we can provide better support for people to people interactions. Emotions are very volatile and can be easily dispersed by a badly designed user interface. Emotions are also highly personal and subjective, which makes it difficult to test in a controlled fashion as they vary widely from one individual to another.

Emotional bonds tie family members together. These emotional bonds are reinforced by "family activities", such as Sunday dinner or vacations together [17]. Our photo-sharing environment within a smart home could enable easy creation and retrieval of memories (in the form of Pictures). This could ultimately reinforce the emotional bonds among family members. Kim et al [3] suggests that women are the primary organisers of photos for storage and display in the home and males share in taking photos with women. Once the photos were taken, it is mostly the women who spent more time preparing and sharing photos with friends and families. Their suggestion is valid as in most societies women are seen as the homemaker and may want to present her lifestyle through pictures.

4 Conclusion

The home of the future will not just be about devices in the home or embedded in the fabric. It will bring together other aspects of technology like wearable computing, smart clothing, multimedia systems, positioning systems, and entertainment computing etc. Sloane [13] also points out problem with large scale of legacy information, which could be in different formats. The legacy data needs to be brought together into the standard format. This digitisation will require time and effort, which may ultimately determine the initial take-up of HIS in the market.

The photo-sharing environment would provide a long-term engagement and satisfaction for the user, as people get bored very quickly of performing the same task over and over again. This could be achieved by involving the user with tasks and activities which are ever changing, and when we look at the relationship between emotions and digital photos it becomes clear that since our emotions change over a period of time, it could be just the factor which will allow the user to be involved with the environment for longer. Miller [4] suggests that products, which give, clear guidance about how they can be used, and allow a sense of control and predictability, will support satisfying interaction.

The aim of this project is to come up with design specifications for a home information system, which allows for the integration of digital media technologies into a seamless, cohesive environment. The research has gone according to the goals set at the beginning. The respondents in the survey have reinforced our initial thought that people want to attach emotions to pictures. We wanted to know about what people want from photo sharing, what they enjoy, how specific design attributes will make them feel, what will delight them and how through this design process their experience might be enhanced. We are now into the development phase of the system, in which we will provide a relaxed atmosphere to view the photos in. We aim to provide the users with photo sharing software where the users can attach emotions to the digital pictures, use personal annotations to store and retrieve pictures from a database, and view then on different viewable platforms.

5 References

1. M. Friedewald, O. Da Costa, Y. Punie, P. Alahuhta, S. Heinonen, Perspective of ambient intelligence in the home environment. *Telematics and Informatics*, 2005.
2. J Barlow, & T. Venables, Smart Home, Dumb Suppliers? The Future of Smart Homes Markets, in R. Harper (ed) Inside the Smart Home, Springer, ISBN 1-85233-688-9, 2003.
3. Jeong Kim, John Zimmerman, Cherish: Smart Digital Photo Frames. Design And Emotion 2006 The fifth conference on Design and Emotion, Gothenburg, Sweden on September 27-29, 2006.
4. Hugh Miller, Mirja Kalviainen, Design for Wellbeing. Design And Emotion 2006 The fifth conference on Design and Emotion, Gothenburg, Sweden on September 27-29, 2006.
5. Friedemann Mattern, Eth Zurich, Wireless Future: Ubiquitous Computing, http://www.vs.inf.ethz.ch/publ/papers/mattern2004_electronica.pdf, (2004).
6. Oliver Liechti, Tadao Ichikawa, A Digital Photography Framework Supporting Social Interaction and Affective Awareness. HUC1999, Karlsruhe, Germany, (1999).
7. Goffman, E. *The Presentation of Self in Everyday Life*. New York: Doubleday Anchor, (1959).
8. http://www.convergex.co.uk/
9. Sondhi G, Sloane A, Emotions And Digital Photo Sharing In A Networked Smart Home, D&E, Gothenburg, Sweden, (2006).
10. Wood T, Next Generation Software User Experience at Eastman Kodak Company, D&E, Gothenburg, Sweden, (2006).
11. Chalfen, R. "Snapshot Versions of Life", Bowling Green State University Press, 1987
12. McAdams D.P. The Stories We Live By. Personal Myths and the Making of the Self. Guildford Press, (1993).
13. Sloane A, Harris A and Huang W (2000b) "Home information systems: the storage problem" in Sloane A and van Rijn F (Eds.) "Home Informatics and Telematics: Information, Technology and Society", Kluwer Academic publishers, Boston MA. ISBN 0-7923-7867-9
14. http://condor.depaul.edu/~elliott/emotion-table.html
15. http://www.confoto.org/home
16. http://www.flickr.com/

17. Darrah, C. N., English-Lueck, J. & Freeman, J. Families at work: An ethnography of dual career families, *Report for the Sloane Foundation* (Grant Number 98-6-21), (2001).
18. J. Macgregor Wise, HOME: TERRITORY AND IDENTITY, Cultural Studies, Volume 14, Number 2 / April 1, 2000, pages 295-310.

Telephone conferences for fun: experimentation in people's homes

Andrew F. Monk [1] and Darren J. Reed [2],
[1] Centre for Usable Home Technology (CUHTec),
University of York, UK
[2] Department of Sociology, University of York, UK

Abstract. The paper illustrates how communication experiments may be carried out in a domestic recreational context. Participants situated in their homes were connected into group telephone conversations and simply asked to "chat and enjoy yourselves". Following the conversation, participants provided Likert scale ratings of the experience. In addition, the conversations were recorded and analysed. A total of 211 participants took part in two experiments. Telephone groups had an average size of five people, each speaking in the same conversation from their individual homes. Comments from the participants and Likert rating scales indicated that it was a positive recreational experience. The primary manipulation in each experiment was intended to encourage spontaneous co-involvement of all of the group. In Experiment 1 this was done by changing the way participants were introduced to the group, in Experiment 2 the group was made more salient by providing each member with a list of names. Open ended responses obtained from telephone interviews with participants in Experiment 1 were used to construct a questionnaire for Experiment 2 to measure presence, involvement and communication efficacy. The measures extracted from transcripts included the average length of utterances and equality of contribution as well as a new measure, the number of lines to the first "flow episode" in the transcript. While neither of the manipulations produced significant effects on Likert scale ratings made after the sessions or the measures extracted from transcripts, the paper is able to recommend the measures used and to provide practical advice for other investigators seeking to run communication experiments in a recreational context.

Please use the following format when citing this chapter:

Monk, A. F., Reed, D. J., 2007, in IFIP International Federation for Information Processing, Volume 241, Home Informatics and Telematics: ICT for the Next Billion, eds. Venkatesh, A., Gonsalves, T., Monk, A., Buckner, K., (Boston: Springer), pp. 201-214.

1   Introduction

1.1 Telephone conferencing for recreational purposes

In the home, communication technologies have an important role in the maintenance of social relationships. One-to-one phone calls, for example, are a common form of socialising. This paper explores the use of many-to-many phone connections for similar, purely recreational and social purposes. The paper also illustrates how field studies and ethnographic analyses can be used to inform the design of experimental studies of possible interventions expected to change the user experience of people socialising in telephone conferences.

People are so used to using the telephone for one-to-one conversations that they can find the notion of several people being connected into the same telephone conversation difficult to imagine. Telephone conferencing, which does just this, is widely used for business meetings but rather more rarely for recreation. There are exceptions to this rule. For example, the RNIB has equipment (telephone switches) that it uses to connect groups of people with visual disabilities for purely social purposes. There are also, of course, the premium rate chat lines that became notorious in the late 1980s when teenagers ran up massive bills on their parents' telephones.

A field study by the present authors [1, 2] looked at a scheme run by the Community Resource Team in Hackney, London. Their befriending scheme supports elderly individuals through recreational telephone conferences and weekly one-to-one telephone contact. The telephone conferencing switch and operator service for this scheme was provided by Community Network, a charity offering telephone conferencing facilities to other charities for business and social purposes. The telephone conferences consisted of four to eight older people with a volunteer facilitator. Most of the volunteers were also older people and were trained by Community Network. These bi-weekly link-ups were greatly valued by the group members. One person interviewed described the scheme as a "Godsend". Another reported that before each call she made herself comfortable in a particular chair with a cup of tea: "it's like waiting for someone to visit"[2].

In order to understand the nature of these multi-person recreational telephone conversations, tapes were obtained with the participants' permission from groups who had been meeting this way for some time. These were transcribed by the second author using Directed Conversational Analysis to describe the conversational structures that could be seen within the detailed transcripts [1]. In particular, one could contrast: (i) the rotating two-person conversations seen predominantly at the start of the transcripts, with (ii) incidents of spontaneous co-involvement, or flow, where the whole group of five or six people took part. The latter were of a quite different character, containing shorter, often overlapping, utterances.

The objectives of this work were: (i) to understand what makes for a good recreational telephone conference, and (ii) to make suggestions about how the technology or the procedures within which the technology is used may encourage such an experience. The results from [1] suggested spontaneous co-involvement as a behavioural indicator of a good recreational telephone conference, as well as various possible manipulations that might encourage it. Many studies would have stopped at this point. However, we were interested to take it one step further and to try out two manipulations designed to encourage spontaneous co-involvement in quantitative experiments. To do this we had to devise a quantitative measure reflecting the behavioural changes we were aiming for. We also needed to develop an experimental procedure that would maintain as many of the important contextual features of mediated domestic socialising as possible while affording the experimental control needed to obtain meaningful results.

1.2 A "six-room" experiment where the rooms are people's homes

There is a tradition of communication experiments going back to the 1970s [3, 4] where people participate in some joint experimental task while in separate rooms using some sort of communication technology. These experiments compare different ways of technologically mediating communication and have become known as two-room experiments (for a summary of this and more recent research see[5]). Very little of this work has looked at mediated communication in groups of more than two people (but see[6, 7]). The aim of the experiments described below was to emulate the recreational telephone conferences pioneered by Community Network and others in an experiment. This would involve connecting six individuals, i.e., a six-room experiment.

It was decided that these experiments should be run using a conventional telephone conference with the participants situated in their own homes. The alternative would have been to bring them in to the laboratory.

One of the reasons that most of the research on mediated communication uses only two rooms is practical, i.e., finding the laboratory space. Connecting people in their own homes with a telephone conference offers a solution to this practical limitation. The other reason for not getting people into the laboratory for these experiments is methodological. While it is reasonable to generalise from experiments in the laboratory to work contexts, this is less reasonable with domestic and recreational contexts. Coming to the laboratory and then doing some task assigned by the experimenter is much like work. Conclusions drawn about technologies designed to support tasks that simulate work can then be (cautiously) generalised to parallel tasks in real work contexts. However, the laboratory is not like the home, even if one sets out a room with domestic furniture and decorations, the context will be artificial and unfamiliar. There will not be the same interruptions and distractions. Any conclusions drawn would be much harder to generalise. Thus while connecting people from their own homes will increase the error variance, it will also make the results more realistic.

When selecting the experimental "task" for these experiments, little attempt was made to influence how the conversations proceeded. In Experiment 1 participants were told "we just want you to chat and enjoy yourselves". In Experiment 2 there were some suggested initial topics and a very short warm up game, but again it was emphasised that they could talk about whatever they liked. This lack of control again makes for more error variance from variation in the way different groups approach the conversation. However, this is natural variance and increases the generality of any conclusions drawn. For another experimental design that successfully confounds context and task with participant in this way see [8].

2. Experiment 1

The Directed Conversational Analysis of the tapes from Community Network (see [1]) identified a possible manipulation in terms of the way participants are introduced to the telephone conference. The effects of this manipulation are examined in this experiment.

2.1 Method

Design

Telephone groups consisted of 4 to 6 individual participants. Each group was randomly assigned to one of two experimental conditions. In the Individual condition participants were introduced to a single individual as they were brought into the telephone conference. In the Group condition they were introduced to the whole group. 92 participants took part in 18 telephone groups run using telephone conferencing switches at Community Network. Participants were recruited by email from the University of York Alumni Database of people willing to be contacted by email about university activities.

Once the instructions for introducing the groups to the conversations had been sent to Community Network we were in the hands of the operators. Examination of the tapes indicate that the assignments we had asked for were not always followed. Table 1 gives the actual allocation of groups by size and condition as confirmed from the tapes. There are two extra groups of size 5 in the Group condition. This equates to a small difference in average size (5.10 vs. 5.13) and so all 18 groups were included in the analysis.

Table 1. Number of groups of each size in the two introduction conditions in Experiment 1.

Size	Four	Five	Six
Individual	2	3	3
Group	2	5	3

Procedure

Starting times for the conference calls were arranged by telephone. In addition, participants were sent instructions indicating that they would be telephoned at the agreed time and date and that they would then be able to talk. To achieve the manipulation that formed the independent variable, the telephone operators at Community Network were asked to follow one of two scripts when introducing participants to a telephone group. In both cases the script involved ringing the first person on the list provided by us and putting them on hold while the next was contacted. Once the operator had the second person on the list connected on their phone they would introduce them to the first and they could talk. At this point the two scripts deviated. In the Individual condition the process was continued with each new group member being introduced to the first person in. The operator would break into the conversation between the participants already introduced and then connect the new group member, e.g., if Anne was the first person to join the call it might go:

"excuse me Anne"

[Anne replies]

"hello Anne it's the Operator, I have Peter joining you"

In the Group condition each new group member was introduced to the group as a whole, e.g.,

"excuse me everyone"

[conversation stops]

"hello everyone it's the Operator, I have Peter joining you"

After approximately 30 minutes the operator broke in and warned the participants that the call would finish in 5 minutes.

After the call the participants were telephoned one at a time by the second author and interviewed about their experience of the conversation. The interview was structured around four statements and the participants' reactions to them:
"It really felt like I was with the other people";
"I was very involved with the conversation";
"This is a great way to get to know people better";
"I was able to speak as much as I wanted".

Each participant was asked for a five point rating on the statement and then to elaborate on their answer. Finally, they were asked for "one good thing and one bad thing about the call". Both the conversation and the interview were recorded, with the participant's permission.

2.2 Results

Ratings and interview data

The sampling unit for the analyses presented in both experiments is the telephone group. The dependent variables derived from the analyses of conversation provide one score per group. While each participant provides a separate score for the dependent variables derived from ratings, these are not independent as, within a telephone group, they are based on the participants' experience of the same conversation. For this reason, ratings from participants were averaged to give a mean rating per group before further statistical analysis in all of the analyses presented in the results sections of both experiments. For this experiment rating data was obtained for all but one participant (Group condition, group size 6).

Table 2. Mean (and standard deviation) ratings on a scale 1 to 5 where 5 is "strongly agree" in Experiment 1.

	Individual (n = 8)	Group (n =10)
1. It really felt like I was with the other people;	3.00 (.71)	3.00 (.35)
2. I was very involved with the conversation;	3.81 (.45)	3.55 (.33)
3. This is a great way to get to know people better;	3.72 (.72)	3.59 (.50)

Table 2 presents mean ratings for the four scales. The predicted advantage for the Group condition is not evident in any of the scales. A 2-way factorial analysis of variance was carried out for each of these mean ratings with condition as one between subjects variable and size of group as the other. There was no significant main effect of condition. There was a significant main effect of group size for statement 2, " I was very involved with the conversation" ($F(2,12) = 8.050$, $p = .006$; means, 4.063, 3.700, 3.360 for group sizes 4-6 respectively). This generally higher degree of involvement might have been expected in the smaller groups. There were no significant interactions.

Analyses of the conversations
The subjective experiences of our participants, as elicited in the post conversation interviews described above, represents their recollection and reconstruction of what happened and how they felt. While this is valuable evidence about the effects of the manipulation, we were particularly keen to assess the quality of the experience through behavioural measures obtained directly from transcripts of the conversations themselves. To this end, the first part of the conversations (about 15 minutes) were transcribed by trained transcribers naive to the experimental manipulation. Each transcript was checked by a second paid transcriber to ensure no utterances had been omitted and that the utterances were accurately attributed to participants. The transcription followed the normal convention in Conversational Analysis of continuing a long utterance on a new line, thus a turn could be more than one line long. All the quantitative analyses that follow use line, rather than turn, as the count indicating progress through the transcript. The length of a line is approximately 60 characters.

Line length as a measure of fluidity: Short mean utterance length has been suggested as an indication of fluency [9]. Here utterance length was measured as the average line length in characters and the percentage of continued lines. These are presented in Table 3. There is clearly no effect of the manipulation on any of these statistics. The same 2-way analyses performed on the ratings revealed no significant main effects or interactions for mean length for all lines, or percentage of continuation lines.

Table 3. Mean statistics (with standard deviation) extracted from the transcripts for the two experimental conditions in Experiment 1.

	Individual (n= 8)	Group (n=10)
Mean line length for all lines	36.2 (4.5)	37.1 (6.6)
Mean percentage of continuation lines	29 (7)	33 (14)
Equality of contribution	.963 (.026)	.942 (.047)
Mean lines to first flow episode	266 (237)	428 (309)

Equality of contribution: One would expect the condition where participants were introduced to the group to result in more equal contributions. Equality was measured using the information theory entropy equation $-\Sigma p \log 2(p)$, where p is the proportion of lines contributed by each participant. This has a maximum value when the proportions are all equal. These maxima depend on the group's size so each entropy was then divided by the maximum entropy attainable for that groups size to give a number between 0 and 1 (see [10]; also [11] for a discussion of similar measures). This statistic is also presented in Table 3. The difference between means was small and in the opposite direction to that expected. The same 2-way analyses performed on the ratings revealed no significant main effects or interactions for this variable.

Flow test: In all the conversations analysed, a pairwise conversational structure was observed to persist, even when all the participants had been connected to the conversation. The pairs would change but the structure is basically pairwise conversation: A talks to B for several turns, then A to C and so on. Reed [1] describes this in terms of Goffman's [12] frame analysis as conversation with a primary frame of seriousness. This primary frame can be broken by activities such as shared and invited laughter. At these points in the conversation the frame changes to one of play and the structure of the conversation becomes fluid and genuinely multi-party. During these states of what Goffman [13] calls spontaneous co-involvement, turns become shorter and there is much overlapping and latched speech. A similar phenomenon is described by Edelsky [14]. The phenomenon might also be thought of as a version of Csikszentmihalyi's flow [15] applied to the group rather than the individual, that is, a period of mutual and strong engagement in the conversation. For this reason we shall refer to these episodes in the transcripts as flow states.

The main hypothesis, derived from [1], was that the groups with introduction to a single individual would be slower to reach flow. Flow is defined as, spontaneous, relaxed and inclusive. It is composed of small turn utterances in close succession ("latched talk"), sometimes overlapping, but when this happens there is no competition. Everybody gets to take part. Topics are light and topic change occurs easily. There are no awkward silences.

To make analysing 18 15-minute transcripts for this first flow event tractable the following procedure was followed. The transcripts were transferred to a spread sheet that was programmed to examine a window of 2n lines from the current line where n is the size of the group. If this window contained a line from all n participants the initial line was automatically flagged by the spreadsheet as the start of a potential flow episode. The second author then examined these flagged 2n windows wherever there were n consecutive flagged lines in a row. This was a three stage process.

1. A sequence was not counted as flow if any of the lines in the 2n window was one of the following:

(i) a long silence (10 seconds or more);

(ii) administrative business, e.g., "who is here", "how many people are expected";

(iii) off call, out of call or about call business, e.g. "who's that in the background", "can anybody hear that noise";

(iv) any part of a routinized turn in the round where there is an expectation everyone should reply, e.g., greetings, "where does everybody live" (and playing the guessing game in Experiment 2).

2. A sequence was not counted as flow if the only line attributed to a participant in the 2n window was:

(i) a non-significant turn utterances or an unrecognisable verbalisations, e.g., a grunt;

(ii) a laughter token or minimal turn utterance such as "mm" or "aha".

3. The content was examined to see if the participants did indeed seem to be enjoying themselves. If they had been arguing, for example, the sequence would have been discounted. In the event, while there was disagreement, there were no potential flow sequences with content of this kind.

If none of these exemptions applied, the starting line was marked as the start of a flow episode.

The number of lines between the introduction of the last member of the group and the start of the first flow episode was then computed. If the group never reached flow the value entered was the line number of the last line in the transcription. The mean lines to the first flow episode are given in Table 3. While there appears to be a relatively large difference between these means it was in the opposite direction to that predicted and the standard deviations were very large. The same 2-way analyses performed on the ratings revealed no significant main effects or interactions for lines to first flow episode in this experiment.

Conclusions from Experiment 1

Changing the way that participants are introduced had no significant effect on the ratings or on the measures extracted from transcripts. While this is a null result, and hence may be due to a lack of sensitivity in the measures used and the experimental design rather than a real lack of effect, one may tentatively conclude that this manipulation probably does not reflect a practically important design consideration.

3. Experiment 2

Experiment 2 looked at the possibility of encouraging flow episodes with visual aids as an addition to the voice channel. For half the groups, instructions sent prior to the session contained a list of the names of the participants, in an attempt to make more salient the fact that they were talking to a group. By making the group more salient in this way we expected to encourage a quicker movement to spontaneous co-involvement.

3.1 Method

Design

Each telephone group of 4 to 6 individual participants was randomly assigned to one of two experimental conditions. In the With List condition participants had a printed list of the participants in the group with their instructions for the session. In the Without List condition the instructions did not include this list. 119 participants took part in 24 telephone groups. 94 were recruited by email from the alumni database of which 50 had taken part in Experiment 1. Five groups were recruited by letter from a database of older adults in Northumbria. There were two of these latter 5 groups in the With List condition, and 3 in the Without List condition.

Again, equipment failures and other misadventures mitigated against efforts to balance the group sizes in each condition. Also there were less groups in the transcript analysis than the ratings analysis as some groups lacked tapes (see table 4). The difference in average size is 4.92 vs. 5.00 for the ratings analyses and 4.67 vs. 5.09 for the transcript analyses.

Table 4. Number of groups of each size in the two instruction conditions in Experiment 2. The reduction in the number of groups providing transcripts is due to equipment failure recording four groups.

	Ratings			Transcripts		
Size	Four	Five	Six	Four	Five	Six
With List	5	3	4	5	2	2
Without List	4	4	4	3	4	4

Questionnaire

A questionnaire was constructed using the recorded interviews data from Experiment 1. These interviews were transcribed and coded using grounded theory analysis [16]. These codes were then grouped into three themes: presence (e.g., how much it felt like one was with the other people); involvement (e.g., how much they had or had not felt immersed in the conversation or how positive an experience it was) and communication efficacy (ways in which mediation affected their ability to communicate, because they could not see each other or recognize each others' voices). Quotes were then selected to illustrate the themes and these quotes converted into agree/disagree statements for use in a questionnaire obtainable on request from the authors.

Procedure

The procedure was similar to that in Experiment 1 (Group condition only). Participants were sent a letter with details of when their call would occur. They were told they could talk about anything but two suggestions were made to get the discussion going: the recent accolades received by the University of York in a Sunday Times poll, and a planned new campus for the university. In order to give both groups a reason to have these instructions in front of them, and thus also a list of participants in the With List condition, each participant was given the name of a different city to use in a brief guessing game. The letter also enclosed the 19 item questionnaire described above to be filled in and returned after the call. The operator introduced each new participant to the group as in the Group condition in Experiment 1 and again warned them when 5 minutes was left.

3.2 Results

Ratings
Mean ratings were computed for three composite scores corresponding to presence, involvement and communication efficacy. These scores were then averaged for the participants in each telephone group, as in Experiment 1, and this mean score entered into the analyses presented below. Not all participants returned their questionnaires. The return rate was 87% for the With List condition and 89% for the Without List condition.

Reliability coefficients for the questionnaire derived from a content analysis of the discussion following Experiment 1 were computed for the three subscales using the averaged group data that was that the basis of the comparisons carried out below (N=24). Presence has an alpha of .64. Involvement has an alpha of .90 and Communication efficacy .55. Together the complete 19 item test has an alpha of .88 and we would therefore recommend it to other investigators needing a measure of conversational experience in mediated communication.

The means of these scores for each condition are given in Table 5. It can be seen that there is very little difference between the two conditions. As in Experiment 1 a 2-way between subjects analysis of variance was carried out with condition and group size as independent variables for each of the three composite scores. There were no significant main effects of condition or group size in any of the three measures.

Both Involvement and Communication Efficacy had significant 2-way interactions ($F(1,18) = 4.483$, $p = .026$; and $F(1,18) = 3.685$, $p = .046$; respectively). This was due to group size 5, showing the expected advantage of making the group salient, whereas the other two groups sizes show the opposite effect.

Table 5. Mean (and standard deviation) questionnaire scores on composite rating scales for Experiment 2.

	With List (n = 12)	Without List (n = 12)
Presence score	2.81 (0.29)	2.83 (0.40)
Involvement score	2.73 (0.80)	2.95 (0.83)
Communication efficacy score	3.08 (0.37)	3.18 (0.30)

Analyses of the conversations
As in Experiment 1 the first part of the conversations were transcribed by trained transcribers naive to the experimental manipulation. The mean length of characters per line and percentage of continuation lines was computed as in Experiment 1 and means for these measures are included in Table 6. The 2-way analyses of these

variables showed no significant main effects or interactions. Finally, the equality of contributions was computed for each group. Here the 2-way analysis showed no significant main effect of condition or interaction, but a significant main effect of group size (F(2,15) = 4.841, p = .024; means, .987, .960, .953 for group sizes 4-6 respectively). This also accords with expectation and replicates the results of Carletta et al. [10] who noted a similar negative correlation between group size and equality using a slightly different statistic (see also [11]).

Table 6. Mean statistics (with standard deviation) for process measures extracted from the transcripts for the two experimental conditions in Experiment 2

	With List (n = 10)	Without List (n = 11)
Mean line length for all lines	30.7 (4.7)	30.0 (7.2)
Mean percentage of continuation lines	23.2 (6.4)	21.8 (11.3)
Equality of contribution	.969 (.030)	.968 (.020)
Mean lines to first flow episode	254 (219)	300 (181)

Mean lines to flow from the line where the last participant entered the conversation were computed as described in the results of Experiment 1. Here the results are in the right direction (see Table 6) but again the standard deviations are large. The 2-way analysis of variance showed no significant main effect of condition, and no significant interaction but this time there was a significant effect of group size with the size 4 groups reaching flow in less than half the number of lines of the other group sizes (F(2,15) = 5.054, p = .021; means, 134, 318, 423 for group sizes 4-6 respectively). One would expect a small group to find it easier to meet our criteria for flow and so this result confirms that the measure has some validity and sensitivity to this manipulation in the experiment.

4. General discussion

4.1 Running experiments in people's homes

The studies described above demonstrate the feasibility of running formal quantitative communication experiments in a recreational setting. A degree or realism was achieved by having the participants join in from home and simply asking them to "chat". As in our earlier studies, participants were connected from their own homes and the conversation was largely undirected. Unlike the telephone conferences in the field studies, however, participants had not met before. Nevertheless, the conversational mechanisms observed were very similar, giving some credence to the idea that there will be a primary frame of seriousness that can be broken with bouts of spontaneous co-involvement in all telephone conferences.

One can also argue that the context was a truly recreational one. Despite the fact that they had been asked to meet with a group of strangers, participants generally enjoyed the telephone conferences. In Experiment 2 the questionnaire included a question to tap into this. The average rating to the statement "I found the call to be an extremely positive experience" was 3.7 in the With List condition and 3.8 in the Without List condition where 1 is strongly disagree and 5 is strongly agree. Given the "extremely" and "strongly" qualifiers, this is a positive endorsement for this recreational experience. Also, as part of the questionnaire used in Experiment 2, participants were invited to make any additional comments they wanted. The large majority of comments were positive about the taking part in the telephone conference. It was 'a most enjoyable exercise' and a 'great experience'.

4.2 The effect of the experimental manipulations

Changing the way that participants are introduced, in Experiment 1, seemed an obvious way of influencing the specific target we had set ourselves, that is to reduce the amount of pairwise conversation and hasten the onset of the first instances of flow. Had the manipulation been successful the results would have had important implications for the running of recreational telephone conferences. In the event it is difficult to know whether the null result obtained is due to the general insensitivity of the experimental design or whether it is really unimportant. The number of groups, 8 in one condition and 10 in the other, should have been sufficient to detect a practically important effect. Tentatively one may conclude that this manipulation has no practically interesting effect on the conversations. The fact that the trend in the results was actually in the opposite direction to that expected leads us to speculate that there may have been two effects working against each other in this experiment. Introducing each new participant to the whole group may have emphasised the group, but introducing each person to the same individual may have made that person a kind of facilitator. If the randomly chosen person to whom the introduction was made facilitated better conversations the result may have been a more rapid move to spontaneous co-involvement. Had they been less effective as facilitators, the other effects may have come through resulting in the large amount of variance observed.

In Experiment 2 the group was made more salient by providing a list of names. The idea was that by being able to see a list of all the group members, each participant would be made continually aware that the current speaker was not the only person there. A number of possible variants on this theme were considered when designing this experiment: making one group anonymous, providing biographies or pictures; they were rejected as all of these variants introduced additional factors and additional practical constraints. The result was a relatively small intervention that appears to have had no effect, although here again the cautions needed when interpreting null results apply. Given different equipment constraints it would be very interesting to explore the use of some of the graphical awareness tools proposed for audio and text conferencing, where the present status of a participant (present/absent, speaking/silent) is graphically represented via avatars.

4.3 Combining field studies with experiments

Perhaps the most important contribution of this paper has been to demonstrate the value of combining experiments with field studies. The benefits work both ways. For example, spontaneous co-involvement (conversational flow) was identified in the field study as a desirable feature of group conversations. The measure, lines to flow, directly resulted from this characterisation. However, in addition, translating the concept into an operationalised quantitative measure that could be used to compare different implementations required a much more clearly defined version of the idea. The scoring scheme identified in section 2.2 can thus be viewed as a clarification of the field studies, resulting from having to design an experiment. The same is true of the experimental manipulations, which, while unsuccessful, do serve to operationalise and hence clarify the design goal we were pursuing.

This paper demonstrates the feasibility of doing communication experiments in the realistic recreational context of people's own homes. It also takes us some way towards the goal of devising practical and sensitive measures for assessing enjoyment directly from user behaviour. Lines to flow is a quantitative measure derived directly from the participants' conversation, reflecting a potentially important aspect of enjoyment. This work is now being extended in this laboratory to examine other measures of group behaviour [17]. Such measures provide new ways of thinking about user experience in addition to the more commonly collected post-experience subjective ratings.

Acknowledgements
This work was funded by grant L328253006 to the first author from the UK ESRC via the PACCIT programme. We are grateful to other participants in the PACCIT programme and members of the HCI group at York who have helped to shape this research.

References

1. Reed, D.J., Fun on the phone: the situated experience of recreational telephone conferences, in *Funology: from usability to enjoyment*, M.A. Blythe, et al., Editors., Kluwer: Dordrecht, the Netherlands (2003) 67-79
2. Reed, D.J. and A.F. Monk, Using familiar technologies in unfamiliar ways and learning from the old about the new. *Universal Access in the Information Society*, 3 (2004) 114-121
3. Short, J., E. Williams, and B. Christie, *The social psychology of telecommunications*, London: John Wiley and Sons (1976)
4. Chapanis, A., Interactive Human Communication. *Scientific American*, 232 (1975, March) 36 - 42
5. Finn, K.E., A.J. Sellen, and S.B. Wilbur, *Video-mediated communication*, Mahwah, New Jersey: Lawrence Erlbaum Associates (1997)
6. Anderson, A.H., J. Mullin, R. Katsavras, R. McEwan, E. Grattan, P. Brundell, and C. O'Malley. Multimediating multiparty interactions. in *Interact'99*. Edinburgh: Amsterdam: IOS Press (1999)
7. Monk, A.F. and L.A. Watts, Peripheral participation in video-mediated communication. *International Journal of Human-computer Studies,*. 52 (2000) 775-960

8. Monk, A.F., E. Fellas, and E. Ley, Hearing only one side of normal and mobile phone conversations. *Behaviour and Information Technology*, 23 (2004) 301-305

9. Daly-Jones, O., A.F. Monk, and L.A. Watts, Some advantages of video conferencing over high-quality audio conferencing: fluency and awareness of attentional focus. International Journal of Human-Computer Studies, 1998. 49(1): p. 21 - 59.

10. Carletta, J., S. Garrod, and H. Fraser-Krauss, Communication and Placement of Authority in Workplace Groups: The Consequences for Innovation. Small Group Research, 1998. 29(5): p. 531-559.

11. Fay, N., S. Garrod, and J. Carletta, Group discussion as interactive dialogue or as serial monologue: the influence of group size. Psychological Science, 2000. 11(6): p. 481-486.

12. Goffman, E., Frame analysis. an essay on the organisation of experience. 1974, Boston: North East University Press.

13. Goffman, E., Fun in games. in Encounters: two studies in the sociology of interaction, E. Goffman, Editor. 1961, Bob Merril: Indianapolis.

14. Edelsky, C., Who's got the floor. Language in Society, 1981. 10: p. 383-421.

15. Csikszentmihalyi, M. and K. Rathunde, The measurement of flow in everyday life: towards a theory of emergent motivation. Nebraska Symposium on Motivation, 1993. 40: p. 57-97.

16. Strauss, A. and J. Corbin, Basics of qualitative research: grounded theory procedures and techniques. 1990, Newbury Park: Sage.

17. Lindley, S.E. Designing interfaces to afford enjoyable social interactions by collocated groups. Proceedings of CHI 2005, Extended Abstracts, 2005, 1122-1123. New York: ACM Press.

Enliven Photographs: Enriching User Experience

Akshay Darbari[1] and Pragya Agrawal[2]

1   Tata Elxsi Ltd., Bangalore, India
2   Infosys Technologies Ltd., Bangalore, India

Abstract. This paper is based on the study aimed at giving a new direction to Photographs, keeping in mind the growing needs of the people and enriching day-to-day experience vis-à-vis paper based photograph. A survey was conducted which revealed few startling but interesting facts as to what more the end-user wants than a mere 'physical paper-based photograph'. This paper talks about the survey, response by the participants, results derived from them, current work and future direction.

1   Introduction

"Ah! Nostalgia…" exclaimed Maya, holding a photograph of her daughter when she was a kid. Maya is trying hard to recollect the moment when her daughter spoke her first words or when her daughter took her first steps and enacted à la Neil Armstrong's giant leap in her own way.

"Pictures that tell their own story maybe worth more than a thousand words". How many of us remember the background of a photograph, long after it's been shot? It's an interesting paradox that with time, people no longer remember the event or context well enough to recollect or relive that moment.

This paper is based on the study aimed at

- Providing a new direction to Photograph, keeping in mind the growing needs of the people and how to meet those,
- Enriching day-to-day experience of people,
- Providing intelligent solutions for improving the quality of life and
- Findings way of expanding boundaries of our personal space and create a world of seamless connectivity.

A survey [2] was conducted where participation of the end-user was encouraged. This survey revealed few startling but interesting facts as to what more the end-user wants than a mere 'Physical Paper Photograph'. The challenge lies in providing solutions to fulfill the end-user's requirements. If this happens, the world of photographs will see a revolution and the way in which we look and handle paper-

Please use the following format when citing this chapter:

Darbari, A., Agrawal, P., 2007, in IFIP International Federation for Information Processing, Volume 241, Home Informatics and Telematics: ICT for the Next Billion, eds. Venkatesh, A., Gonsalves, T., Monk, A., Buckner, K., (Boston: Springer), pp. 215-219.

based photographs as of now will also change. The photographs won't be the same again.

2   The Study

The survey was conducted on randomly chosen user base of 100, with people from different age group, gender, and location. Each participant was asked a carefully defined set of seven questions. The participants were asked to answer the following questions online as part of the survey:

1. What is the significance of photographs to you?
2. Do you prefer viewing photographs as a paper based activity or watching it on screen?
3. What do you think of sharing photographs on screen rather than on paper?
4. Do you feel something is missing in the photographs? What is it?
5. What other media do you like to augment with photographs? Text/handwriting/audio/short video/others
6. How do you think this media will enhance the status quo of photographs?
7. Would you like photographs to be interactive? What is your idea of interacting with the photograph?

3   The Response

The response received from the participants, is compiled as follows:

- **What is the significance of photographs to you?**
  Photographs in general are a treasure trove of memoirs for all and encompass mood, emotions, and feelings that influence reflexes, perception, cognition and behavior. Majority of the participants replied that they view photographs to recollect past events and refresh their memories followed by Fun/recreation, Hobby, Miscellaneous respectively as shown in figure 1.

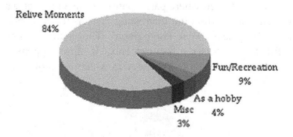

Fig. 1. Significance of photographs to people in percentage

- **Do you prefer viewing photographs as a paper based activity or watching it on screen?**
  In this digital age, even the viewing experience has changed from paper based to digital photographs on screen. The users attribute this change to the ease of editing and sharing of photographs, which is not possible in case of paper-based photograph. But the survey shows that even though users are inclined towards digital photographs, people still enjoy viewing photographs as a paper-based activity rather than on screen. Users associate this with the nostalgia attached with the paper based photographs.

- **What do you think of sharing photographs on screen rather than on paper?**
  As mentioned in the above section people find it more convenient to share the photographs on screen than on paper. Digital photographs can be shared on screen or Internet and can be edited easily without any hassle. Creation of multiple copies of the same photograph is also simple, less time consuming and without any investment.

- **Do you feel something is missing in the photographs? What is it?**
  Though the question sounded a bit out of place to the participants, but when explained most of them felt that the answer is 'yes'. The participants feel that with time the context attached with the photographs is lost and it is difficult to recollect and relive that moment.

- **What other media do you like to augment with photographs? Text/handwriting/audio/short video/others**
  This was another complex question for the participants. Maximum people opted for audio as a media, which will help in annotating the photographs and enhance the value of the photograph the most, followed by video, text and others respectively.

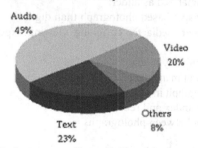

Fig. 2. People choice of Media Augmentation with Photograph

- **How do you think this media will enhance the status quo of photographs?**
  These media are going to indirectly increase the value of the photograph. The viewing experience will enrich the user's viewing experience and help them to relive the moment.

Another interesting finding from the survey is that, the effect of different media is different for different people. Therefore, different people prefer different media to help invoke emotions.

- **Would you like photographs to be interactive? What is your idea of interacting with the photograph?**

The participants were extremely creative and gave interesting answers to this question. A few of the responses are replicated in this paper to give a feel of what the participants want:

- "Interactive...Yes... if it means that suppose I want to know more about the background and surroundings of a particular location being shot..."
- "Why not? Image maps as in HTML, links to other image libraries...eg clicking on A's pic (in, say a family photo) takes one to an album containing A's pics..."
- "ya that will definitely be useful to handle bad or dated or damaged copied or to selectively view photos, through voice."
- "...I couldn't comprehend how could a photograph be interactive... If the only implication derives from the fact that the same picture can be viewed from multiple angles... "

And the replies on the lighter side:
- "You should invent something like star trek such that when I see a photograph Mr. Spock just presses a button and I can be with the person...."
- "Kissing it goodnight and tucking it under the pillow..."

4   Results

Results After the survey a wish list was prepared. The wish list was based on the survey responses and what normally people would expect if the solution were based on a digital photograph.

The wish list is summarized as under:
- Preference for paper based photograph than digital
- Augmenting other media for enriching viewing experience and help relive the moment
- Annotations using any media
- Better photograph management
- Restoring photograph in case of wear out
- Search, browse, index and retrieve
- Communication between photographs

This wish list was shared with the participants and was asked their opinion. The participants found it hard to visualize how the wish list can be realized.

5 Future Directions

Perhaps, if the wish list is to be implemented for digital photographs the problem might not be that complex. The challenge lies in offering solutions for the survey outcome of user preference for paper based physical photographs.

The participants feel that if not fictitious, this is quite a futuristic solution and question its viability. The authors disagree and are of the opinion that the time has come to provide such user-friendly solutions to enrich common day-to-day experiences.

The authors are currently working towards providing solution for the paper-based photograph. So far, they have been successful in generating enough interest in the idea from all quarters and intend to bring a revolution in the world of paper-based photographs.

Acknowledgement

We express our deep sense of gratitude to those who participated in the 'Enliven Photographs' survey and replied back whenever we wanted their feedback. We would also like to thank our Parents, who always stood by us whenever we were in need of them. We regret any inadvertent omissions.

References and Citations

1. Enliven Photograph; http://home.graffiti.net/akshay.darbari:graffiti.net/html/ep.html
2. Enliven Photograph Survey

Changing only the aesthetic features of a product can affect its apparent usability

Andrew Monk and Kira Lelos

Centre for Usable Home Technology (CUHTec), University of York, UK

Abstract. Three experiments were conducted to investigate the relationship between usability and aesthetics with students and older people. A common mechanical domestic appliance, the can opener, was chosen as a proxy for future digital products. The experiments involved comparing the rated usability of can openers that had been painted to make them more or less aesthetically pleasing. Experiment 1 tested students' ratings of beauty and usability. Experiment 2 similarly tested an elderly population on their ratings before and after use. In general, the products rated more beautiful were rated as more usable. To avoid the possibility that rating a product for its aesthetic qualities could somehow affect its subsequent rating for usability, Experiment 3 repeated Experiment 2 but products were only rated for usability. In Experiments 1 and 3 the manipulation of product features associated only with aesthetic qualities of the product (painting the can openers) also significantly affected ratings of usability. The results are related to Hassenzahl's model of user experience, and interpreted in terms of the holistic evaluation of product features in judgements of hedonic and pragmatic attributes. The results confirm and extend previous findings and highlight the importance of aesthetic considerations as well as usability in all forms of design.

1 Introduction

Home oriented IT products bring to the fore different user requirements to those traditionally considered for work oriented IT products [1]. In particular, requirements related to the aesthetic qualities of objects we bring into our homes are quite different to those in the workplace. This has led to an upsurge in research on beauty as a topic within the Human Factors and Human-Computer Interaction (HCI) communities. One theme within this research has been the relationship between aesthetic quality and the traditional requirement for usability. An early study by Kurosu and Kashimura [2] demonstrated a strong correlation between ratings of usability and ratings of beauty. They had 156 students rate 26 layout drawings for a bank ATM. Averaging over participants and correlating across layouts they obtained a correlation of 0.6 between ratings of usability and beauty. This finding is

Please use the following format when citing this chapter:

Monk, A., Lelos, K., 2007, in IFIP International Federation for Information Processing, Volume 241, Home Informatics and Telematics: ICT for the Next Billion, eds. Venkatesh, A., Gonsalves, T., Monk, A., Buckner, K., (Boston: Springer), pp. 221-233.

potentially important because it questions the traditional conception of usability in Human Factors and HCI which is based on performance measures such as time to completion or learnability. If two products are similar in objective usability but the more attractive product is judged more usable then it would seem that the user has a different concept of usability to that implied by the objective criteria. This questioning of the concept of usability has resonance with a new emphasis within the HCI community on emotional response (e.g., [3]) and user experience (e.g., [4]).

Of course, the Kurosu and Kashimura [2] result is open to criticism, in particular, that the participants rating these products had not actually used them. With little else to go on, it is possible that they fell back on attractiveness when making their ratings of usability. This possibility was addressed by Tractinsky et al. [5]. Nine ATM layouts from the [2] study were selected as high, medium or low aesthetic quality. Screen simulations of ATM functionality were added so that participants could use them to simulate eleven tasks such as withdrawing cash or making an account enquiry. The ATMs were rated for usability and beauty before and after use and the post-usage ratings yielded the same apparent effect of aesthetic quality on usability ratings as the pre-usage ratings.

Both [2] and [5] are open to the further criticism, that one cannot assign a causative interpretation to a correlation [6]. The high aesthetic quality layouts were selected from the complete set on the basis of aesthetics ratings. It could be that this selection of layouts are indeed more usable in terms of their objective ease-of-use and ease-of-learning. The experiments to be described here address this issue by manipulating the appearance of otherwise identical products. A causative link would be demonstrated if this manipulation has an effect on perceived usability.

1.1   Hassenzahl's model

Hassenzahl [7] makes a plea for a more explicit model of what is going on in the studies described above. His model will be used to frame the experiments described below. He sets out three entities: Product Features; Apparent Product Character and Consequences (see Figure 1, A). Product Features are the results of design, content, presentation, functionality, etc.   The Apparent Product Character is the user's perception of the products. Finally, the Apparent Product Character leads to Consequences, the product's general appeal ("goodness"), pleasure in its use, and behavioural consequences such as time spent using it. Consequences depend on the situations the users find themselves in, for example, a product that is a pleasure to use at work may not be judged so at home (Hassenzahl's diagrammatic depiction of the effect of context has been left out of Figure 1 for the sake of simplicity).

A.

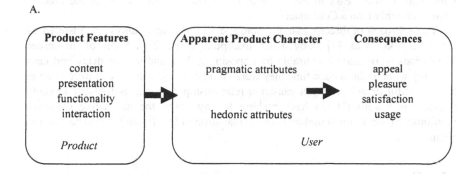

B.

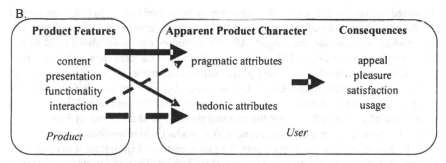

Fig 1. A. Hassenzahl's (2003) user experience model. B. Proposed causative relationships, dotted arrows represent a prediction of the effect of the aesthetic manipulation used here, solid arrows represent the effect of Tractinsky et al.'s (2000) manipulation of usability.

Hassenzahl's [7] model assumes that when a participant in an experiments is asked to rate a design they imagine themselves in a particular situation and make some evaluation of Apparent Product Character and then what the Consequences of this judgement might be. He has encapsulated this theory in a questionnaire (see [6]) measuring different aspects of Apparent Product Character in terms of hedonic and pragmatic quality. Pragmatic quality corresponds to usability. Hassenzahl [6] provides support for his model using data from a study using a range of MP3 player skins. Support for the independence of three elements of product character, hedonic-stimulation, hedonic-identity and pragmatic quality, is provided by identifying four skins that vary quite differently on these three dimensions.

The experiments described below directly manipulate Product Features associated only with aesthetic qualities of a product, that is, its hedonic attributes. The hypothesis is that this manipulation will also affect its pragmatic attributes supporting a holistic view of the evaluation of hedonic and pragmatic attributes in the perception of Apparent Product Character (see dotted arrows in Figure 1, B). Note participants in these experiments were asked to rate the extent to which they agreed with the statement "this can opener is easy to use" rather than the seven semantic differentials suggested by Hassenzahl to measure pragmatic quality. However, Hassenzahl's pragmatic quality score has been shown to correlate highly with "hard to use - easy to use" and in Hassenzahl's terms is part of the Product Character rather than a Consequence.

The approach of directly manipulating specific product features was inspired by the Tractinsky et al. [5] study which manipulated usability. Some of the screen simulations were made less usable by imposing a 9 second system delay and keys that only worked the second time they were clicked. These simulations were rated as less beautiful demonstrating a causative relationship between usability and beauty ("usable is beautiful") but have nothing to say about the alternative causative relationship ("beautiful is usable"). The explanation of this finding is also depicted in Figure 1 , B.

1.2   The can opener as a proxy for future digital products

As stated above, the purpose of the experiments described here is to demonstrate that the direct manipulation of aesthetic Product Features affects ratings of usability when the product is otherwise unchanged. All of the studies described above used screen simulations of products, ATM designs rendered as line drawings and decorative graphic designs in the form of MP3 player skins. Hassenzahl [6] criticises the use of ATM designs because they are not objects owned by the user. He also criticises the use of engineering students as being unrepresentative of the general public. To give a strong test of our hypothesis that the manipulation of aesthetic Product Features can affect the experience of usability, we needed a product where aesthetics and usability were both important to the participants. To make aesthetics important it needed to be a product that they might own and keep in their homes. To make usability important it needed to be a product whose function could be understood readily by the participants, which in these experiments were psychology students and members of the general public attending a drop in centre for older people. It was hard to find an electronic product that (a) met these requirements and (b) could easily be manipulated (rather than selected) to look more or less visually appealing. For this reason we chose to use can openers as a proxy for the many portable electronic devices that are gradually making their way into our homes (e.g., phones, music players and hand held web browsers). Two of each of four models of can opener were purchased ranging from the simplest and cheapest to more expensive ergonomically designed models (see Figure 2 at end of paper).

Enamel paint was applied to alter the aesthetic qualities of the can openers. Pre-rating of the can openers by a small sample of students showed that, when unmodified by painting, Model 1 was rated very low given the statement "this can opener is appealing to look at" whereas Model 4 was rated very highly. Accordingly, the handles of the modified version of Model 1 (row 1 column 2 in Fig. 2) were painted red (Metallic Deep Red) to make it more attractive compared with the unpainted version. Models 2, 3 and 4 (rows 2-4 column 1)were painted a rather unpleasant blotchy green (Pea Green) to make them unattractive. Model 4 (row 4 column 2) was left unpainted in the attractive condition, Models 2 and 3 (rows 2 and 3 column 2) were painted red. It is difficult to see how this manipulation could have affected the objective ease-of-use of the can openers.

2. EXPERIMENT 1

The general procedure in each of the three experiments described here is similar. Each participant rated either the four attractive, or the four unattractive, can openers. This way the participant saw only one version of each model and was never asked to directly compare the attractive and unattractive conditions. This was to minimise the possibility of the participant guessing the purpose of the experiment. To test the effectiveness of the manipulation participants rated the statement "this can opener is appealing to look at". They were also asked to try the can openers with some washed empty food tins before rating the critical statement "this can opener is easy to use".

2.1 Method (Experiment 1)

Participants
These were 20 male and female undergraduate students from the University of York studying various subjects, and ranging in age from 19 to 26. They were not rewarded for their participation.

Procedure
Each participant was randomly assigned to one of the two groups Ugly, rating the four ugly can openers, and Pretty rating the others. Each of the four models was presented to each participant in a randomised order. Half of the participants rated aesthetics first followed by usability, while the other half rated usability first followed by aesthetics. For aesthetic ratings, the participants were able to hold and study the can opener, while for usability ratings the participants were instructed to use the can opener on a tin by turning the handle and partially opening it. For the aesthetic ratings they were read the statement "this can opener is appealing to look at" and given a card with a five item Likert scale printed on it where "1" was labelled "strongly disagree" and "5" strongly agree". For the usability ratings the statement read was "this can opener is easy to use".

2.2 Results (Experiment 1)

Manipulation check - aesthetics ratings
If the manipulation of Product Features has been successful one would expect the aesthetics ratings of the Pretty Group to be higher than those of the Ugly Group. This is a strong test of the manipulation as the participants were not able to directly compare the two versions of each model. The results confirm that painting the can openers had the desired effect. The overall mean aesthetic rating of the Ugly Group was 1.90 (Std. Dev. 0.13) and that for the Pretty Group 3.45 (Std. Dev. 0.13). A split-plot analysis of variance where the between subjects effect was Group (2 levels) and the within subjects effect Model (4 levels) showed a significant main effect of Group ($F(1, 18) = 75.209$, $p < 0.05$) and Model ($F(3, 54) = 36.818$, $p < 0.05$) but no significant interaction.

Criterion variable - usability ratings

The critical comparison comes from the usability ratings. As predicted, these closely mirror the aesthetic ratings. The difference between the overall means for the two groups is smaller but still very reliable ($F(1, 18) = 13.157$, $p < 0.05$). The overall mean rating of the Ugly Group being 2.53 (Std. Dev. 0.12) and that for the Pretty Group 3.13 (Std. Dev. 0.12). Again, there was a significant main effect of Group ($F(1, 18) = 75.209$, $p < 0.05$) and Model ($F(3, 54) = 88.105$, $p < 0.05$) and no significant interaction. Manipulating the aesthetic Product Features of the can openers alone, i.e., leaving other Product Features normally associated with usability unchanged, had a direct effect on the Apparent Product Character usability as measured by our rating scale. It would appear that the predictions of the model depicted in Figure 1, B (dotted arrows) are supported. The experience of usability is influenced by aesthetic Product Features as well as those Product Features associated with objective definitions of usability such as time to completion or task completion.

Another notable feature of these results is the way that the usability and aesthetics ratings strongly parallel one another. In both cases there is a large effect of Model with the cheapest, least sophisticated models being rated lowest and the more expensive and more sophisticated models being rated highest (see Figure 3, A and B). Again, this is consistent with a holistic judgement of Apparent Product Character where Product Features interact when a judgement is made. Alternatively, it may be that we have just happened upon a set of products with Product Features that co-vary in this way.

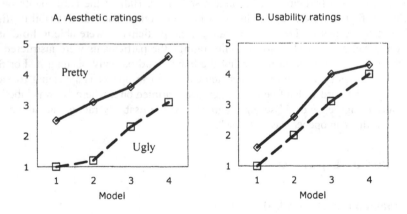

Fig. 3. Experiment 1, students' ratings of Aesthetics and Usability for each model from Pretty and Ugly groups

3. EXPERIMENT 2

In order to test the generality of the results from Experiment 1 a new user population was selected. To make this as different as possible from the students used in

Experiment 1, and most experiments in this area, this was people visiting a drop-in centre for the over 60s. We expected this to make the usability features more salient. The more expensive models were designed for people with poor grip and hence older people were expected to appreciate them more. In addition, it was decided to add a pre-use rating of the can openers to make the experiment directly comparable to [5].

3.1   Method (Experiment 2)

Participants
Participants were 32 citizens from the St. Sampson's Drop-In Centre located in York. They were a mixture of male and female (22 female and 10 male) and various ages from 60 years to above 80 years (modal range 60 to 65). They were not rewarded for their participation. Permission was gained in writing from the manager of the centre and verbally from the participants.

Procedure
The procedure used was the same as in Experiment 1 except that participants rated the aesthetics and usability of each of model, then used them, then rated them again for both aesthetics and usability. The order of rating (usability-aesthetics or aesthetics-usability) and the order the models were presented were both counterbalanced.

3.2   Results (Experiment 2)

Manipulation check - aesthetics ratings
Again the overall mean aesthetic rating of the ugly group was significantly lower (2.44, Std. Dev. 0.15) than that for the pretty group (2.98, Std. Dev. 0.15). A split-plot analysis of variance was carried out where the between subjects effect was Group (2 levels) and there were two within subjects effects, Time of Test (2 levels, before and after) and Model (4 levels). This showed a significant main effect of Group ($F(1, 30) = 6.354$, $p < 0.05$). While statistically significant, this effect was much smaller for this population of older people than it was for the students in Experiment 1 (0.54 scale points rather than 1.55 respectively). This could be because the colours used were selected using ratings from students, i.e., they were not colours that were particularly attractive or unattractive to older people. Another possibility is that older people are less influenced by colour in general.

Time of Test was also significant ($F(1, 30) = 29.138$, $p < 0.05$) and Model ($F(3, 90) = 17.347$, $p < 0.05$). The Time of Test effect was due to the second set of ratings after using the product being slightly higher than the before ratings. Much to our surprise the very significant effect of Model was in exactly the reverse direction to that observed with the student raters. Model 1 the cheapest and simplest product was rated highest and model 4, the most expensive and ergonomic lowest (see Figure 3, A). There were no significant two- or three-way interactions.

Criterion variable - usability ratings
Usability ratings again closely mirror the aesthetic ratings, except that there was no significant effect of Group. The overall mean usability rating of the Ugly group was only marginally lower (2.87, Std. Dev. 0.13) than that for the Pretty group (2.98, Std. Dev. 0.13). The analysis of variance applied to the aesthetic ratings was applied to the usability ratings. This showed a non-significant main effect of Group (F(1, 30) < 1, n.s.), but significant effects of Time of Test (F(1, 30) = 28.200, p < 0.05) and Model (F(3, 90) = 21.434, p < 0.05). There were no significant two- or three-way interactions.

As with the aesthetic ratings the Time of Test effect was due to the second set of ratings after using the product being slightly higher than the before ratings. The effect of Model in the usability ratings closely followed those of the aesthetic ratings, i.e., they were also the reverse direction to that observed with the student raters (see Figure 4 A and B). Model 1 the cheapest and simplest product was rated highest and model 4, the most expensive and ergonomic lowest.

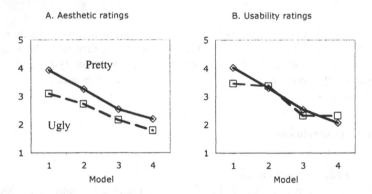

Fig. 4. Experiment 2, older people's ratings of Aesthetics and Usability for each model from Pretty and Ugly groups averaging across before and after.

Experiment 2 then does not replicate the key result found in Experiment 1. There was not a significant effect of Group. Of course, this is a null result. It could be that there is no effect of manipulating aesthetic Product Features on usability ratings with this user population. Alternatively, it may be that the experimental design was not sensitive enough to detect such an effect. As noted above, while still statistically significant, the effect of painting the can openers on aesthetic ratings was very much smaller than in Experiment 1.

The reversal of the effect of model and the way it is seen both in aesthetic and usability ratings is noteworthy. One hypothesis is that the older people were strongly influenced by the familiarity of the models considered. Model 1 is commonly found in many homes while the more expensive designs represented by the other models less so. The higher ratings for model 1 may reflect subjective estimates of the objective usability criterion, time-to-learn. Many older people have a quite reasonable scepticism about learning to use unfamiliar tools that would not be a concern to students. Whatever the cause of this reversal of effect it is most interesting that it is reflected equally in the aesthetic and usability ratings, further bolstering the case for holistic judgements of Apparent Product Character from a variety of Product Features.

4. EXPERIMENT 3

It is possible that asking for ratings for aesthetics and usability for the same object somehow confused the participants in our experiment. To simplify the procedure we kept the before-after element but only asked for ratings of usability. The same set of can openers were used.

4.1 Method (Experiment 3)

Participants
A new set of 32 citizens were recruited from the St. Sampson's Drop-In Centre who had not participated in the previous study. The participants were a mixture of male and female (19 female and 13 male) and various ages from 60 years to above 80 years old (modal range 66 to 70).

Procedure
The procedure used in this experiment was the same as in Experiment 2, except each participant was only asked about usability and was not questioned about aesthetics.

4.2 Results (Experiment 3)

Criterion variable - usability ratings
There were no ratings of aesthetics in this experiment. The usability rating confirm the results from Experiment 1. The overall mean usability rating of the Ugly group was significantly lower (2.80, Std. Dev. 0.08) than that for the Pretty group (3.08, Std. Dev. 0.08). The analysis of variance used in Experiment 2 showed a significant main effect of Group ($F(1, 30) = 6.551$, $p < 0.05$), a non-significant effect of Time of Test ($F(1, 30) = 2.899$, n.s.) and a significant effect of Model ($F(3, 90) = 36.882$, $p < 0.05$). The effect of Model was as in Experiment 2: Model 1, the cheapest and simplest product, was rated highest and model 4, the most expensive and ergonomic, lowest. However, in these data there was a significant Group by Product interaction ($F(3, 90) = 5.510$, $p < 0.05$), see Figure 5. It would seem that the effect of Group is mainly seen in the ratings for Model 1, the simplest and aesthetically preferred can opener for this group. This interpretation is confirmed by a simple main effects analysis which show a significant effect of Group for Model 1 ($F(1, 120) = 19.248$, $p < 0.05$) but none of the other models.

This then is a partial replication of the key effect observed in Experiment 1 for the model showing the largest effect of the aesthetics manipulation as evidenced in the aesthetics ratings in Experiment 2. Manipulating the aesthetic Product Features of this model and leaving other Product Features normally associated with usability unchanged, had a direct effect on the Apparent Product Character usability. The result is striking given: (i) the limited nature of the manipulation as evidenced by the manipulation check in Experiment 2; (ii) the fact that the participants did not have the two versions of the can opener to compare, and (iii) that they were only asked to rate the can openers for usability.

Fig. 5. Experiment 3, older people's ratings of Usability for each model from Pretty and

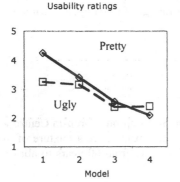

Ugly groups averaging across before and after.

5. GENERAL DISCUSSION

Three experiments have been presented comparing ratings of usability and aesthetics for products whose aesthetic Product Features had been manipulated. The results of Experiment 1 conformed closely to the predictions of the model represented in Figure 1, B. The manipulation had the desired effect on aesthetic ratings, and was also reflected in usability ratings. The results of Experiment 2 were less clear cut. The effect of the manipulation on aesthetic ratings was much smaller and was not reflected in a significant effect on usability ratings. However, Experiment 3, which only required ratings of usability, did show a significant effect of the manipulation on usability ratings for Model 1.

In Experiment 1, the participants were students, whereas in Experiments 2 and 3 they were older people attending a drop-in centre. That these two populations have different values and aesthetics is dramatically demonstrated in the reversal of the effect of model. The cheapest and most familiar model obtained the lowest ratings from the students but the highest ratings from the older people. Serendipitously, this provides further evidence for a holistic judgement of Apparent Product Character as the ratings of usability completely paralleled the ratings of aesthetics.

Implications for Hassenzahl's model:
Hassenzahl's [6] model only contains the two rightward facing arrows depicted in Figure 1, A. No predictions are specified as to the interaction of individual Product

Features with pragmatic and hedonic character. It is however assumed that several elements of Apparent Product Character will interact to determine Consequences (see also [6], Figure 6).

Overall the prediction in Figure 1, B (dotted arrows) are upheld. Taken with [5] demonstration of the effect of a manipulation of usability on aesthetic ratings, there is a strong case that Product Features influence aspect of Apparent Product other than those they are obviously associated with.

Figure 1, B is convenient for considering alternative explanations of the findings. For example, [6] explains the correlation between beauty and usability observed by [5] in terms of an effect in the Consequences column. He states that "ugly-beautiful" has a general evaluative function as a rating scale. That is, the semantic differential "ugly-beautiful" taps into the Consequences as well as hedonic character. The effect of manipulating Product Features normally associated with objective usability on ratings on "ugly-beautiful" then is explained as occurring in the causative link between Apparent Product Character and Consequences.

It is harder to make such a case with the findings presented here as "this can opener is easy to use" would seem much less generally evaluative. However, it would be interesting to repeat the study with Hassenzahl's full questionnaire to directly test this assumption. This would also permit analysis of covariance to test the goodness of fit of alternative models of causation.

Methodological and practical implications:
There are clearly some advantages in sampling from different populations of potential users. The participation of older users extended the generality of previous findings in this area and a new effect of Model was observed. However, the effect of the aesthetic manipulation was small for this sample. Further research is required to determine what governs ratings of hedonic and pragmatic quality in the older population and to repeat the experiment with more successful manipulations of aesthetic features. Given the differences observed with these two user populations, it would also seem to be imperative to repeat the experiment with different products and different imagined or actual contexts of use.

This paper started by contrasting objective measures of usability, such as time to completion or ease of learning, with subject user experience. The results confirm previous findings that highlight the importance of aesthetic considerations in determining many aspects of user experience. The question remains as to how objective measures of usability should be factored into this equation. We have not assessed the objective usability of our can openers and whether this differed for older people and students, but if we had, it is not clear exactly how such data should be interpreted in the general model of user experience. Instantiating Hassenzahl's (2003) model in these experiments has thus exposed important theoretical and practical questions that need to be addressed in future research.

REFERENCES

1. Monk, A.F., User-centred design: the home use challenge, in Home informatics and telematics: information technology and society, A. Sloane and F. van Rijn, Editors. 2000, Kluwer Academic Publishers: Boston. p. 181-190.
2. Kurosu, M. and K. Kashimura. Apparent usability vs. inherrent usability. in CHI 1995. 1995: ACM Press.
3. Norman, D.A., Emotional Design: Why We Love (or Hate) Everyday Things. 2004, New York: Basic Books.
4. McCarthy, J. and P. Wright, Technology as experience. 2004, Cambridge, MA: MIT Press.
5. Tractinsky, N., A.S. Katz, and D. Ikar, What is beautiful is usable. Interacting with Computers, 2000. 13(2): p. 127-146.
6. Hassenzahl, M., The interplay of beauty, goodness and usability. Human-Computer Interaction, 2004. 19(4): p. 319-349.
7. Hassenzahl, M., The thing and I: understanding the relationship between user and product, in Funology: from usability to enjoyment, M. Blythe, et al., Editors. 2003, Kluwer: Dortrecht. p. 31-42.

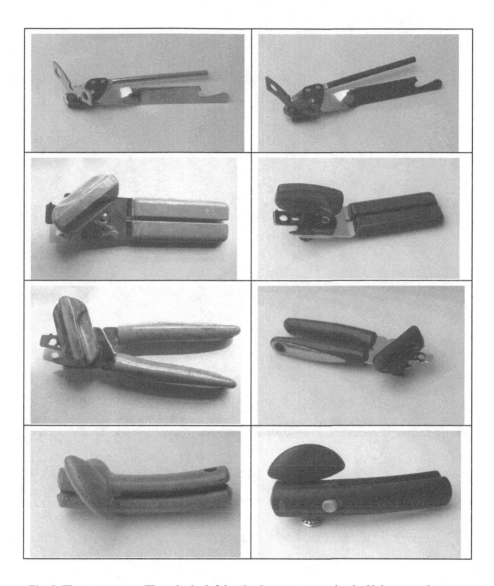

Fig. 2. The can openers. Those in the left hand column were seen by the Ugly group, those on the right by the Pretty group. The first in each column is model 1 and so on down to model 4. (see text for description). This figure is in colour. Please contact the authors if you only have access to a printed copy of the paper.

Exploring technology influences between home, work, school: implications for managing ubiquitous technologies in the home

Geraldine Fitzpatrick and Mark Stringer
Interact Lab, Department of Informatics, University of Sussex, UK

Abstract. Understanding current issues and experiences with technologies in the home, and the relationships with work and school in how technologies are managed in the home, can be useful for anticipating issues with next generation technologies. This paper contributes to this understanding through in-home studies with ten UK households. Case data is presented that both reinforces current understandings about access to expertise in the workplace and school, and presents new understandings that further unpack the ways in which the technology in the home influenced by work and school. We also discuss the more subtle ways in which technologies get into the home, and how they are managed and maintained through people's exposure to technologies, skills and expertise outside of the home. Given the increasing interest in ubiquitous technologies for the home, as played out in next generation home automation and home monitoring scenarios, we argue that such discussions are timely reminders, raising interesting questions about how these future technologies will come into the home and how people will gain the exposure and experience to help manage them.

1 Introduction

The home is increasingly becoming a site of interest as researchers look to understand, with a view to supporting, the practical accomplishment of home 'work' and home life e.g., [1, 2]. The home is also of growing interest for other fields such as ubiquitous computing where current advances in technology open up new possibilities for augmenting and supporting social life and work in the home. To this end, various studies have sought to explore home life in different ways, e.g., [3, 4, 5, 6, 7]. Many of these studies implicitly bound the limits of their concerns to the home as an entity in its own right or consider the occupants as consumers or as managers

Please use the following format when citing this chapter:

Fitzpatrick, G., Stringer, M., 2007, in IFIP International Federation for Information Processing, Volume 241, Home Informatics and Telematics: ICT for the Next Billion, eds. Venkatesh, A., Gonsalves, T., Monk, A., Buckner, K., (Boston: Springer), pp. 235-249.

of family life. Others explore the relationships between home and places such as work and school e.g., [8, 9, 10].

This paper contributes to this literature around home-oriented technologies by further unpacking the ways in which the home is situated within a network of influences and relationships between home and work and home and school. While these influences and relationships are clearly bi- directional, our particular focus here is on influences into the home, and on how people's experiences and expectations derived from their work/school lives can have a powerful if subtle effect on the kinds of technologies that are brought into their homes and how they are managed there.

We explore these issues through in-home studies with ten UK households. We argue that such discussions are timely reminders and pose interesting questions for future ubiquitous technologies in the home. This picks up on some themes of influences in home life, e.g., of Venkatesh [11] and Molotoch [12] who argue for a more general socio-historical overview to explain behaviours and technologies in the home. As the field of ubiquitous computing is maturing to a point where we can seriously start thinking (technically at least) about deploying distributed wireless sensor-based technologies in 'everyday' households, where will the influences and expertise and exposure come from that will enable the people in the home to acquire and manage these new technologies, given experiences with current technologies?

The paper is structured as follows: we first discuss related work in the area of domestic technology and the effect of technology on the interplay between home and work. We then give an account of our study of domestic technology use in 10 English homes and discuss our findings with respect to the influence of work on technology in the home. Finally we discuss the implications of these findings for next generation technologies in the home.

2 Related Work

While there is a diversity of work focusing on the home, here we look at the following strands relevant to the study of the relationships between home, work and technology: the work of home life, new technologies for the home, smart homes, and the role of work and school in relation to technology at home.

There is a growing body of literature drawing attention to the sociality of home life and to the practical accomplishment of home life as a legitimate form of work. Many of these studies are oriented towards possible technical support. The research focus tends to be similar to studies of the workplace, such as: the role of artifacts and spaces for the coordination of home life [13, 14, 15]; the flow of information around the home [6]; the way that routines are constructed as a means to achieve this work [6, 34]; and the negotiation of practices around technologies in the home [6]. This type of work can be seen as taking within-home life as its unit of analysis with an implicit focus on the 'core' occupants of the home, i.e., those who are part of the family or who would describe themselves as permanent residents, and on the coordinative and informational aspects of home life. Where technologies figure in the studies it is often to understand how they help regulate home life [13] or how their use is negotiated [6, 16].

Some research has moved to the development and deployment of prototype technologies for the home, often based on findings from the above studies. Communication in and out of the home is a common theme of this work [17, 18, 7]. Other work takes more of a 'ludic' perspective, as with Gaver et al's drift table [19]. Crabtree et al [20] also argue for a focus on the ludic aspects of home life. With the recent advances in pervasive technologies, including wireless sensor networks, there is growing interest in how to instrument home settings to automate aspects of the home, as per a 'smart home' scenario, e.g., [3, 21], and to monitor activities, often with a concern for the care and safety of older people in the home, e.g., [22]. Here the focus is much more on the home as a site for technology deployment to aid home management via automation or occupant management via activity monitoring.

However, while maturing, many of these technologies are still at early prototype stage. There are few examples of long-lived deployments in 'everyday homes' rather than purpose built smart homes. Often where everyday homes are used, there is still access to considerable expertise from the university or research lab undertaking the deployment e.g., [23]. Grinter et al's [5] findings about the work to make home networks work, where people with advanced expertise are involved, and our own studies of routine problems with current technologies in the home [24], suggest that there will be many practical issues to be solved for yet more advanced ubiquitous applications in the home.

Complementing the focus on the home as a unit of analysis, there is also considerable work looking at the interplay of work and home [25, 26], and indeed school and home, around technology use. For example, Venkatesh and Vitalari [27] contribute to the literature on teleworking/telecommuting by studying patterns of supplemental working at home often out of hours and at the weekends and that this was positively related to personal computer ownership and the portability of work. Sellen et al [9] refer to these as "crossover activities" and further point to the ways that home also permeates work as well as work permeating home. Others have looked at the relationships around technology between home and school. Downes [8], for example, looks at the different discourses around computer use in the home and school and the their implications for learning practices.

Work and school, along with informal peer networks, have been identified as key resources for learning about consumer technologies currently in the home. In particular the home is noted as being an important site of informal learning about technologies. Downes [8] notes the home as providing "opportunities for spectatorship and apprenticeship within the family [...] mainly available to children who had older brothers and sisters". Selwyn [10] also notes that "formal learning in the workplace also appeared to be inherently entwined with informal follow-up learning at work and home". He goes on to talk about "sustained informal learning networks" and "warm experts" that can include extended family and friends/social networks as well as co-workers who can act "as sources of help when using a computer at home".

The study that we will discuss here also finds many cases of such informal networks and use of "warm experts". However, the findings also suggest that there are much more subtle influences and diffusions from work into the home based on what people are familiar with, what skills they develop in the workplace and what skills they can access from the workplace. School provides yet another diffusion path. These result in a set of informal influences across work, school and home that are directly implicated in what technologies get brought into the home and how they are managed. Given the directions that technology research for the home is taking, it also raises interesting questions for where future influences and learnings will come from. We go on now to introduce the study and to review the findings around the influences of work/school on home technologies.

3   Study Overview – Participants and Methods

A series of in-home studies were undertaken as part of a larger research program to design novel ubiquitous applications for domestic environments. The goal of the studies was to establish a baseline understanding of the homes and people we wanted to design with and for. In the process we also wanted to gain a better understanding of the current practical issues surrounding everyday technologies. We have reported elsewhere on the routine troubles people have with everyday technologies and sensors in the home [24]. Here we focus on unpacking the influences and interdependencies created between home and work and home and school in terms of diffusion paths and exposure to technologies, skill development and expertise.

We recruited 19 people from 10 UK households, via mailing lists and connections of friends and colleagues, to participate in this study (see Table 1 for an overview of the households). Participants were remunerated £25 for their involvement. All the adult participants were middle class by English standards – they were professionals or worked in clerical roles in support of professionals and had a university education.

Table 1. Profile of participant households (Pseudonyms used)

House-hold	Primary occupants (Ages)	Adult professions
1. Megan & James	Couple, mid 30's, two children 6 and 8	Teacher, technology company director
2. Emily & Thomas	Couple, late 20's	Admin assistant, software developer
3. Chloe & Jack	Couple, late 50's	Admin assistant, teacher
4. Charlotte & Joshua	Couple, mid-30's, four children 3, 5, 10, 12	Human rights consultant, homemaker
5. Sophie & Daniel	Couple, mid 60's	Retired astronomer, homemaker
6. Lauren & Harry	Couple, late 30's, three children 8, 10, 14	Technology company director, homemaker
7. Lucy & Sam	Couple, in 60's	Retired engineer, homemaker
8. Greg & Jane	Couple, in 40's, 1 boy, 13	School assistant,

		charity worker
9. Gladys	Woman, in 60's	Retired clerk
10. Dora & Owen	Couple, in 30's two boys, 8 and 15	School assistant, software engineer

A study session with each household consisted of an in-home tour and interview with one or two of the adult family members (subsequent in-home design sessions were also held with participants but are beyond the scope of this paper to discuss). Each session lasted approximately 90 minutes and was conducted by two researchers and captured on video. A study protocol was developed focusing especially on the current relationship of participants to the technology in their homes. Participants were asked to give the interviewer a tour of the house and discuss the technology in each room. The participants were asked how each piece of technology came to be there, what it was used for, and if there were any problems or issues with it. (As it turned out, these tours are similar in approach to that used in other home studies [28, 29].) As interviews were informed by literature from other ethnographic studies on the home, e.g., [13], we also asked questions about areas, activities and artifacts that had been identified in these studies as potential candidates for digital augmentation. Analysis of the videos was conducted through transcription, repeated viewing and identification of recurring themes, using a grounded theory approach [30].

4. Work/school influences on technology into the home

We focus our discussions here on findings related to the effect that work (or indeed, its absence) and school have in deciding the kinds of technologies, practices and expertise that are present in the home and the networks of people involved in managing those technologies. These findings contribute further detail and cases to the growing understanding of technologies in the home and the influences between home, work and school [8, 9, 10, 25]. They also provide a timely basis to reflect on the implications of such influences for emerging ubiquitous technologies in the home. We present the findings in the following themes: technology paths into the home; influence of implicit external requirements; standards and expectations; work as a source of expertise and skills; and what happens when you don't work.

4.1 Technology paths into the home

Hindus [1] argues that one of the key differences between home and the workplace is that people are consumers not knowledge workers. While we certainly saw many examples of consumer-like behaviour across our participants in their choice of technologies for the home [24], i.e., making "purchases based on aesthetics, fashion and self-image" [1], work also created another set of factors in those choices, factors that are often not foregrounded in a 'consumer-driven' view. Hindus [1] also suggests that "the diffusion path for technology is from workplaces to home". While more recent studies suggest that there is also a diffusion path from the home to the workplaces, as with instant messaging (IM) [31], for the discussions here we focus on the paths into the home and how this worked out for the participants in our study.

In many cases, the diffusion path from work to home is based simply on familiarity. Often the work people did put them in contact with specific products which served to 'bias' or influence their own choices of technology. Problems can be created though when that familiarity isn't shared by others in the household. For example, Lauren's husband Harry ran his own company that installed wireless networks. Knowledge and enthusiasm for wireless networking had encouraged him to install an 802.11-based music system but Harry was the only person who could actually operate this, and it needed to be done from his work laptop. In another case, James ran his own mobile marketing company. He was therefore interested in having the latest 3G (third generation) mobile phone as his work handset and included a handset for his wife as part of the contract. Only after he had been using the handset for several months did he realize that 3G handsets actually performed poorly in an area of poor 3G coverage, as with where they lived, compared to a GSM handset. His wife Megan was not even aware that she had a 3G handset.

Familiarity was also sometimes associated with a perverse loyalty even when that loyalty created problems because of commitments to technologies that weren't actually performing as required. For example, Joshua worked as human rights consultant. He bought Acme [pseudonym] printers only because Acme was one of his clients, even though he had persistent problems with another of their products.

Joshua: I had to send it back to the factory and it had to be fixed. [Acme] Corp are one of my clients actually, so one of the reasons I buy their stuff, even though they're not doing very well at the moment, I sort of have a brand loyalty for the companies that I work with on the human rights front.

The above are examples of work-influenced consumer choices. People also had technologies in the home where they had little choice in selecting the technology because it was work-allocated. For example, the laptops in houses 3 & 8 were acquired or given to the person as part of their job.

Chloe: That laptop is Jack's work laptop... and also he's just discovered today that he might be able to get a computer under this new computers for teachers scheme, we might not even have to pay for it.

Greg: The laptop is a loan-stroke-purchase, well it's got a purchase option on it. It came as a result of me doing a university degree that was partially subsidized by [...] a government organization. And the deal is that I can have it for three years and then at the end [...] I've got the option to buy it.

Unsurprisingly, even though laptops and other technologies were acquired for work purposes, once in the home, they were often put to a range of uses by others and became a shared resource.

Greg: My son uses it [laptop]. He talks to his friends on MSN... he mainly uses it for social reasons, really. He does do some homework on it. My wife uses it for all sorts of different things: photography, letter writing, things like that. And I use it – the bulk of my university work is on it.

Influence of implicit external requirements
While some diffusion paths into the home were more explicit, either by individual influence and choice or by work allocation, others were more subtle, often by virtue

of implicit external expectations or to take advantage of opportunities for interactions between the home and work or school.

External bodies often set up priorities and requirements for certain technologies in the home but these were not formalized in some contract. Instead they were requirements implicitly entailed in the practical achievement of their work. These often served to set certain timeframes and standards for the technology and had financial implications in the provision of the technology and ongoing maintenance implications. In the following, for example, work and work-related education is cited as a reason for needing to have broadband installed:

Greg: We've just recently had broadband installed because… I have to look up research papers etc. I have to access, part of my course, is via the internet where we have virtual tutorials and seminars which I have to contribute to.

The interactive whiteboards at Megan's school have direct implications for how she prepares her lessons. Given that a lot of her preparation work happens at home, they also have implications for how she makes use of her personal technologies:

Megan: We do all our planning on computers, in school we've got interactive whiteboards. I'd often plan a lesson, and then take it, put it on a memory stick and then plug it into the laptop. It's a real laborious thing because I can't get my laptop to work with the interactive whiteboard for some reason.

Technology standards and expectations set at schools can create other implicit pressures about technology provision in the home and create home 'work' to acquire and maintain that technology in the home. While schools provide students with access to the technologies that they expect them to use, students will also want to work from home. Hence even though the school might not explicitly require every household to have a computer and internet connection, there is strong, albeit implicit, pressure to have them. Electronic homework submission is one example. Joshua and Charlotte's youngest daughter was expected to submit her latin homework by email, which she wanted to do from home once she had completed it. This class, with small numbers, was only possible because it could be taught across several schools using distributed computing technologies.

Work issues can also influence technology being brought into home life in other more subtle and indirect ways. The following examples are about technology choices being made to support the 'invisible' work of maintaining family relationships as a consequence of the time demands of work life. For example, Lucy cited other people's school and work schedules as a reason for wanting to use new communication technologies such as web cams. Lucy's son worked six days a week and so Lucy did not feel comfortable intruding on the scarce family time that her son had with his children. Instead she decided to use a webcam to enable her to still 'see' her grandchildren even if she couldn't physically visit them:

Lucy: Because now the [grand]children are at full time school and they're [twenty miles away] you're really sort of reliant on weekends or school holidays whereas I'd like to see them once a week and to be able actually to have a conversation and be able to see them rather than via the telephone.

Similarly James (house 1) cited the fact that he was regularly not home from work before his children went to bed as a reason for buying video-capable mobile phones for himself and his wife so that he could 'see' his children in the evenings.

Standards and expectations

Work was also a source of expectations for the basic standards of how technologies should work, also serving as drivers for upgrades in technologies. Chloe, for example, found that she could not put up with the poor performance of email from home over a dial-up connection because she was used to a well-supported fast email service at her workplace and now had a low tolerance level for poorly functioning services at home; this became one of their primary motivations for acquiring (their problematic) broadband.

Work influences on technology choices in the home can become problematic though when there are multiple often competing influences and 'standards'. This can particularly play out with software tools. One source of tension was the conflicting requirements of different home and work calendar systems, and the conflicting needs of being able to see across these calendars but also maintaining some separation between home and work. The other was when there were different systems that needed to interoperate. These were the case for Joshua. He worked with several different groups of people who all had different calendar systems and who all wanted to have networked systems:

Joshua: A big issue for me is I used to work for a company and they had a networked calendar system. I sort of went to computer-base calendar for appointments and I've kept that going although what I've never done is network that with different people that I work with all round the world. Although there's a lot of pressure on me from two of the organizations that I work with to network with their calendars.

Int.: So why is it an issue? You don't want to network with their calendars?

Joshua: [Laughs] Well, there's an element of that. And also, they have different systems. One company that I partly own has a web-based system...at the moment I still can't synchronize that with outlook. So that's an issue. The other people in Sweden would like me to do that [synchronize appointments in outlook] but I need to upgrade – I think – to Microsoft Office Professional to do that and I also have to open an MSN relationship with them,. But then I'm also slightly worried about them seeing my private calendar because it's got stuff on that's not to do with them, basically. That's an issue.

4.2 Work as a source of expertise and skills

Perhaps even more important than work/school being influential in the choices of certain artifacts being in the home is the influence of work and school on the management and support of technology in the home by virtue of exposure to technologies in these settings. This plays out both in the skills that people in the home have as a result of their work, or the skills they are able to access in the workplace - Selwyn's 'warm experts' [10].

As also noted by Grinter et al [5], those people who had experience of working with technology as part of their jobs were often expected, by default, to be the one who 'knows how' to do the trouble shooting and management of technology in the home. In house 8 it was Greg's employment that resulted in the laptop being brought into the home but it was his wife, whose job was the distribution and maintenance of technologies such as laptops and projectors for a local charity, who was expected to do the majority of maintenance of the laptop, along with their teenage son.

Greg: I'm not that technically minded, my wife's much more technically minded because she works much more on a daily basis with computers than I do, it's part of her job. So technical stuff tends to be sorted out by her.[...] I tend to use it specifically for what I'm doing... I think it's the amount of exposure, both my son and my wife are much more technologically minded than I am because they're both exposed to it a lot more than I am in my job and they both need it more in their jobs and schooling that I do in my job. So it falls – that's the order, Jane deals with most difficulties, my son has got very good insight into it and I just sit and listen basically [laughs].

Some of the other ways that workplace skills and knowledge play out in the home can be downright quirky. In house 2 Thomas has added a cardboard flap to the central heating control (as shown in Figure 1) to discourage his partner Emily from pressing the button that changes the central heating program. His idea to use the flap came from his experience working in the aviation industry:

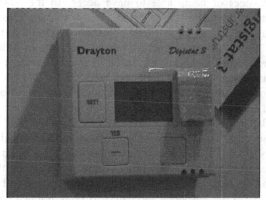

Fig. 1. Heating control modified using principles from aircraft cockpit design

Thomas: This is my safety interlock. I quite like this feature. It's borrowed from the aviation industry where in cockpits in flight simulators and in aircraft they have gates to stop pilots accidentally flicking switches. And the idea is something like "Dump All the fuel" is obviously quite a last measure to take so that will have a gate round it and what I found is that Emily was controlling – [to Emily] you don't mind me saying this? Was controlling the central heating by switching the mode from the standard five times throughout the day into night setting or day setting. So what I did was, rather than just tape over it I put this cardboard flap here so that if she wanted to push that button she had to consciously lift that up. And the act of doing so makes her think – I think – that actually maybe I'd be better off pressing the temperature button.

Emily: Yeah – that has stopped me pressing that button.

Even when the people in the home did not have the skills themselves, work was still often used as a source of exposure to others with expertise. We saw numerous examples of people accessing informal work networks to help them with home problems. For example, Chloe frequently asked her technically-savvy work colleagues for help though sometimes in vain as was the case when they tried unsuccessfully to fix the problems with her broadband.

Family and friends were other sources of help for managing technology in the home. Here again, work was a factor in who they asked because the people they targeted were people who tended to have the necessary skills by virtue of their work or school experiences. For example, Sam who was retired asked his brother who was still working for help trying to get his webcam to work. Rode et al [16] discuss this in terms of a 'trade' where those who do not have these technical skills will require social skills in order to trade with those members of the family who do have the technical skills. This might not be a bad thing, as access to technical support from family and friends also functions as a kind of gift exchange and social 'glue' [32].

When you don't work – not 'keeping up'
All of the above point to the importance of 'exposure' in the workplace or at school for acquiring skills and experiences or being able to have access to the 'warm experts' with the skills. This raises the interesting question then of what happens if you don't work and don't have access to experiences or experienced others for keeping up with technologies. The following examples illustrate the ways in which retirement and staying at home to care for children can result in a certain amount of isolation from technical expertise that is not easily redressed.

At a very basic level, we can see the impact of a lack of a diffusion path from work to home - the two retired couples were the only households in the study not to have a wireless network and a laptop in the home.

However, the diffusion from work into the home isn't just about the technologies per se but also about the ability to keep up to date. Daniel retired five years ago and Sophie has been a homemaker for 20 years. Even though there was a PC in the house, Sophie did not know how to use it: "I'm completely ignorant, I'm ashamed to say"; she still made extensive use of the telephone and letters to keep in touch with people rather than email or IM. Her husband Daniel, a retired astronomer, was now faced with the problem that, in retirement, he no longer had access to technical support for the non-standard partitioning of his home PC.

Daniel: What else do I use it [PC] for? Well, I used to use it for my work, when I first retired, it was partitioned with a linux section, with all my programs that I used to use, which were put on computer for me. In fact that's going to be a crisis for me now because I have to have that done specially by somebody I know, because the computer people [at the local computer store] didn't know anything about linux or partitioning it for linux.

Lucy and Sam are also both retired, and found that they relied on either (expensive) dedicated professionals or Sam's brother to provide technical support:

Sam: He [brother] still works and he's a bit more up on the technology 'cos I retired... ten years ago it left me all behind. I had an old MSDos computer, so I'm learning windows again and just coming up to speed. And coming up to where I was ten years ago I suppose.

This wasn't just an issue for retired people. As a full-time mother/homemaker Charlotte felt that she was faced with the task of assessing the risks of the new technologies that her daughters were getting familiar with at school but was aware that she was struggling to keep track of the latest developments in internet communication technologies such as chat programs. This particularly became an issue when the older daughter, Jenny, setup a personal website.

Joshua: The thing that really worried us was the website...there's a picture of our twelve-year-old daughter with you know, images that she's found on the website but you know "Sexy babe" and all these other things and it's really quite – whoa! Does she know what she's doing here?

Similar to people who are retired, Charlotte didn't have access to a professional workplace to gain exposure to such technologies; for her it was her children who often performed this role.

Charlotte: It's just that MSN is the fashion at her age – talking on there and setting up your own website...she's our oldest so we don't know how new this is. I'd never heard of MSN.

Even though Joshua worked outside the home and was the one who eventually addressed the issue of the website, he was also aware that they didn't really know how to deal with it. In the end, Charlotte and Joshua could only manage to take down the offending website with the help of their younger daughter, using her expertise gained from friends at school to access the website, and then leaving a warning message pretending that it had come from the site administrator.

Scenarios such as this create interesting tensions in families. As has been discussed by Grinter and Eldridge [33], it is the work of teenagers (or as in the case we discuss here, pre-teenagers) to maintain their social-life and in support of that to understand the in-vogue methods of communication. However, parents also see it as a fundamental part of the work of parenting to restrict access to technologies that they feel produce a negative effect on their children [6]. Both of these kinds of 'work' can come into conflict and can shift the balance of power between parents and children when children have more 'know-how' surrounding the technology and parents are learning from their children. If parents haven't been able to gain the knowledge in advance from another source (such as their own workplace), they are always playing 'catch-up' and often resorting to work-around solutions.

5. Discussion

The studies just discussed build on others' work about the diffusion path into the home [1] and indeed, while beyond the scope of this study to report, complement work about the diffusion path from the home to work [31]. Through illustrative examples, we have discussed a range of different ways in which the technological landscape of work and school permeate and influence the technological landscape of the home, both in terms of how technologies get into the home and how technologies are managed once in the home. While the general principle of the influences between home and work and home and school is not new, the studies here provide further data for how these play out and also point to more nuanced and subtle ways that exposure to work/school can influence technologies in the home.

It is interesting to reflect here on the role of recent technology advances around portable mobile technologies and wireless networks as enablers of these changing relationships and blurring boundaries. When computers are fixed to an office desktop location, the sphere of influence is more likely to be limited to the mobility of people rather than technology, e.g., through the skills and know-how people bring home. Now the technology can also be carried between home and work and others at home can use it directly, developing their skills and experiences with new types of technology. The easy availability of networking also sets up implicit requirements that people should be able to connect out to work/school from home with the inherent requirements for new technologies to do this.

These new capabilities create implicit but very real 'invisible work' demands (involving time, money and skill) on people in the home because of decisions being made in workplaces or schools. If you want your child to be able to submit homework electronically or do research on the web, there is the invisible work, and the financial commitment, to purchase, install and maintain a working technology environment; the equivalent technical set-up some years ago in an office environment would have had people with specialized skills to do this work. In the home, there is no designated IT department and it becomes a similar story to that of "more work for mother" [34] where increasing technological sophistication perversely can result in more not less work: implicit, unaccounted and highly skilled work for which there is no formal training or support structure.

More generally though, and with a view to future trends, the technologies in the homes we have discussed are relatively stable consumer technologies and services: PCs, laptops, calendar systems, chat tools, email, websites, webcams, broadband networks. Further they are generic technologies, equally 'at home' in the office as well in domestic environments. While they are adaptable enough to be put to very different purposes in the different settings, the core aspects of the technologies enable skills and experiences to be transferred between settings.

What happens then when we start to look at the next generation of proposed technologies for the home? If we take the visions of the 'home of the future' seriously, as characterized by some of the 'smart home' work [35] as well as some of the 'aging in place' work [22], homes will be places with hundreds of sensors, wireless networks, and interacting devices and displays.

Many of these home applications, while using emerging toolkits and components [36], are nonetheless relatively bespoke for the particular domain problem, e.g., to monitor activities of daily living of an older person with cognitive impairment [22] or to enable remote interactions with the appliances of the home [23]. Where will people gain the exposure to, and experience with, similar technologies to help them choose and manage these technologies in their homes? Apart from manufacturing settings that make use of technologies such as RFID etc, it isn't clear that there will there be similar applications of the same ubiquitous technologies in the workplace as an avenue for exposure and learning. To date very little ubiquitous computing research has been targeted at workplaces. Instead, home and public spaces have been the settings of choice. Further, many applications have more ludic and playful purposes than those one would expect to be useful in a workplace. Will there be analogous applications of ubiquitous computing in the workplace, as has happened for example with the move of chat from home to work settings? And will such applications become 'ubiquitous' enough that there is critical mass of skills and expertise among 'warm experts' [10] to call upon or will these be niche areas?

Early explorations show that schools rather than workplaces may well be the first places that people have exposure to, and can gain experience with, next generation ubiquitous technologies. The Ambient Wood [37] and Chawton House [38] projects, for example, make use of ubiquitous ensembles of mobile wireless networks, sensors and handheld devices for novel interactive learning experiences in outdoor environments and so it is easy to imagine that children will have greater familiarity with these technologies. As with the case of Charlotte and Joshua's website problem, this may well exacerbate shifts in know-how and control within families.

6. Conclusion

Understanding current experiences with technologies in the home, and the relationships between home and work and home and school, can be useful for anticipating issues with next generation technologies. This paper has contributed to this understanding by presenting case-based data that both reinforces current understandings about access to expertise in the workplace and school, as well as further unpacking the ways in which the home is situated within a network of influences and relationships with work and school. The ubiquity of experiences with common consumer technologies between work, school and home provides a foundation for influences to move between work and school into the home. These influences can be quite explicit in terms of what technologies people buy or have use of but can also be more subtle in terms of the expectations people have or the implicit requirements set up by the capabilities of technologies and the different ways that work and school lives integrate with home life.

Given the increasing interest in ubiquitous and tangible technologies for the home, as played out in next generation home automation and home monitoring scenarios, interesting questions arise about how future ubiquitous technologies will come into the home and how people will gain the exposure and experience to help them manage these technologies in the home. Where will the future influences and learnings come from? We suggest that future prototype deployments of ubiquitous technologies in 'everyday' homes need to take these questions as part of the research agenda so that such deployments are not just about whether a certain application is acceptable in that setting but what are the skills and resources required to manage and maintain that application in the home and where will these come from.

Acknowledgements

We would like to thank the participants in the study and the anonymous reviewers for helpful comments. This work was funded by the UK EPSRC through the Equator IRC Project (EPSRC GR/N15986/01).

References

1. D. Hindus, The Importance of Homes in Technology Research, *Proceedings of CoBuild '99*, (October 1999), pp 199-207.
2. P. Tolmie, J. Pycock, T. Diggins, A. MacLean, and A. Karsenty, Ubiquity: Unremarkable computing. *Proceedings of CHI 2002*, (Minneapolis, ACM Press 2002), pp. 399 - 406.
3. F. Aldrich, Smart Homes: Past, Present and Future in: *Inside the Smart Home*, edited by R. Harper (Springer-Verlag, London, 2003)
4. A. Crabtree, T. Hemmings and J Mariani, Informing the Design of Calendar Systems for Domestic Use, *Proceedings of ECSCW'03*, (Helsinki, Finland: Kluwer, 2003)
5. R. E. Grinter, W. K. Edwards, M. Newman, and N. Ducheneaut, The work to make the home network work, *Proceedings of ECSCW'05* (Paris, Springer-Verlag, 2005) pp. 97-119.
6. J. O'Brien, T. Rodden, M. Rouncefield, and J. Hughes, At home with the technology: an ethnographic study of a set-top-box trial, *ACM Trans on Computer Human Interactions* **6**(3), 282-308 (1999).
7. K. O'Hara, R. Harper, A. Unger, J. Wilkes, B. Sharpe and M. Jansen, TxtBoard: from text-to-person to text-to-home, *CHI '05 Extended Abstracts on Human Factors in Computing Systems* (Portland, OR, ACM Press, 2005) pp. 1705-1708.
8. T. Downes, Blending play, practice and performance: children's use of the computer at home, *Journal of Educational Enquiry*, **3**(2), 21-34 (2002).
9. A. Sellen, J. Hyams and R. Eardley, The everyday problems of working parents: Implications for new technologies, Hewlett-Packard Labs Technical Report HPL-2004-37. (March 13, 2007) http://research.microsoft.com/~asellen/publications/everyday%20problems%2004.pdf
10. N. Selwyn, The Social Processes of Learning to Use Computers, *Social Science Computer Review* **23**(1) 122-135 (2005).
11. A. Venkatesh, Computers and Other Interactive Technologies for the Home, *Communications of the ACM*, **39**(12), 47-54 (1996).
12. H. Molotch, *Where Stuff Comes From: How Toasters, Toilets, Cars, Computers and Many Other Things Come to Be as They Are*, (Routledge, New York, 2003).
13. A. Crabtree, T. Rodden, T. Hemmings and S. Benford, Finding a Place for UbiComp in the Home, *Proceedings of Ubiquitous Computing*, (Seattle, Springer, 2003) pp. 208-226.
14. L. Swan and A. S. Taylor, Notes on Fridge Doors, *CHI '05 Extended Abstracts on Human Factors in Computing Systems*, (Portland, OR, ACM Press, 2003), pp. 1813-1816.
15. A. S. Taylor and L. Swan, List making in the home, *Proceedings of CSCW '04*, (Chicago, IL, ACM Press, 2004), pp. 542-545.
16. J. A. Rode, E. F. Toye and A. F. Blackwell The Domestic Economy: a Broader Unit of Analysis for End User Programming, *CHI '05 Extended Abstracts on Human Factors in Computing Systems* (Portland, OR, ACM Press, 2005), (Portland, OR, ACM Press, 2005), pp 1757 – 1760.
17. J. D. Herbsleb, D. L. Atkins, D. G. Boyer, M. Handel, and T. A. Finholt, I Think, therefore IM: Introducing instant messaging and chat in the workplace, *Proceedings of CHI 2002*, (Minneapolis, ACM Press, 2002), pp 171-178.
18. H, Hutchinson, W. Mackay, W. Westerlund, B. B. Bederson, A. Druin, C. Plaisant, M. Beaudouin-Lafon, S. Conversy, H. Evans, H. Hansen, N. Roussel, and B. Eiderbäck, Technology Probes: Inspiring Design for and with Families, *Proceedings of CHI '03*, (ACM Press, New York, NY, 2003), pp 17-24.
19. W. Gaver, J. Bowers, A. Boucher, H. Gellerson, S. Pennington, A. Schmidt, A. Steed, N. Villars and B. Walker, The drift table: designing for ludic engagement, *Proceedings of CHI '04 extended abstracts*, (Vienna, Austria, ACM Press, 2004), pp 885-900.

20. A. Crabtree, T. Rodden, and S. Benford, Moving with the Times: IT Research and the Boundaries of CSCW, *Computer Supported Cooperative Work,* **14**, (2005) 217-251.
21. S. Helal, W. Mann, H. El-Zabadani, J. King, Y. Kaddoura, and E. Jansen, The Gator Tech Smart House: A Programmable Pervasive Space, *Computer*, **38**(3), 50-60 (2005).
22. E. M. Tapia, S. Intille, and K. Larson, Activity Recognition in the Home Setting Using Simple and Ubiquitous Sensors, *Proceedings of PERVASIVE 2004*, Vol. LNCS 3001, (Berlin Heidelberg: Springer-Verlag, 2004), pp. 158-175.
23. M. Mozer, The Neural network house: An environment that adapts to its inhabitants. In Intelligent Environments, *Papers from the 1998 AAAI Spring Symposium,* number Technical Report SS-98-92 ,(AAAI, AAAI Press, 1998) pp. 110-114.
24. M. Stringer, G. Fitzpatrick, and E. Harris, Lessons for the Future: Experiences with the Installation and Use of Today's Domestic Sensors and Technologies, *Proceedings of Pervasive 2006,* (Dublin, Springer-Verlag, 2006) pp. 383-399
25. C. Salazar, Building boundaries and negotiating work at home, *Proceedings of GROUP 2001,* (Boulder CO, ACM Press, 2001), pp 162-170.
26. C. Nippert-Eng, *Home and Work: Negotiating Boundaries through Everyday Life*, (Chicago, University of Chicago Press, 1996).
27. L. Baillie, and D. Benyon, Investigating ubiquitous computing in the home, *Proceedings of 1st Equator Workshop on Ubiquitous Computing in Domestic Environments,* (Nottingham UK, 2001); http://www.mrl.nott.ac.uk/~axc/equator_workshop/Baillie.pdf (accessed March 13th 2007).
28. A. Venkatesh, and N. Vitalari, Emerging distributed work arrangement: An investigation of computer supplemental work at home, *Management Science,* **38**(12), 1687-1706 (1992).
29. M. Mateas, T. Salvador, J. Scholtz, and D. Sorensen, Engineering Ethnography in the Home, *Proceedings of CHI'96,* (Vancouver, Canada, ACM Press, 1996), pp. 283-284.
30. B. Glaser, and A. Strauss, *The Discovery of Grounded Theory,* (Aldine, Chicago, 1967).
31. J. D. Herbsleb, D. L. Atkins, D. G. Boyer, M. Handel, and T. A. Finholt, Introducing Instant Messaging and Chat in the Workplace, *Proceedings of CHI'02,* (Minneapolis, USA, ACM Press, New York, NY, 2002) pp. 171-178.
32. A. Woodruff, and S. Mainwaring, Everyday Practices in Great Rooms, *Ubicomp 2005 Workshop: Situating Ubiquitous Computing in Everyday Life; Bridging the Social and Technical Divide*; http://filebox.vt.edu/users/mae/ubicomp2005/woodruff_ubicomp05.pdf (accessed 13th March 2007).
33. R.E. Grinter, and M. Eldridge, y do tngrs luv 2 txt msg? *Proceedings of ECSCW'01,* (Bonn, Germany, Kluwer Academic Publishers, 2001), pp. 219-238.
34. R. S. Cowan, *More Work for Mother*, (Free Association Books, London, 1989).
35. S. S. Intille, K. Larson, J. S. Beaudin, J. Nawyn, Munguia E. Tapia, and P. Kaushik, A Living Laboratory for the Design and Evaluation of Ubiquitous Computing Technologies, *CHI '05 Extended Abstracts on Human Factors in Computing Systems*, (New York, NY: ACM Press, 2005), pp 1941-1944.
36. T. Rodden, A. Crabtree, T. Hemmings, B. Koleva, J. Humble, K-P. Åkesson and P. Hansson, Between the Dazzle of a New Building and its Eventual Corpse: Assembling the Ubiquitous Home, *Proceeding DIS2004,* (Cambridge MA, ACM Press, 2004) pp. 71-80.
37. Y. Rogers, S. Price, C. Randell, et al. Ubi-Learning Integrates Indoor and Outdoor Experiences. *Communications of the ACM*, 48(1), 55-59 (2005).
38 J. Halloran, E. Hornecker, G. Fitzpatrick, M. Weal, D. Millard, D. Michaelides, D. Cruickshank, and D. De Roure. The literacy fieldtrip: using UbiComp to support children's creative writing, *Proceedings of Interaction Design for Children '06,* (Tampere Finland, ACM Press, 2006), pp.17-24.

Designing for Co-located Social media use in the home using the CASOME infrastructure

Marianne Graves Petersen[1], Martin Ludvigsen[2], Kaj Grønbæk[1] and Kaspar Rosengreen Nielsen[1]

1 Center for Interactive Spaces, Department of Computer Science, University of Aarhus, Denmark

2 Center for Interactive spaces, Aarhus School of Architecture Denmark

Abstract. . A range of research has pointed to empirical studies of the use of domestic materials as a useful insight when designing future interactive systems for homes. In this paper we describe how we designed a system from the basis of lessons from such studies. Our system applies the CASOME infrastructure (context-aware interactive media platform for social computing in the home) to construct a system supporting distributed and collaborative handling of digital materials in a domestic context. It contains a collective platform for handling digital materials in the home and also contains a range of connected interactive surfaces supporting the flow of digital materials around the physical home. We discuss applications and use scenarios of the system, and finally, we present experiences from lab and field tests of the system. The main contribution of the paper is that it illustrates how insights from empirical studies can be realized in a concrete system design, and it highlights how co-located, connected and social media use is an area which needs further exploration in concrete systems design.

1 Introduction

Currently, there is an ongoing process of massive digitization of domestic materials, e.g. pictures, movies, recipes, news, bank papers, messages etc. A range of research have pointed to the need to learn from the nature of the home in the design of future interactive applications for the home [1, 2, 3]. The argument is that in the transfer from physical to digital materials, we need to learn from the inherent valuable qualities of physical materials. What is particularly striking about the use of physical materials in the home is their widely distributed character and how the social organization happens through the household members' interactions with a host of

Please use the following format when citing this chapter:

Petersen, M. G., Ludvigsen, M., Grønbæk, K., Nielsen, K. R., 2007, in IFIP International Federation for Information Processing, Volume 241, Home Informatics and Telematics: ICT for the Next Billion, eds. Venkatesh, A., Gonsalves, T., Monk, A., Buckner, K., (Boston: Springer), pp. 251-267.

materials distributed around the home [4]. This is in marked contrast to the limited number of interactive displays typically available in homes. Accordingly, Crabtree and colleagues have raised the need for working with networks of ecologically distributed displays in the home [ibid].

In this paper, we describe how we have worked from the body of empirical research on use of domestic materials to inform the design of a future interactive media system for the home. We describe the design of the system and the rationales behind, and how in particular, existing research and systems have led us to focus on designing for co-located and social media use in the home. Intentionally, the system supports a family in integrating digital media in daily, informal interactions in the home. Designing the system has been a process of negotiating insights from empirical studies with technological possibilities. Finally, we report our experiences from lab and field tests of the system, which involved four interactive displays providing various means of interaction

2   Empirical Studies of Domestic ICT Challenges

Taylor et al recommend to artfully combining heterogeneous displays in the home [3]. Similarly, Crabtree and colleagues have raised the need for working with networks of ecologically distributed displays in the home [4]. They develop a taxonomy for places for communication in the household including 'Ecological Habitats', 'Activity Centers', and 'Coordinate Displays' [ibid]. Ecological habitats are places where communication media live and where residents go in order to locate particular resources. Activity centers are places, where media are actively produced and consumed and where information is transformed. Coordinate Displays are places where media are displayed and made available to residents to coordinate their activities. However, until now there has been little research into how these specific lessons can inspire concrete design solutions for future interactive homes. One of the challenges of concretizing these concepts is to design the appropriate means of interaction for the different situations and areas of the home. With physical materials, as e.g. Crabtree et al have studied [ibid], the possible means for interaction is given per se. However, when moving to digital materials, the interaction needs to be designed explicitly and carefully. Thus an ecology of interaction must be designed.

Recently, researchers have pointed to the potential in supporting social experiences in the form of co-experiences [5] and shared experiences in the home around for instance photo collections [1]. Places of the home, where people typically gather, e.g. sofas and tables have also been identified as interesting sites for ubiquitous computing for the home [4]. However, few interfaces and infrastructures support collaborative and social experiences around digital materials in the home. One exception though is a recent interest in interactive tables due to their qualities in terms of supporting face-to-face collaboration and coordination [6]. This is a really interesting development, as the physical setting of a table presents unique opportunities for supporting collaborative activities among co-located users, in a way which integrates well with the existing physical furniture of the home. However, as discussed earlier, there is also a need to consider how an interactive table is linked to other devices in the home in an artful way [3], and with few exceptions, interactive tables are developed as stand-alone systems, and their relations to other displays are not considered.

Moreover, a strand of research has looked into the different values which underlie design of systems for the home [2]. Different people value different qualities and we also see that clearly different systems and infrastructures give priority to different values. E.g. range of visions for future home life and actual systems and infrastructure value individual power and control [7,8], whereas few support social experiences in the home. But this is an issue which is rarely discussed explicitly [9].

With our design, we wish to point to the need for designing for social experiences around digital materials in the home, and for exploring how the insights from the ethnographic research can inspire concrete future designs for the home. This work is one attempt to concretize these insights into a system.

2.1 Recommendations from empirical studies

To summarize, we have set out to develop a Domestic Media System which realizes the recommendations from empirical studies:

- Combining and linking heterogeneous devices
- Designing activity centers supporting production, manipulation, and organization of household media clips
- Designing coordinate displays which support for coordination of activities and presence
- Designing ecological habitat, that is means for people to locate resources
- Social sharing of media amongst co-located users in a home
- Linking media clips to specific places in the home
- Designing Interaction experiences tailored to place and context

In the following section we will describe how our system realizes these recommendations.

3 The CASOME enabled home

3.1 CASOME Infrastructure

The infrastructure depicted in **Figure 1** connects a number of heterogeneous media surfaces through tailoring of the application layer components.

The applications from the CASOME Application layer can be tailored to specific configurations as discussed below. For instance a MediaTable typically runs the Organizer application as the default interface, and various MediaDisplays may run either VideoPlayer or ImageViewer as the default interface. The instance we developed contains four specializations of this interface. These are MediaTable, MediaDisplay, MediaBoard, and MediaMobile.

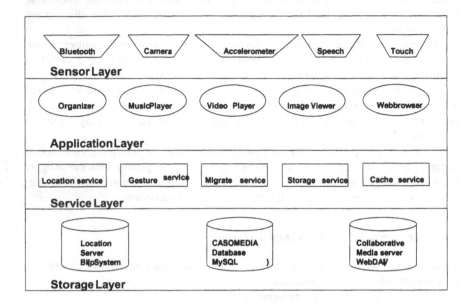

Figure 1: CASOME infrastructure

To give a flavor of the potential of the system, we provide a scenario of use before we move on to describe the concrete instances in turn.

Scenario of use

    Sarah and Peter are about to plan their family's summer holiday. They sit down at the MediaTable and start to browse for different possibilities. Sarah is most interested in going to a city having cultural experiences and Peter is more interested in hiking. They each find stuff and show to the other negotiating where they should go. They pool all the materials into a collection. After an hour Sarah needs to leave for a meeting, she pushes a picture from London to the ceiling display in their bedroom to remind Peter about her preferences as he goes to sleep a little later. Peter continues to browse and he finds a great picture of a hiking landscape and sends this to the display in the hallway for Sarah to see as soon as she comes home from the meeting. Meanwhile their daughter Kathrin comes home and sees the pictures and asks her father what that is about. They sit down together and browse for more information, including some Scottish music which they have much fun listening go. They decide to meet up the next evening all 3 of them to discuss and make more plans around their holiday.

    Adopting a metaphor well-known in a domestic context, the system has a chest of drawers. The left-most part of the screen in **Figure 2** shows the contents of the currently open drawer. Drawers are opened through clicking the knobs in the vertical bar. The series of portraits indicate personal drawers. Each family member has a drawer and the family may have a shared one. The series of letters TV, B, K are references to places in the home, in this case the TV in the living room, the interactive table, and the display in the kitchen respectively. Each place is also associated with a drawer. In the grey area materials can be manipulated, copied, deleted, played and organized into collections. In the rightmost vertical bar it is possible to shift between players where materials are played in full screen and an organizer mode where materials can be manipulated, as can be seen in **Figure 3**. Technically, all materials are stored on a home-server and only references to materials are manipulated.

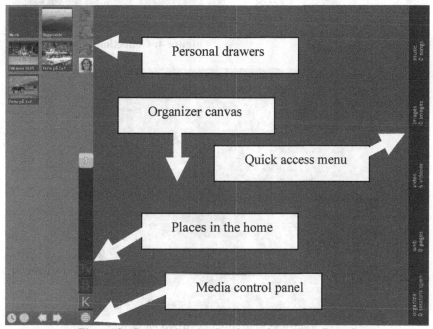

Figure 2: Generic Media Surfaces Organizer Interface.

Inspired by empirical research [3], we use collections as the prime means for organizing materials. Collections may hold heterogeneous materials. In our current implementation this includes pictures, movies, music and websites. Exploiting the advantages of digital materials there are different modes of viewing the contents of the collections. They can be sorted by name, by date but also notably by their persistent spatial position within the collection as they were originally placed herein. In this way, we make it possible to organize collections spatially whenever this is the most appropriate given the specific contents and purpose. **Figure 4** and **Figure 5** illustrate how the same materials can be viewed sorted by date in a grid, and clustered in persistent piles as they are formed by users.

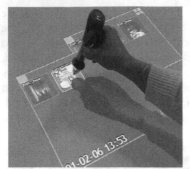

Figure 3: Managing contents of collections

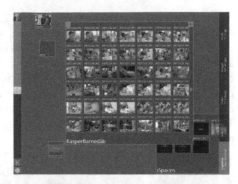

Figure 4: Collection sorted by date

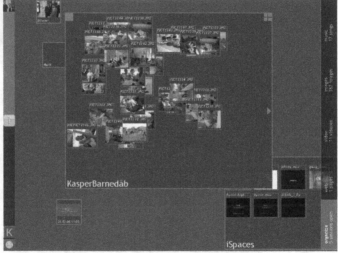

Figure 5: Spatially organized collection

The generic Connected Media Surfaces interface is instantiated in a number of different forms in order to reflect the nature of the different places of the home. This is to some extent inspired by the work of Crabtree et al. [4]. We explored the taxonomy of ecological habitats, activity centers, and coordinate displays to shape the forms of socially organized production and consumption of communication media in the home. Using the same graphical interface across different platforms we design for recognition at the same time as we provide different types of displays. In the following the different instances of MediaSurfaces we have developed are described and motivated.

3.2 MediaTable

At our interactive MediaTable, the generic interface in **Figure 2** is made available on an interactive table top as illustrated in **Figure 5**. The current design consists of a top projected screen with Mimio [10] pen interaction, or in a newer version with true multiuser interaction using a multilight tracker technology [11], however the latter were not the implementation we evaluated as reported in section 4. We envision the table to be placed in common rooms, and preferably at the dining table itself.

Figure 6: The MultiLightTracker [11] technique in use on a MediaTable

The table holds characteristics of all three types of displays depicted by Crabtree et al [4]. It is the site of locating information (ecological habitat), i.e. materials can be taken out of the different drawers and put elsewhere. It is the site of collaboratively producing and manipulating materials (activity centre), and finally it works as a coordinate display in that materials can be left persistently on the surface for other family members to view.

A key issue in designing interactive tables is that of the orientation of the materials on the table [6, 12]. At the MediaTable we provide support for manual orientation. In this way we wish to support easy and manual transitions, not so much between different modes of viewing materials as in e.g. [13], but rather to support for easy transitions in group sizes and positions as we expect this to be a characteristic of the use of a domestic interactive table.

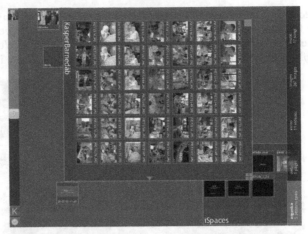

Figure 7: Materials oriented towards left side of screen

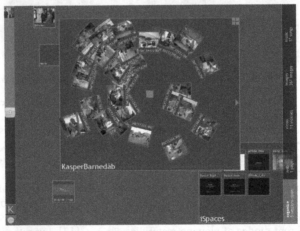

Figure 8: Materials oriented in a circular display for equal accessibility from all sides.

In homes, people come and go and continuously leave in social situations unlike e.g. planned meetings in workplaces where a fixed number of participants gather around a table to solve a task. **Figure 7** and **Figure 8** illustrates how the anchor, i.e. the small rectangle in the top right corner of the collection in **Figure 7** is the key to shift between different orientations. Thus **Figure 8** is established from **Figure 7** though simply dragging the anchor to the center of the collection. Equivalently, placing the anchor in the top left corner results in the orientation depicted in **Figure 4**.

3.3 MediaDisplays

We developed the form of MediaDisplays to support the casual viewing and browsing of information materials throughout the home. Thus this kind of display is more in the form of an ecological habitat [4]. Ecological habitat being places where communication media live and where residents go in order to locate particular resources. At MediaDisplays media collections can be browsed using an eMote, which is a gesture-based remote control. Flipping to the sides with the remote supports flicking through a pile of materials currently associated with the place of the display. The remote control further enables pick and drop of materials between displays. Thus a movie, piece of music, web site etc. can at any time be picked up from a display with a gesture and subsequently dropped on another display with a gesture. Depending on the specific placement of the display in the concrete home, MediaDisplays may also work as coordinate displays. E.g. a display at the entrance would in many cases be a central place for communicating coordinate messages between family members [ibid].

Figure 9: Gesture-based interaction at a MediaDisplay

In our current design of MediaDisplay we have adopted a minimal mode of interaction supporting flick trough materials and pick and drop materials. We envision a range of MediaDisplays to be distributed around the home in order to make the digital more prominent throughout the home inspired by the rich distribution of current physical materials.

3.4 MediaBoard

As opposed to MediaDisplays, which are placed around the home showing images or other types of content and interacted with at a distance, the MediaBoard is placed in the kitchen and has other forms of interaction associated with it. The Collective

Media Surfaces system is used through a touch interface for the detailed manipulation of collections and through a speech interface for changing website or song or for bringing up the recipe that you need for tonight's dinner party. Speech interaction in the kitchen is motivated by situations of cooking where the hands are busy with other things, and possibly filthy and wet.

MediaBoards have the same generic interface as on the other surfaces, and as was the case with the MediaTable, the MediaBoard is a place for organizing and directly manipulating collections of materials, i.e. an activity centre. The MediaBoard is placed within reach in a place where we assume that a closer and more detailed interaction form is preferable.

One might argue that the MediaDisplay and the MediaBoards are the same thing, but the main difference is how they are placed in their immediate surroundings and how the are presented to the users. MediaBoards are placed within reach and in places where users would need some of the abilities that e.g. the browser interface and the organizer present. Therefore the MediaBoards support and create a very different opportunity for interaction than the MediaDisplays.

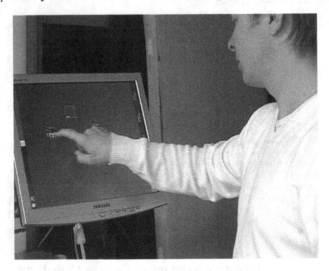

Figure 10: MediaBoard with touch interface

3.5 MediaMobiles

The last part of our interactive home system is the integration of the mobile phones of the family into the system. Phones with bluetooth connectivity and camera can upload images onto a Table or Board running CASOME applications. Each media surface is equipped with a bluetooth receiver and with the mobile phone each member of the family or anyone coming for a visit can upload images or films to the surface they are closest to. This opens the entire media infrastructure to several levels of use. As with the physical home people can be invited and participate in interaction and the distinction between participants, users and non-users is open and dynamic as opposed to strictly discreet. You do not have be registered as a user or download a software component or the like in order to put images into the system. In this way, visitors to the home can bring digital content and share it or give it to people in the home. In a sense this reflect the current hospitality of the ordinary home where you can be invited in by the residents, and you can follow the social norms about conduct and interaction or you can choose to breach these norms. The system in itself does not have a parenting or gate keeper function, as we choose to leave these sensitive social issues in the hands of the people in the social situation.

4 Experiences and Reflections

In the study we combined two evaluation methods. We first did a laboratory evaluation with four families. After this round of evaluations we spend two weeks adjusting details in the interaction design, before we installed the system in the home of a family for a period of two weeks. In both the laboratory and the in-situ evaluation we conducted qualitative, open-ended interviews. In all evaluations, we put an effort in putting the families' own materials in the system for them to deal with.

Figure 11: A family around the MediaTable in a lab evaluation

4.1 Evaluation in Lab

In the laboratory study, we invited four families in. The families have children in the age between 6 and 20. We asked the families to perform certain tasks, and we discussed with them the implications of having such a system in their home. All the families found the possibility to gather around the table extremely appealing, they pointed to a number of scenarios that they saw as obvious. Holiday Planning is a theme which three of the four families mentioned. Playing games, preparing music collections for parties, viewing pictures together with friends, looking up more information on the web regarding a theme which comes up during conversations at dinner. E.g. a mother in one of the families argued that they often first sit around the table, but suddenly they find themselves in the office, because they want to look up something, and that this is extremely annoying since they cannot all look at the screen at the same time and they have to leave the nice context of the living room in order to get the information. A woman doing accounting in her job argued that it would also be a really attractive platform for her to work from home. Further, planning and negotiating the logistics of family life was seen as an obvious activity to perform between the family members around the table.

In two of the sessions the families started to play around with pushing materials between two locations. I.e. in one situation the father and daughter pushed some pictures from the 'kitchen display' to the mother, son and another daughter who sat at the table. They found this really funny, even though, or perhaps because they at the same time were able to shout to each other that something was coming – "check this out".

Further several argued that they liked the easy way of pushing materials between places. One man argued, that in principle he can move stuff between the different computers in their home now, and often do so, but as it is now this is a very time consuming and troublesome task.

4.2   Evaluation in a Private Home

The family involved in the in-situ study consists of a father aged 46, a mother aged 47, one daughter aged 22 living away from home, and two children living at home: a boy aged 13, and a girl aged 15. They live in a suburb outside a medium sized city. We installed the system described above in the home for a period of two weeks. Inherently, the system leave traces of activities in the form of new collections made. We used these traces of activities to interview them about what they had done with the system over the two weeks of use.

At the installation of the system in the home, the family was a bit concerned that they would not engage much with the system, as they are busy, each having their own agendas throughout the week. It turned out however, that the family gathered in a number of ways around the system during the two weeks the system was installed. The first time was when the son invited his friends over for playing games on the Table, in the living room and on his own computer. This happened several times during the first week. The second time was when the oldest daughter came home from boarding school bringing pictures on her digital camera. Here the family gathered around their Table to see the pictures, organizing them in a collection and watching them together in the kitchen. They did comment however, that some of the pictures were overwhelming to see on the table in full size, and they would have liked to be able to push them to a vertical display besides the table. Thus where the table was useful for organizing materials, they preferred a vertical display for viewing large-scale images together. This is a concrete example of what kinds of heterogeneous displays people wishes to have in their home and for which purposes.

The father pointed out that it brought the family together in a new way when the boy sat at the table in the common room and played with his friends. In this situation, the parents saw more than the back of their son, which they are used to when the boy sits in his room and play at the computer, and the parents had more awareness of the son's activities. The mother argued that at times it was also a little overwhelming to have so many children in the kitchen, and in the home. Nevertheless, this points to a second quality arising from the attraction of an interactive table in a common room, namely the possibility to have awareness about each others' activities with digital materials, even though they are not directly engaged in the same activity.

In line with the suggestions of the families in the lab evaluation, this family had also been browsing for possible places for their next holiday.

The mother had an interesting comment as we took down the system, as she suddenly realised an unexplored potential of the display in the hallway: "oh, yeah I see that (...) then we could put holiday pictures up there (...) and make people jealous (...). Can we keep it a week more?" Over the two weeks there had not been much activity on this display. The father had posted some pictures of relatives there, but he suggested that this was mostly done to explore the system. Instead of pictures, he requested a SMS gateway making it possible to post sms messages on this display

5 Designing for Collaborative, Heterogeneous, and Connected Interaction

With CASOME we have designed for collaborative, heterogeneous, and connected interaction in the home. To discuss how we have accomplished this it is useful to revisit the requirements coined in section 2.1

Combining and linking heterogeneous devices
With the CASOME home prototypes we have constructed a home environment which indeed contains heterogeneous devices. Our way of realizing this has been to design a range of connected platforms which allows for doing different things, different places. We have supported the full range of situations of the home ranging from single user to multiple users working collaboratively and co-located. We have supported casual on-the-fly interaction in terms of e.g. pick and drop on MediaDisplays as well as long-term concentrated activities around the MediaTable
In the experiences from the evaluations we see how they different devices certainly have different roles. Our studies suggest that some displays are more appropriate for some things than others, e.g. table for organizing, complemented with a nearby wall display for viewing. Also our studies confirm the value of combining devices supporting easy push and pull of materials between people and places.

Designing activity centres supporting production, manipulation, and organization of household media clips
The evaluations suggest that a tabletop is a potentially really interesting site for designing activity centers in the future. Our evaluations also point to the need for developing new applications beyond what CASOME currently supports, e.g. collective game-playing around a table.

Designing coordinate displays which support for coordination of activities and presence

In our approach of realizing this, information materials can be kept and distributed explicitly amongst *people* and *places* of the home. The evaluation suggested the hallway display as a potentially useful site for coordination activities as well as the table for collective planning activities

Designing ecological habitat, that is meant for people to locate resources

Our evaluations did not investigate this much as they were performed with a limited set of test-data

Social sharing of media amongst co-located users in a home

The evaluation points to a number of ways this may happen. Several people may collaborate on the same tasks at e.g. a table setup. Materials may also be seen at a different place, but at the same time, as when people start to push materials to each other while also shouting to each other. Furthermore, larger, collective displays may also promote more awareness between family members' activities and be the scene of shared experiences with materials.

Linking media clips to specific places in the home

Our study point in particular to the entrance area and the table in the commonroom as interesting sites for specific place-references to be made.

Designing Interaction experiences tailored to place and context

In our setup we have developed some new alternatives for interacting with digital materials in the home, e.g. multilight tracker [11] and eMote. The excitement around the table platform suggests the need for supporting multiuser interaction mechanisms like multilight tracker. Further, several were pleased with the possibilities for touch interaction and requested this for the table too.

Obviously, more research is needed in this direction to further elaborate these very generic qualities and explore different strategies for realizing them. Clearly, there is also a need for keyboards and mice in a home-environment, but with CASOME, we have complemented these instruments to investigate how new qualities of interaction can emerge in this way.

6   Comparison to Related Work

While others have conducted research into future interactive home environments, our work differs in various ways from previous work. Compared to related design concepts, we focus on supporting the collaborative handling of media among people who actually live in the same home, rather than supporting awareness between people living in different physical locations, which has been investigated by other projects [14,**Error! Reference source not found.**]. Moreover, we focus on handling of digital materials broader than photos [16] and we challenge the position that experiences of handling digital photos in homes can be limited to searching, wandering and recommending [ibid]. In contrast, we suggest that digital photos may be important material in shaping the ambience of homes, provided that interaction mechanisms are supported that respect the qualities of the homes. Our first suggestion is in the form of collective and playful experiences around a MediaTable, which supports collective handling of materials, which is in opposition to the prevalent, more individualized concepts [ibid].

In [7] a software infrastructure for supporting personalized interaction in the home is presented. CASOME shares many of the same features, however, our focus is on going beyond the personal experience supporting the social experiences, thus we provide applications for large shared displays, rather than small personal devices, like PDA's as the main focus in [ibid].

Compared to the Jigsaw domestic component system [17], we have taken a material centered approach. We have focused on the organization of domestic material and on how we can provide a seamless folding between the physical and digital material spaces. Where Humble et al. [ibid] focus on supporting transformations between digital and physical material, we focus on linking and integrating the digital media and the physical environment.

LiMe [18] is a Philips project among other things developing a CafeTable and Public Screen concept with access to digital material and the ability to relate it to RFID tags. Compared to LiMe, CASOME focuses on the collaborative interaction with home materials, and the distributed management of materials on heterogeneous displays in the home.

7 Conclusion

This paper has presented results from empirical studies and discussed how the CASOME infrastructure can be used do design social interaction for future home environments. The design of the CASOME home prototypes is based on empirical studies of home activities. Empirical studies and literature studies have outlined a set of recommendations for home systems. The CASOME addresses the empirical challenges and recommendations, and compared to related work CASOME is unique in its support for co-located social interaction in the home. Among other things it supports the Activity Center concept put forward by Crabtree et al [1,4] in support for a multiuser table for uploading and organizing of home produced media such as photos and videos, and it supports connected surfaces allowing for easy flow of materials between different surfaces in the home.

CASOME supports context dependent handling of home media, and depending on the type of and placement of the display it supports multimodal and/or multi-user interaction. Thus it points to how an ecology of interaction can be designed for the home. The paper discusses applications and use scenarios as well as experiences from lab and field tests.

Acknowledgements

This work has been supported by ISIS Katrinebjerg, Center for Interactive Spaces. We wish to thank all our center colleagues. In particular, we would like to thank Søren Boll Overgaard for his work on the project. We would also like to thank the industrial partner B&O A/S, in particular we would like to thank Experience Designer Jannie Friis-Kristensen, and finally our thanks go to the families who participated in the evaluations of the system.

References

1. Crabtree, A., Rodden, T., and Mariani, J. (2004) Collaborating around Collections: Informing the ContinuedError! Reference source not found. Development of Photoware. In Proceedings of CSCW 2004, ACM Press, pp. 396-405

2. Petersen, M. G., Ludvigsen, M., Jensen, H. F., and Thomsen, A. (2004) Embracing Values in Designing Domestic Technologies. In Proceedings of European Conference on Cogni-tive Ergonomics, ecce'12, York, September 2004

3. Taylor, A., and Swan, L. (2005) Artful Systems for the Home. In Proceedings of CHI 2005. ACM Press, pp. 641-650

4. Crabtree, A., Rodden, T., Hemmings, T., and Benford, S. (2003) Finding a Place for Ubi-Comp in the Home. In Proceedings of the 5th International Conference on Ubiquitous Computing. Springer-Verlag.

5. Forlizzi, J., and Batterbee, K. (2004) Understanding Experience in Interactive Systems. In Proceedings of DIS 2004. ACM Press, pp. 261-268.

6. Kruger, R., Carpendale, M.S.T., Scott, S.D., & Greenberg, S. (2003). How People Use Orientation on Tables: Comprehension, Coordination and Communication. Proc. Of GROUP'03, 369-378.

7. Nakajima, T., and Satoh, I. (2006) A software infrastructure for supporting spontaneous and personalized interaction in home computing environments. In Personal and Ubiqui-tous Computing (2006) vol 10 no 6: Springer Verlag, pp. 379-391

8. Ruyter, B. de, and Aarts, E. (2004) Ambient Intelligence: Visualizing the future. In Pro-ceedings of AVI, ACM Press, pp. 203-208.

9. Petersen, M.G. (2004): Remarkable computing: the challenge of designing for the home. In Proceedings of CHI'2004, ACM Press, pp. 1445-1449.

10. Mimio http://www.mimio.com/

11. Nielsen, J. & Grønbæk, K. (2006): MultiLightTracker: Vision based simultaneous multi object tracking on semi-transparent surfaces. In proceedings of the International Confer-ence on Computer Vision Theory and Applications (VISAPP 2006), 25 - 28 February, 2006 Setúbal, Portugal.

12. Matsushita, M., Iida, M., and Ohguro, T. (2004) Lumisight Table: A Face-to-face Col-laboration Support System That Optimizes Direction of Projected Information to Each Stakeholder. In Procedings of CSCW 2004, ACM Press, pp. 274-283.

13. Shen, C., Lesh, N.B, Vernier, F., Forlines, C., and Frost, J. (2002) Sharing and Building Digital Group Histories. In Proceedings of CSCW 2002, ACM Press, pp. 324-331.

14. Hutchinson, H., Mackay, W., Westerlund, B., Bederson, B. B., Druin, A., Plaisant, C., Beaudouin-Lafon, M., Conversy, S., Evans, H., Hansen, H., Roussel, N., Eiderbäck, B. (2003) Domesticated Design: Technology Probes: Inspiring technology design with and for families. In proceedings of CHI 2003. ACM Press, pp. 17-24.

15. Mynatt, E. D., Rowan, J., Craighill, S., and Jacobs, S. (2001) Digital Family Portraits: Supporting peace of mind of extended familiy members. In Proceedings of CHI2001, ACM Press, pp. 333-340

16. Teixeira, D., Verhaegh, W., and Ferreira, M. (2003) And Integrated Framework for Sup-porting Photo Retrieval Activities in Home Environments. In Lecture Notes in Computer Science. Issue 2875. Ambient Intelligence. Springer-verlag, pp. 288-303.

17. Humble, J., Hemmings, T., Crabtree, A., Koleva, B. and Rodden, T. (2003) "'Playing with your bits': user-composition of ubiquitous domestic environments", Proceedings of the 5th international Conference on Ubiquitous Computing, pp. 256-263, Seattle: Springer.

18. Philips, LiMe project, http://www.design.philips.com/smartconnections/lime/

Usability – Key Factor of Future Smart Home Systems

Gerhard Leitner, David Ahlström and Martin Hitz
Department for Informatics Systems, Klagenfurt University, Austria

Abstract. A framework of usability factors is presented which serves as a basis for the thorough research of usability issues in the context of smart home systems. Based on well accepted approaches taken from the literature, various aspects related to usability are identified as significant for the implementation and future development of smart home systems. Finally, the partly existing prototypical installation of a smart home system is discussed and scenarios for future investigations are presented.

1   Introduction

The widespread of smart home devices has increased within the last few years and has now reached the level of a mass market. The increased application of such systems will probably lead to problems well known from other areas – problems related to bad usability. Personal computers, websites or VCRs are intensively discussed examples of sub-optimal usability. Smart home systems include multiple factors which are potentially relevant in relation to usability, both as singular aspects and in a combination. Besides simple functionality, such as switching the lights on or off, smart home systems also support networked operation, the definition of macros, and the usage of diverse, mostly GUI-based devices. All these components may cause severe problems when usability is not considered.

In this paper, integration of important usability aspects which could be relevant in relation to smart home appliances in future is attempted. After an overview of the theoretical background and related work in the field, a framework comprising aspects derived from various usability models and theories is discussed which may serve as a conceptual basis for future research activities. Examples of possible research topics and research methods are given afterwards, followed by a description of relevant parts of the prototypical installation of a smart home system which serves as an infrastructure for usability investigations. The paper concludes with a discussion on future research topics.

Please use the following format when citing this chapter:

Leitner, G., Ahlström, D., Hitz, M., 2007, in IFIP International Federation for Information Processing, Volume 241, Home Informatics and Telematics: ICT for the Next Billion, eds. Venkatesh, A., Gonsalves, T., Monk, A., Buckner, K., (Boston: Springer), pp. 269-278.

2 Background

The times have passed when smart appliances have been seen merely as either a hobby of persons fascinated by technical gimmicks, or as necessary tools for the maintenance of public or company buildings. The electronic industry has already focussed on the private person as a potential mass consumer of smart home technology. There are many indicators showing that smart home appliances are already an issue for the broad public. For instance, almost each do-it-yourself store has at least one system available, and advertising in television or magazines is also intensively dealing with that subject. The offered smart home systems range from stand-alone switching components to networked systems (either wired or wireless), depending on the intended purpose of the system. Because of the high availability, solutions had to be found to support a side-by-side operation of different devices. This has been accomplished by the definition of standards, like the U.S. X10 standard and the EIB/KNX standard developed in Europe, cf. e.g. [1]. These standards provide an infrastructure including detailed interface specifications on the basis of which different manufacturers can develop and release devices.

An important development came with the widespread of smart home appliances: the users of devices are no more only specialists with technical skills, like company technicians responsible for the electrical equipment in an enterprise. Moreover, training of end users, which is usual e.g. when a new system for building automation is deployed, seems not to be very realistic. The other possibility to overcome usage problems would be to provide guidelines and specifications for the design of the user interfaces, available for different computer platforms and operating systems. However, such documentation is only partly considered in standards like X10 and EIB/KNX.

The missing consideration of issues of the user interface and the neglect of end user needs is very similar to situations consumers have been confronted with in the past. When VCRs came on the market, consumers had to struggle with bad usability. The next hurdles came with the appearance of the personal computer and more recently with the widespread of the Internet.

In relation to usability, smart home appliances add new dimensions to our lives which are important to consider, because complex smart home systems include a combination of devices and, therefore, a combination of potentially severe usability problems. Indeed, it had been annoying when recording a movie had not been possible with the new VCR, or bad usability of websites or software programs led to aborted online purchases or cumbersome text processing, but these symptoms do not have critical impact on our lives. Considering smart home appliances, bad usability could have more severe effects, e.g., if one cannot switch on the heating in winter, cannot get into one's apartment, or – even worse – is trapped inside a building. Especially novice users or elder persons are a target group for smart device marketing and the benefits of an increased ease of life when everything works by pushing a button on a remote control are illustrated in high-gloss brochures. But how realistic are these scenarios when considering all the usability problems related just to single devices such as mobile phones?

2.1 Related Work

Usability aspects of smart home appliances have been investigated under different viewpoints. Beginning with the very early discussion of "the psychology of everyday things" as Norman [2] terms it, where bad usability of quite simple devices was critically observed, long before smart home systems reached the market. Usability aspects of smart home devices have been researched, e.g. by [3] who investigated usability problems related to the user interface of a smart home system. Schoeffel [4] describes a usability engineering oriented design approach for a smart home end user interface. Ringbauer & Hovfenschioeld [5] investigated the emotional aspects related to the usage of such systems. Investigations regarding the utility and usability of smart home systems for the elderly were done e.g. by [6] and long term usability observations have been conducted at the Philips Homelab [7].

The work in this area is characterized by punctual investigations which do make sense in answering specific questions. However, as discussed, smart home systems include very different components which could show interaction effects. These effects cannot be considered and measured with singular methods. Therefore, a comprehensive model including the most relevant dimensions seems necessary. Such a model is presented in the following.

3 Usability Oriented Framework of Smart Home Interaction

The investigation of usability aspects related to smart home appliances is difficult because several areas of usability research are linked together in one problem domain. One common shortcoming of the related work presented in the previous section is that only singular aspects have been addressed, focused on the user interface. However, smart home appliances affect at least two areas of usability: real world usability issues, e.g. the ergonomics of door handles, wall mounted switches [8] as well as usability issues related to software or Web interfaces. Furthermore, if mobile system components are in use, additional aspects regarding mobile usability have to be considered.

Thus, ensuring usability in smart home environments is a difficult and multidimensional task. To address all relevant dimensions, it is necessary to specify a framework which serves as the basic structure for usability research related to smart home appliances. Complex smart home systems are integrating distinct paths of manipulation and feedback, e.g., one user is switching a device with a power switch while another user who is accessing the system via Internet is retrieving feedback on the current system status. Figure 1 illustrates the possibilities of interaction between a user and a smart home system. To keep the model simple, only the most immediate switching and feedback loops are presented.

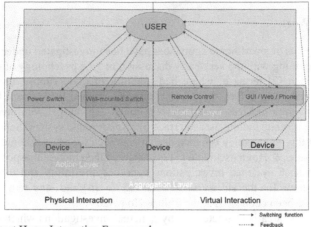

Fig. 1. Smart Home Interaction Framework

Physical Interaction:

A user can switch a device by activating a control directly on the device or a wall-mounted switch which e.g. closes a circuit to an attached device. Feedback is given by the device itself (e.g., the light goes on), or by the switch – which is giving tactile and/or visual feedback. In some cases the feedback is given by some indirect feedback mechanisms, e.g., when the central heating in the basement is switched on, feedback can be observed via the increasing temperature of the radiators.

Virtual Interaction:

A user can press a button on a remote control, and feedback is given by the switched device (if the user is in the same room he sees that the lights went on). This case seems to be similar to physical interaction, but due to the involvement of at least two parts of the system (electrical wiring and remote system) the situation is categorized as virtual. If the user is pressing a button on the remote control, but is not in the same room, he cannot see the status of the switched devices and has to rely on feedback given by the remote control or on feedback provided by other devices, e.g., a building layout equipped with status LEDs.

When a user is accessing the system over a desktop computer, a handheld device or a mobile phone, the device is switched indirectly. The system involved in this switching process can include diverse technical and interaction related dimensions, e.g., wireless or wired infrastructure, interface features of the used device (PC, handheld or mobile phone). As the manipulation is performed remotely, the switched devices themselves cannot provide feedback to the user, therefore feedback representation is given by software components like graphical symbols or similar means. Another possibility would be that a system-independent device can provide feedback, e.g. the user can observe over a webcam whether the lights are on.

The three layers (Action Layer, Interface Layer and Aggregation Layer) in the framework are symbolising the usability dimensions of relevance are discussed below.

Action Layer – In the context of physical interaction, many aspects play a role. The interaction model of Norman [2] and the model of Abowd & Beale [9] define different aspects of interaction between a user and a system. The two models include functional- and feedback components. Additionally, of interest are the characteristics of the interaction with "everyday things" postulated by Norman:

- Visibility – The system should not hide important interface components.
- Affordance – Controls should animate the user to use them (the right way).
- Mapping – The system should have a representation with affinity to the real world.
- Feedback – The user should be able to observe if and how the system is working.
- Constraints – The system should be adapted to the users' capabilities and circumstances of the usage.
- Conceptual model – This characteristic is considered within the Aggregation Layer (cf. below).

Additional aspects of relevance can be taken from the theory of action regulation (cf. e.g. [10]) which adds e.g. unconscious or automated actions, or "habits", as Raskin [11] terms it. To give an example what could be a relevant problem on the level of action is the switching of a wall switch which is designed as a standard switch (affordances) – but is wirelessly steering a remote device. In such situations questions are to be answered, like: "Which usability aspects do play a role? Does the switch give tactile or optical feedback regarding the status of the switched component?" When more than one switch is there – which switch belongs to which device (see Figure 2 containing illustrations of smart home switching components)? More difficult is the analysis of the device represented on the right side of the figure. Tactile components like buttons are used for the regulation of the device, a character based display is giving information on the chosen values. These components of a smart home system have to be analysed in relation to both the Action and the Interface Layer.

Fig. 2. Examples of smart home switching components (sources: http://www.moeller.at, http://www.eib-home.de/gepro_knx-eib-tableau_2006.htm, 2007-03-17)

Interface Layer – This can be conceived as the layer containing classical usability issues. Singular aspects of the interface are of relevance, but also the interaction of different interface components has to be considered. This is the most researched segment of the model. An abundance of literature exists, ranging from different collections of usability heuristics to relevant standards and norms, e.g. the ISO 9241 series. The characteristics to be analysed within this level are, e.g., usability factors of the ISO 9241-11 Guidance on Usability [12] , i.e.:

- Effectiveness – Can a user accomplish a task?
- Efficiency – Can the task be accomplished with acceptable effort in acceptable time?
- Satisfaction – Is the performance of the task satisfactorily?

As these factors are parts of a theoretical construct which cannot be observed directly, measurable attributes have to be identified. Literature regarding factors influencing usability is rich, models are discussed e.g. by [13,14,15]. One of the newest and therefore most complete list of basic principles for interface design is the one published by Tognazzini [16] shown in Table 1.

Table 1. Usability Principles in Interaction Design

Anticipation	Fitts´ Law
Autonomy	Human Interface Objects
Color Blindness	Latency Reduction
Consistency	Learnability
Defaults	Metaphors
Efficiency of Use	Protect Users work
Explorable Interface	Readability

An example question regarding the Interface Layer could be: "Are the criteria of usability fulfilled in an existing interface? What can be improved?". Figure 3 shows a layout of a smart home control desktop software on the left, and another example of a GUI interface based on a tablet PC on the right.

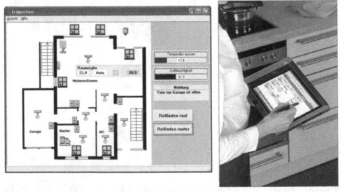

Fig. 3. GUI based systems of smart home appliances (sources: Contronics and Siemens).

Aggregation Layer – This level contains aspects related to different components of the multi-tasking, multi-device interaction (as shown in the interaction framework). The content of this layer is least known at the moment. The idea behind the Aggregation Layer is a kind of "Gestalt" in the nomenclature of psychological

Gestalt Theory. The central postulation of this theory is that the whole is more than the sum of its parts. The central question to be addressed within this level is how the different aspects of interaction in smart homes influence each other, what are the criteria which influence the "homeostasis" of the system. Is it the chosen technology, be it human factors like personality, age or gender.

3.1   Research Methods

As difficult as the development of a conceptual model is the selection of appropriate methods to investigate the different aspects of usability of smart home appliances. Our approach is to use a set of methods pertinent to the different layers. Physical action can be observed and investigated with usage analysis protocols used in industrial psychology, e.g. VERA [17], but also methods usually applied in the analysis of ergonomics are considered. The outcome of the investigations based on such methods is information regarding the tactile sensory features of the devices.

For the investigation of aspects related to the Interface Layer, a broad range of user interface analysis methods is available. These contain focus groups, structured interviews, contextual inquiries, usability questionnaires, usability expert methods and usability tests (an overview is given e.g. by [14] and [18]). Questions to be answered by the applications of these methods are e.g. to what degree the interfaces investigated reach the requirements of standards, fulfil the user needs and are satisfactory for the users regarding design and functionality.

The methods mentioned in relation to the Action Layer and the Interface Layer have been used in different other contexts and can be successfully adapted to the new domain of smart home systems. The investigation of aspects related to the Aggregation Layer is a bigger challenge. The major difficulty is that a punctual evaluation of factors related to single actions or the singular usage of an interface is not suitable for the identification of relevant aspects influencing a continuous usage of a smart home system. Therefore, longitudinal observation methods have to be used. Such longitudinal observations have already been successfully used, e.g. by [7], however in artificial environments. Other approaches were based on the observation of groups of people for a short time period combined with questionnaire data [5]. Thus, the most suitable approach to investigate long-term usage aspects seems to be based on the participant observation method (often applied in psychology and sociology) which is characterized by the fact that the researcher is concurrently observer and part of the topic of investigation. This approach has both advantages and disadvantages. The major advantage is that it is possible to conduct observations in a natural environment if the investigations are performed in the home of the participants (one of which is the researcher himself) which guarantees realistic situations and surrounding conditions. A second advantage is that the researcher, as part of the setting, can therefore perform the observation without massively influencing the behavior of the observed persons. However, the latter advantage can also be a major disadvantage since the participation of the researcher can highly influence the study outcome.

3.2   Prototypical Installation

Currently, a prototypical implementation of a system of smart home appliances is installed at two different locations. The first location is an experimental lab, where punctual investigations can be performed. The second location is a one-family house, where the longitudinal studies can be carried out. In the latter location a test set has already been installed and first investigations were already carried out. These first investigations served the purpose of a pilot study to collect more detailed and complete requirements for a realistic implementation of the system in use. The outcome resulted e.g. in the decision for a system which is open for the integration of different devices and – more importantly – provides an interface for the development of customized software components. Figures 4 and 5 show a sketch of the test installation. Figure 4 shows a set of devices already in use in relation to the presented framework. For instance, a remote control can be used to switch attached devices (like a garage door or a lamp). With a desktop computer or a smart phone the status of the system can be observed. The camera shown in the figure serves as an additional feedback channel. All the devices mentioned are part of the Interface Layer. Other devices like wall mounted switches or switches on the device itself can be used to switch devices more directly. These devices are part of the Action Layer.

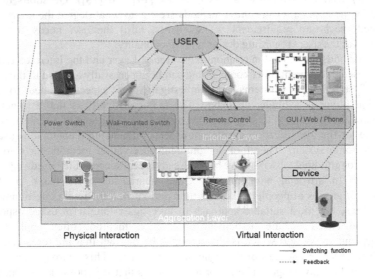

Fig. 4. Example Devices in relation to the Layers of the Framework

Figure 5 on the next page includes an overview of the whole infrastructure installed so far on the basis of a floor plan.

Fig. 5. Installed Devices on the One-family House Floorplan

4 Future Work

The framework for the investigation of usability of smart home appliances which has been put forward in this paper will serve as the basis of our future research projects. The very next step is to complete the prototypical installation and implement software components, like logging tools or statistics programs which provide the possibility of detailed analysis of the behaviour of the users interacting with the system. Several research questions on different levels are planned to be addressed,. The following list represents some of the questions formulated so far:

- Ergonomic factors of switching components – e.g., how can feedback be realised when the switched device is not visible?
- User Interface Factors – is it possible to apply standardized GUI-widgets or is the primary user group not familiar with computers?
- How do smart homes change habits, rituals or behaviours of the persons using them?

5 References

1. G. Westermeir, Der Europäische Installation Bus EIB, http://www.hfs.e-technik.tu-muenchen.de/ext/d12/eib2.pdf (March 17, 2007).

2. D.A. Norman, The Design of Everyday Things (Doubleday, New York, 1988).

3. B. Ringbauer, F. Heidmann and J. Biesterfeldt, When a House Controls its Master - Universal Design for Smart Living Environments", in: Proceedings of HCI International, Vol. 1, pp. 1228 – 1232. (2003).
4. R. Schoeffel, Usability Engineering am Beispiel des Home Electronic System von Siemens und Bosch. in: Software-Ergonomie '97. Usability Engineering: Integration von Mensch-Computer-Interaktion und Software-Entwicklung, pp. 37–53. (1997).

5. B. Ringbauer and E. Hofvenschiöld, Was macht es denn jetzt? - Emotionale Faktoren bei der Akzeptanz von Smart Home Lösungen, in: Usability Professsionals 2004, Tagungsband des 2. Workshops des German Chapters der UPA, pp. 87-89. (2004).

6. T. Erkert, T and A. Koenig, Neue Medien zur Alltagserleichterung von Seniorinnen und Senioren. http://www.swz-net.de/infoserver/download/index.htm (March 17, 2007).

7. B. de Ryter, 356 Days – Ambient Intelligence in HomeLab, http://www.research.philips. com/technologies/misc/homelab/downloads/homelab_356.pdf (March 17, 2007).

8. M.J. Darnell, http://www.baddesigns.com (March 17, 2007).

9. G.D. Abowd and R. Beale, Users systems and interfaces: a unifying framework for interaction'. In: HCI'91: People and Computers VI., pp. 73-87. (1991).

10. M. Frese and D. Zapf, Action as the Core of work psychology – a german approach. in: Handbook of industrial and organizational psychology. Vol. 4 (Consulting Psychologists Press, Palo Alto, CA, 1994).

11. J. Raskin, The Humane Interface: New Directions for Designing Interactive Systems. (ACM Press/Addison-Wesley Publishing Co, New York, 2000).

12. ISO 9241-11, Ergonomic requirements for the work with visual display terminals (VDT) ± Part 11 Guidance on usability. (1998).

13. M. van Welie, G. C. van der Veer and A. Eliens, Breaking Down Usability, in: Proceedings of INTERACT 99, pp.613-620.(1999).

14. J. Nielsen, Usability Engineering. (AP Professional, Boston, MA, 1993).

15. B. Shneiderman, Designing the User Interface. (Reading: Addison-Wesley, 1987).

16. B. Tognazzini, First Principles in Interaction Design. http://www.asktog.com/ basics/firstPrinciples.html (March 17, 2007).

17. E. Ulich, Arbeitspsychologie. (Poeschel, Stuttgart, 1991).

18. M. G. Helander, T. K. Landauer, P. Prabhu, and P. V. Prabhu, Eds. Handbook of Human-Computer Interaction. (Elsevier Science Inc., North-Holland, 1997).

Lessons from the Life of Domestic Objects:
Design Considerations for UbiComp Devices for Home

Youngmi Choi

Faculty of Architecture, Building and Planning and Department of
Information Systems (Interaction Design Group)
The University of Melbourne, Victoria, Australia

Abstract. Domestic Objects are emerging as a source for embedding ubiquitous computer technologies. The current focus on single objects or a singular function neglects people's diverse functional use of domestic objects and their cultural significances at home. Based on ethnographic interviews, this paper reports how people utilize domestic objects in relation to activities and domestic spaces. The paper concludes with some design considerations for ubiquitous computer devices.

1 Understanding the Domestic Environment

Ubiquitous computer technologies signify a transformation of the traditional form of computers into diverse objects that make up our everyday environment. The discussions on ubiquitous computer technologies initially focused on the work environment until the late 1990s when a call emerged emphasizing the need for exploring the home environment [1, 2]. Together with the growing industry interests in so-called smart home technologies, the home environment has emerged as a new source of design opportunities for ubiquitous computer technologies. At the same time, as the discourse in human-computer interactions expanded beyond the domain of computer related disciplines, researchers in the field began to unleash particular considerations necessary for designing ubiquitous technologies for home.

Three particular research approaches are worth mentioning in the area of designing ubiquitous computer technologies for home thus far developed: (1) understanding people at home as users, (2) designing to support routine activities, and (3) substituting existing functions of home objects with computational devices.

Understanding People at Home as Users

Initially from the work environment and later within the domestic environment, the use of technologies was initially studied from the perspective of technology

Please use the following format when citing this chapter:

Choi, Y., 2007, in IFIP International Federation for Information Processing, Volume 241, Home Informatics and Telematics: ICT for the Next Billion, eds. Venkatesh, A., Gonsalves, T., Monk, A., Buckner, K., (Boston: Springer), pp. 279-290.

adoption and then their influence on the things people do. A range of studies explored the adoption and use of technologies within the domestic environment including technologies for cooking and cleaning [3], telephone [4], entertainment [5] and computers & Internet [6]. The adoption of computers is one area widely researched with a particular focus on its social implications including the use by older people [7], people with a disability [8], young people or people from rural or city location [9], and women [10] as well as the issues exploring the digital divide [11]. In some technology studies exploring the home environment, people are narrowly defined as users with active purchasing power while investigating social and cultural meanings of possessing technological goods [12], how one modifies their use of technologies to suit their likings or purposes [13, 14] and changes that occurred in the life at home, derived from the use of new technologies [6].

Designing to Support Routine Activities

Domestic activities have been studied from a single dimensional perspective, led by extensive investigations into routines activities[15]. A strong focus on understanding the routine nature of domestic activity, though important, risks missing two significant points. Firstly the reactive and adaptive nature of use can be overlooked. For example the introduction of the VCR enabled users to rearrange or change radically their routine activities at home to stretch and distort time. Secondly, it can fail to realize that the ways routine activities are performed and delivered have changed as new ways and means have been introduced to people in the domestic environment. Consider what we have for and how we have breakfast. Over many centuries, we have been having bread and milk for our breakfast while the processes and the forms they get on to our breakfast table might have changed, not to mention the introduction of other ways we resolve our breakfast meals. Hence, identifying routine activities can be a rather inadequate approach to designing ubiquitous computer technologies. This is simply because computerizing these activities by producing a technological device can only be a short term solution to today's ways and means of carrying out our routine activities. As a result, a demand has emerged for a broader viewfinder that lets us see what occurs at home and how we can understand this without limiting or resorting to routine activities.

Replacing Functions of Home Objects with Computational Devices

Another trend in the studies into the domestic environment for technologies is a tendency of investigating the functions of the objects with an intention to convert them into the technological device. This resolute focus on functions can result in overlooking other significant elements influencing the way we relate or utilize objects at home. In addition, this can include objects' multiple functions and invisible relationships with people and their neighboring objects, and how they are related in the space they are placed in.

Essentially supported by activity theory, technology researchers began to explore the domestic life focusing on practical activities in the social and cultural context [16]. Studying the user experience in conducting practical activities has a direct connection with operating objects (referred to as tools or artifacts) including studying the context of graspable (or tangible) objects [17]. Nonetheless, one potentially significant aspect is overlooked by the researchers taking this approach: While objects are seen as mediating the user activities, they are perceived mainly in their primary functions in many studies. In other words, single objects or singular functionalities of domestic objects are at the centre of these studies.

This view neglects the possibility of other functions it may play, including those modified by users. Highly personal domestic objects may have a multi-dimensional relationship with their owners, and perform 'multiple functions', functions that grow from the user's experience and extend the object beyond its original given roles. The roles played by domestic objects can be heavily influenced by users due in part to the complex social and physical settings of use [18]; use that is rooted in personal and family rituals and defined by powerful emotional attachment within the home environment [19, 20].

The consideration for environment and spatial issues is another aspect being neglected. By concentrating on their primary function, it is easy to neglect the objects' invisible relationship with the way neighboring objects are located and how and where the activities associated with the objects are taking place. The interconnection of space, form and activity is widely discussed in the field of architectural design, which pursues a social analysis of the interfaces between user experience of space and its social context [21, 22]. Neglecting the spatial and environmental aspect, therefore, may lead to overlooking the wider and invisible structure or relationship beyond the objects the user is engaged with. In turn, this approach may fail to articulate the functionalities beyond the primary role of objects originally designed by the designer. Consequently, a need arises for exploring the objects in a deeper contextual manner including their indirect and intangible relationship with their users in order to come up with something that can be utilized in seamless orchestration with their local environment at home and with user activities.

All three of these developments somewhat contribute to building ways of identifying design opportunities and furthering the fit of ubiquitous computer technologies for the home environment. These approaches, however, can be in conflict with how people consider and utilize the meanings and functions of the domestic environment and/or domestic objects. For instance, it is not often that we perceive our life at home as a source for a great improvement through embedding technologies. Hence, taking one of the three developments may lead to a narrow pathway for HCI research into the home environment. Consequently, a need exists for a new direction for a fundamental groundwork about people at home that can suggest a holistic and contextual framework.

Taking this as a departure point, our paper unfolds an investigation into the domestic furniture and its diverse functional use at home. Based on analysis of the field data collected via ethnographic interviews, observation and photography, we discuss four particular furniture pieces –dining table, coffee table, chairs and sofa – and how diversely people utilize them within the physical and social context of home.

2   About the Study

As discussed, future ubiquitous computer solutions need to support more than just the function previously provided by desktop PC in order to accomplish calmness in use. How can this be achieved? This study explored our unremarkable everyday activities centered around domestic objects with an intention to understand functions and meanings in a social and personal context. The aim is to aid the design of ubiquitous technologies for home that can be 'invisible in use', just like those everyday objects at home. Considering that activities never take place in isolation and they are interwoven with other activities that deal with the same or connected objects, we believe that a deeper understanding of user object relationships needs to be obtained in order to learn about the structure and implication of neighboring objects. To achieve this, we initially concentrated on furthering our knowledge of home activities and how people draw out multiple functions from some domestic objects.

We conducted ethnographic interviews and observations with 14 adults (couples or singles) living in metropolitan Melbourne without any children. In each household, we spent minimum of half a day to one day and data was recorded using field notes, photography and mini digital disks. Eight out of 14 were living in a rented property while the rest owned a home. Using ethnographic interviews, observation and photography, we identified significant objects from the participants and analysed their relationship with activities in a particular space. During the analysis process, we kept close eyes on the context of the social and personal meanings of the objects in use and people's spatial experience as well as the participants' meaning of home.

3   Significant Domestic objects

The data from the field revealed interesting insights into the participants' relationship between co-occupants, creating a personal space and performing activities. No strong evidence was shown that home ownership influences the participants' attachment to home as no significant difference were shown in the way the renters and the home owners utilize their home objects and spaces. On the other hand, differences were identified when they placed a stronger meaning or happiness in a certain phase of their life. For instance, amongst the people whose current home is a rental property, they still showed a strong attachment to their current home. All of these people indicated that the meaningfulness of their current homes is because these places are the places they began a couple life with their partners.

In terms of technology objects, the meaningfulness seems to have developed in association with particular people, including themselves or someone associated with the objects or a particular user activity. Most technology objects at home tend to maintain their originally designed primary function. The cases of user-modification in these objects, therefore, were found when users applied the primary function in new contexts aiming for different results. Also, the social, personal or educational value the technological objects generate seemed to give new social functions to them.

The data revealed four general characteristics in the way people utilized significant objects at home and how the meanings impact on home activities. Initial patterns in the relationship between significant objects, activity and space emerged from the field and helped shape further analysis and they include:

- The participants place some significant objects together to create a personal space in order to support personally significant activities.
- Personal space is a place with a sense of connectedness.
- The routine or habitual activities at home communicate messages to co-occupants.
- Patterns of utilizing domestic furniture are influenced by user activities, neighboring objects and the design of the objects.

Based on these characteristics, we further recorded activities taking place in and around the significant domestic objects in the context of their meanings and functions and those of the participants' home. What emerged from this analysis were five noteworthy themes that exhibit roles and implications of the significant objects at home and how people interact with them. The five themes are: Homely ambience, personal relevance, responsiveness to neighbouring objects, multiple functions and user appropriation and meaningful space.

3.1 Homely Ambience –Perceived Suitability for Home

In the two pictures below, we can easily identify that they are showing someone's home because of their 'homely settings'. (Fig 1 & 2 are two different living rooms owned by one person.) An even closer look into one of the pictures can also effortlessly reveal that something is not or may not be quite right for the inside of a typical home: In the picture on the right, two camping chairs are placed in the middle of a living room and most of us would feel that they are unsuitable for a home or 'homely setting.'

Fig 1   Fig 2

Homeliness or homely ambience is hard to define. Judging a place homely or not is a complicated, multi-layered and even personal decision, involving the materials, design appearance or styles and so forth. Comparing the two pictures provide one descriptive case showing how the suitability of home objects can be identified and the reasons for the judgement can be illustrated. In this fashion, we summarize six ways homeliness is judged by our participants and they include:

- Size and materials;
- Perceived usefulness;
- Perceived values attached to the objects – its functions or its meanings;

- Perceived ease of use ;
- Relevance to personal values, identity or history; and
- Objects' possibility of contributing to creating a meaningful space

People develop subjective and personal meanings, beliefs and ideas in making judgements on whether or not an object is suitable for home. To be perceived as suitable for home, an object has to give homely ambience through whichever channel described here. As instantaneous as the judgment may be, the perceived suitability for home environment gives a clear leverage in being accepted by people. This means that a new object for the domestic environment must not rub off the feel of homeliness.

3.2   Personal Relevance

Home is a complex domain represented by a range of social, cultural and personal values. It is a place where one can exercise values such as authority, freedom and privacy [23]. Home is a place consisting of objects and furniture. It can also be the feelings that come from the objects and the spaces composed by these objects. At a first glance, onlookers find it hard to recognize the embodiments of these values at home as they are private so often undisclosed to others. For this very reason, the patterns and effects of how some objects are utilised can reveal values particularly relevant to the owner. The sources for the relevance appear to come from four aspects including personal habit or routine, personal biography, identity and self image. Consequently, the significant objects are embodiments of personal values in real life and the embodiment contributes to the life of the objects at least in four ways:

- They help lengthening the lifespan of objects.
- They provide a trigger for changing the pattern of utilisation.
- They offer mental and emotional interactions to users.

Some domestic objects are shadows of personal values connected to personal identity or an articulation process expressing personal identity. This is the connection, according to Wise, we confirm our territorial ownership of homes that gives the feeling of homogeny of our home and is a representation of us [24]. Consequently, seeking to enhance personal relevance in objects can present new design opportunities as well as leading to designs that can offer a possibility of diverse use, multiple interaction channels and emotional relevance to individual users.

3.3   Responsiveness to Neighbouring Objects & Rituals

A house accommodates various domestic objects that have both physical functions and personal meanings. Some domestic objects, more than other objects, convey cultural values preferred by individuals [25] and provide functions that aid user activities. Studies into domestic objects in the field of human and computer interactions frequently set out from either functions or meanings. While a scarcity can be seen in the number of HCI studies into the domestic objects that attempt to bridge functions and meanings [26], there already exists an established body of contextual inquires from social and cultural studies [27, 28]. Comparable to these contextual inquires in the field of HCI can be seen in the studies exploring routine activities and lived experience [15, 29]. However, routine activities are fragile to changes triggered by the introduction of new domestic objects. For this reason, they have some vulnerabilities as a design source for emerging ubiquitous computer applications [30]. Alternatively, a contextual approach can lead to designing domestic objects, aligned with the meaning and roles of the home environment and habitual user activities. One way of looking into this complexity is by placing a focus on a ritual situation where objects and activities occur in a particular place and to examine the interactions between the three-objects, activities and place.

How then can we characterise different types of interactions occurring within home? The field work findings reveal four ways people arrange and utilize objects at home and they include:

- On the pathway of an action flow: Objects are arranged and utilized as the user conducts a stream of activities.

- Enjoying the benefit of a house fixture: Objects are arranged in a way the user can take advantage of certain house fixtures such as windows, TV or heater.

- Offshoot of a fleeting action or situation: Objects are utilized to cope with a temporary situation or spontaneous activity.

- Budding up the experience of habitual activities: Objects are placed in a close proximity to a particular activity to strengthen the experience of conducting the activity.

Drawn up from the way people utilising objects within a particular space, the above four ways address the ways that the domestic objects are utilized. They bring two suggestions for designing of any emerging devices for home: one) objects need to be responsive to objects in a close proximity, and two) objects need to be responsive to a stream of activities.

3.4 Multiple Functions and User Appropriation

People are known for their capability of making and using tools since the discovery of the earliest bipedal hominids, Australopithecus. While people have continued to develop tools for their activities, discussions around people and objects they use have also continued. In the area of technology research, a noteworthy endeavour was made to design what better supports human activities by shifting its focus from end products to end users. This shifting focus on end users began to emerge amongst some researchers by the CSCW (Computer Supported Collaborative Work) movement [31] and study of technology adoption and domestication [12] during the period when personal computers began to appear in the work environments. At the centre of this focus is a claim that objects, particularly those well-designed ones, are complementary to human activities [32]. Consequently, designing with an emphasis on the fit of objects in people's everyday life illuminates ways and means of naturalising object's intrusion into people's private domains. One vital way to achieve this is to understand how people cultivate and utilise objects in their everyday life.

Fig 3   Fig 4   Fig 5-1   Fig 5-2

My fieldwork data revealed some evidence of people's appropriation in two ways—drawing up multiple functions by adding new functions, and replacing the originally designed function with a new personalised one. Objects used with new functions included Fred's dining table, GuangWu's tea table. As shown in picture 3, Fred places books and notes on a chair placed next to the entry so that he can be reminded to take them when he goes out. He says that he uses it as if it were an '*in-tray*' and '*out-tray*' (See Fig 3). GuangWu uses his plastic container with a lid as a tea table by covering it with an orange colour cloth and placing it between two armchairs in the living room (See Fig 5-1 & 5-2). In terms of introducing new functions, Fred was utilising his dining table as a study desk accommodating a PC (See Fig 4). Previously introduced in the earlier pattern, Alex's use of a blue mobile phone cradle also falls into this category.

Results of the field observation can be summarised as follows:

- In the case of drawing up multiple functions, objects are used on the basis of either temporary or habitually repetitive use. They maximise a personal experience within a certain locus and can be utilised spontaneously.

- On the other hand, the newly replaced functions appeared to be permanent until a new object or activity is introduced. They also appeared to have been accepted on the grounds of emotion and the relationship.

- Some objects perform single functions only and electric appliances primarily perform single functions.

- Ten factors appeared to be influencing user introduced functions and they include: time and occasion of use, physical location, shape and material, user's habitual tendencies & ritual activities, original function, influence of co-occupant's activity or behaviour, personal and social meaning and function of the accommodating space, user's social and cultural intention, use of other/ significant objects, and personal and social meaning of the objects.

- User introduced functions when it can be socially justifiable.

An object designed in consideration of the above list will have a longer lasting life span beyond its novelty affect and accurately meet user activities and the context of use.

3.5   Meaningful Space

Home plays both physical and psychological functions. Within this structure, people organise domestic objects to meet activities or images particularly important to them. This was an evident development in the bourgeois interior since the 19th century: a private and individualised interior was seen by choosing and arranging of objects than by the physical nature of space [33]. This adds complexities in the understanding of the domestic environment by presenting double layers for meaningfulness and practical functions to both home as a physical structure and a place that accommodates personally meaningful objects. The meaningfulness is a symbolic representation that counteracts a notion of mere passive consumers in the modern world. It is rather an evidence of cultural consumption, Hugh Mackay explains, that balances between constraint and creativity and the role of consumption [34]. What this tells us is that both home and objects perform physical and psychological functions to users that add complexity in understanding the domestic environment. This complexity can be overcome by placing a central focal point in how people create a particular space within home including reasons for and elements constructing the space. Consequently, there is a need for examining domestic objects in relation to spatial placement and user activities both in the physical and psychological functions they perform.

My field data revealed the four cases where significant objects contributed to construction of a meaningful place:

Arm chair I: Brian uses his armchair as a central piece in constructing a place where he can replace his experience of personal space and freedom he used to have in his old garage.

Dining table: Fred currently uses his dining table as a study desk to accommodate his PC.

Sofa: Ian studies from his sofa in the living room where he can overlook the outside. He enjoys looking out and the feel of being in the air by watching his apartment from the 5th floor.

Armchair II: Fiona set up a corner where she placed her red armchair for reading. She also placed other objects to enhance her experience of reading such as books and a bookshelf, a reading lamp and incense.

Extracted from the field data, three distinctive characteristics of meaningful places were witnessed:

- Users create a personal space with home to accommodate personally meaningful activities & the significant domestic objects that supports those activities.

- The personal space is a place with a sense of connectedness.

- Routine or habitual activities are a proxy communicator amongst family/close people

Based on the field data, a meaningful space is constructed for performing a particular activity. In other words, meaningful space is an activity centre for a personally meaningful activity. Construction of meaningful space appears to be based on three triggers: domestic fixture, user's social & psychological activity, and routine or ritual driven.

This understanding contributes to designing objects that meet both practical and psychological functions and that meet the context of ritual usage. It can also help direct to potential design opportunities by adding or combining functions, identifying user behaviour patterns in a particular physical setting, and providing a clue for mapping the domestic objects in relation to user activities and other objects in a particular domestic space. Finally this understanding can also help evaluate the fit of new designs for home.

4   Design Considerations for Home Ubiquitous Computers

The findings provide useful considerations for the design of ubiquitous computer technologies for home, in particular when embedment of computer technologies involves utilization of existing domestic objects. The lessons from the field can aid initial design ideas and evaluating the appropriation of interface design.

The five themes that emerged from the field work can help generate initial design ideas that fit the user perceptions and the current usage patterns of significant objects at home. Theme three and four, for instance, reveal how people use objects to construct a personal space in order to conduct activities significant to their everyday life. They show how a collection of objects are accommodated in a close proximity and, in some cases, how their functions are manipulated in order to support a stream of activities to enhance personalised user experiences. The amalgamation of different objects in a personalised space can also inspire initial design ideas. Initial design ideas can be derived from the way people appropriated the functions of existing objects by introducing new functions or replacing existing functions.

The five themes can be used for evaluating the appropriation of interface design. The details presented in the five themes portray the types of interactions people have with the domestic objects. The theme, responsiveness to neighbouring objects, for instance, shows people's attempt to experience a core stream of activities underpins the type of objects amalgamated in a physical space. It shows that, in order for people to maximise their experience, objects need to be designed in the context of objects and their associated activities in the neighbouring area. In some cases, a sequence of user activities needs to be considered in the design process to enhance the user experience. Personal relevance people find in domestic objects are also seen as important in shaping interaction patterns as it is an embodiment of social cultural values. This highlights a need to incorporate ways and means for people to create personal relevance.

The findings of this study help answer the question of the 'what and how' in designing ubiquitous computer technologies for home. This was done by collecting and analyzing empirical data on people's everyday life at home beyond the currently prevalent problem-solution paradigm in HCI design. The study demonstrates that everyday life at home needs to be understood in the context of domestic activities and the use of objects to better assist the designing of ubiquitous computer technologies.

5. References

1. Hindus, D.: The Importance of Homes in Technology Research. In: N. Streitz, J.S., V. Hartkopf, S. Konomi (ed.): The Second International Workshop on Cooperative Buildings (CoBuild'99). Cooperative Buildings - Integrating Information, Organizations, and Architecture, Pittsburgh (1999)
2. Harper, R.: Inside the Smart Home: Ideas, Possibilities and Methods. In: Harper, R. (ed.): Inside the Smart Home. Springer, London (2003)
3. Shove, E.: Comfort, Cleanliness and Convenience. Berg, Oxford (2003)
4. Marvin, C.: When Old Technologies were New: Thinking about Electric Communication in the Late Nineteenth Century. Oxford University Press (1990)
5. Barnouw, E.: Tube of Plenty: The Evolution of American Television. Oxford University Press (1992)
6. Venkatesh, A.: An Ethnographic Study of Computing in the Home. Working paper. University of California, Irvine, Irvine (1996)
7. Crabtree, A., Hemmings, T., Rodden, T., Cheverst, K., Clarke, K., Dewsbury, G., Hughes, J., Rouncefield, M.: Designing with Care: Adapting Cultural Probes to Inform Design in sensitive Settings. OZCHI 2003: New Directions in Interaction: Information Environments, Media & Technology. University of Queensland, Brisbane, Australia (2003)
8. Dewsbury, G., Clarke, K., Rouncefield, M., Sommerville, I., Taylor, B., Edge, M.: Designing Technology in Homes to Meet the Needs of Disabled People. Technology and Disability (2003)
9. NOIE: The Digital Divide. Vol. 2004. NOIE (National Office for Information Economy), Canberra (2003)
10. Zimmerman, J.: The Technological Woman: Interfacing with Tomorrow. Praeger, New York (1983)
11. Selwyn, N.: Apart from Technoogy: Understanding People's Non-Use of Information and Communication Technologies in Everyday Life. Technology in Society **25** (2003) 99-116
12. Mackay, H.: Consuming Communication Technologies at Home. In: Mackay, H. (ed.): Consumption and Everyday Life (Chapter 6). Sage Publications Ltd, London (1997) 259-308
13. MacKenzie, D.A., Wajcman, J.: Introductory Essay. In: Mackenzie, D.A., Wajcman, J. (eds.): The Social Shaping Of Technology. Open University Press, Milton Keynes UK (1999) 3-27
14. Carroll, J., Howard, S., Peck, J., Murphy, J.: From adoption to use: the process of appropriating a mobile phone. Australian Journal of Information Systems **10** (2002)
15. Crabtree, A., Rodden, T.: Domestic Routines and Design for the Home. Computer Supported Cooperative Work (2004) 1-30
16. Bannon, L., Bodker, S.: Beyond the interface: encountering artifacts in use. In: Carroll, J.M. (ed.): Designing Interaction: Psychology at the Human-Computer Interface. Cambridge University Press., Cambridge (1991) 227-253
17. Fitzmaurice, G.W.: Graspable User Interfaces. Department of Computer Science. University of Toronto, Toronto (1996)

18. Moore, J.: Placing Home in Context. Journal of Environmental Psychology **20** (2000) 207-217
19. Tuan, Y.-F.: Space and Place: The Perspective of Experience. University of Minnesota Press, Minneapolis (1977)
20. Csikszentmihalyi, M., Rochberg-Halton, E.: The Meaning of Things: Domestic Symbols and the Self. Cambridge University Press, Cambridge, UK (1981)
21. de Certeau, M.: The Practice of Everyday Life. University of California Press, Berkeley (1984)
22. Goffman, E.: The Presentation of Self in Everyday Life. Allen Lane, Penguin, London (1969)
23. Morley, D.: Home territories: media, mobility and identity. Routledge, London (2000)
24. Marcus, C.C.: House as a Mirror of Self: Exploring the Deeper Meaning of Home. Conari Press, Berkeley (1995)
25. Bourdieu, P.: Distinction: A Social Critique of the Judgement of Taste. Routledge and Kegan Paul, London (1984)
26. Dourish, P.: Where the Action is: The Foundations of Embodied Interaction. MIT Press (2001)
27. Seigworth, G.J., Gardiner, M.E.: Rethinking Everyday Life: and then nothing turns itself inside out. Cultural Studies **18** (2004) 139-159
28. Van Loon, J.: Social Spatialization and Everyday Life. Space and Culture **5** (2002) 88-95
29. Nagel, K.S., Hudson, J.M., Abowd, G.D.: Between Dinner and Children's Bedtime: Predicting and Justifying Routines in the Home. Vol. 2006 (2005)
30. Choi, Y., Howard, S., Dave, B.: The Secret Life of Domestic Objects: their multiple functionalities: understanding their triggers & influences from the user context. OZCHI, Canberra, Australia (2005)
31. Greenbaum, J., Kyng, M. (eds.): Design at Work: Cooperative Design of Computer Systems. Lawrence Erlbaum Associates, Hillsdale, NJ (1991)
32. Norman, D.: Things That Make Us Smart: Defending Human Attributes in the Age of the Machine. Addison-Wesley, Reading, Massachusetts (1993)
33. Perrot, M., Guerrand, R.-H.: Scenes and Places. In: Perrot, M. (ed.): A History of Private Life, Volume IV, From the Fires of Revolution to the Great War. Harvard University Press, Cambridge, MA (1990)
34. Mackay, H.: Consumption and Everyday Life. Sage, London (1997)